The Democratisation of Disempowerment

The Problem of Democracy in the Third World

Edited by Jochen Hippler

Pluto Press

with

Transnational Institute (TNI)

First published 1995 by Pluto Press
345 Archway Road, London N6 5AA
and 140 Commerce Street,
East Haven, CT 06512, USA
in association with
the Transnational Institute (TNI),
Paulus Potterstraat 20, 1071 DA, Amsterdam

British Library Cataloguing in Publication Data
A catalogue record for this book is available from the British Library

ISBN 0 7453 0977 1 (hbk)

Library of Congress Cataloging-in-Publication Data
The democratisation of disempowerment: the problem of democracy in
    the Third World / edited by Jochen Hippler.
        p.   cm. – (Transnational Institute series)
    Includes bibliographical references and index.
    ISBN 0–7453–0977–1.
    1. Democracy—Developing countries. 2. Developing countries—
Politics and government. I. Hippler, Jochen. II. Series.
JF60.D46   1995
320.9172'4—dc20   95–4121
                                                                            CIP

Designed and produced for Pluto Press by
Chase Production Services, Chipping Norton, OX7 5QR
Typeset from disk by Stanford Desktop Publishing Services
Printed in the EC by TJ Press, Padstow, England

Contents

Preface

With the end of the Cold War, democracy and democratisation of the Third World have moved, amidst a great deal of fanfare, from the soap-box and the pious wish to the realm of practical politics. Left- and right-wing politicians in the North, business people, political elites and generals in the South, non-governmental organisations in both North and South, social movements, the media and academics are all agreed: not only is democracy important and necessary, there is now a veritable 'wave of democracy'. Governments in Washington, Paris and Bonn, as well as the European Union and the World Bank have all decided to make democratisation a priority in their policies towards the South. These aren't just empty words: if particular governments refuse to introduce democratic reforms, the donor countries of the North threaten to cut off all economic assistance.

Almost everyone today is in favour of democracy. But such a degree of harmony makes one suspicious, especially when it is to be found among individuals, organisations, groups and governments better known otherwise for their mutual animosity. In Algeria, 'The Solution is Islam' is a popular slogan. In a similar vein, one hears everywhere 'The Solution is Democracy'. That may well be the case, but the solution to which problem? Is democracy the solution to *every* problem? And if so, why wasn't this discovered earlier?

Democracy provides the instruments to solve the problems of dictatorship and autocratic rule and, to a certain extent, the problem of oppression. But the use of democratic procedures in the election or replacement of governments doesn't automatically mean that human rights are respected. India and Colombia are two obvious examples of this. And what can democratisation of the Third World do to relieve hunger, poverty or economic stagnation? This is at least an open question.

All the authors in the present volume are in favour of democracy and democratisation, and not only in the South. But they share the view that democracy has to be more than just a formula that one invokes, that, in itself, it does not solve all the problems in the world. Hidden beneath the label, 'democracy', one not infrequently finds egoistic particular interests that are simply making tactical use of the concept. Democratisation is not just a solution; quite often it is also a problem. It is difficult to envisage how one could bring together, in one concept, the very different notions of democracy that are held by, for instance, Islamic clerics, rural movements in the Third World, the World Bank, governments of Northern countries, one-time liberation movements, reformist military leaders and the ethnic militias involved in some of today's civil wars. And would it be even desirable to do so?

Democracy and democratisation are also concepts quite frequently instrumentalised by various sides to further their own interests. 'Not everyone talking about heaven is actually going there' is a saying that applies equally well to democracy. Democratisation doesn't always and automatically aim to give people the chance to determine their own destiny. It not infrequently aims to legitimise existing power structures or is part of an ideological offensive aimed at establishing one group's hegemony. One particular notion of democracy, held by elites in the North and the South, aims precisely at excluding the poor and marginalised sectors of Third World populations from any possible share in the exercise of power, while developing ostensibly democratic forms.

In 1993, the Transnational Institute began a number of projects concerned with democratisation in the Third World. These projects will study external influences, from Northern governments, for instance, and the role of elites and social movements in the Third World. As a prelude to this work, in November 1993, the Institute organised in Cologne a joint conference with the Buntstift e.V. of Göttingen. The main theme of this conference was the way that democratisation in the Third World can be instrumentalised as a technique of domination. The papers presented to the conference are published in this book. With very few exceptions, the speakers at the conference have revised their papers in the light of the discussion and some new authors have contributed additional material to the collection.

The present volume is meant to be the starting point for future work on the theme of democratisation. The main purpose of the book is to make some suggestions, and to propose ideas and analyses that might stimulate political discussion and further scientific analysis. The contributions, therefore, are at very different levels of abstraction, and they come from different regions of the Third World as well as from the Northern countries.

One of the goals of the Transnational Institute has been not just to discuss the Third World from a distance but to bring together experts from both North and South to discuss the North-South problem. It is therefore no accident that roughly half the contributions in the present volume were written by authors from the South: from Nigeria, the Philippines, Trinidad, Nicaragua, Zimbabwe and the Israeli occupied territories. The Northern authors come from Finland, the USA, France and Germany. Together, they cover a wide range of the problems of democratisation in the Third World: Jochen Hippler looks at how democratisation is ideologically and politically instrumentalised or ignored by the Northern countries. Joel Rocamora looks at how progressive elites in the South have dealt with democratisation since the end of the Cold War, while Peter Schraeder analyses the democratisation policies of the African elite. Claude Aké develops this theme and asks why, in spite of democratisation, the powerlessness of people in Africa has actually increased. Niala Maharaj is very sceptical in her assessment of the chances of the democratic system in Trinidad, while Achin Vanaik and Praful Bidwai observe the influence of Hindu nationalism (communalism) on the stability of Indian democracy. Xabier Gorostiaga complements his analysis of the chances of democracy in Central America with proposals as to how these could be improved. Joe Stork looks at US policy in the Middle East and its effects on the development of democracy in that part of the world. Azmy Bishara analyses the link between democracy and religion in the Middle East, in particular the question of Islamic 'fundamentalism'. Basker Vashee examines the basic attitude of the World Bank, the European Union and the USA to democratisation in the Third World and Susan George looks at the concept of 'good governance' in the context of the discussion of democratisation. Liisa Laakso deals with the link between capitalist rationality and the instrumentalist view of democratisation in the South. Finally, Franz Nuscheler cautions against the fashionable tendency to regard democracy as something that can be exported.

This book would not have been possible without the support of the Buntstift e.V. in Göttingen. FINNIDA, the developmental assistance agency of the Finnish foreign ministry, also played an important supporting role. We would like to thank both for their cooperation and support. Without this kind of commitment, this joint effort of scientists from the North and the South would not have been possible.

Thanks also to Gus Fagan who translated the German contributions into English.

Jochen Hippler

1

Democratisation of the Third World After the End of the Cold War

Jochen Hippler

Whether democracy is advanced, weakened or abolished in the Third World is a question that will be decided, in the first instance, in the Third World itself. Internal political structures can be influenced, promoted or undermined from the outside, but they can not be artificially created. However, since many Third World societies lack secure foundations, have fragile institutions, and are economically dependent on other countries and on the world market, external influences play a particularly large role.

A discussion of democracy in the Third World, therefore, can not overlook the role played by governments of the North. Democratisation in the Third World always takes place within the context of the North-South relationship as well as within the context of an internal dynamic in which different factions of the power elite are in struggle both with each other and with different sectors of the population that are, by and large, excluded from power. In the economic field, in particular, but also in the political, cultural, technological and military fields, the North carries such overwhelming weight that it exercises a decisive influence on the internal power dynamics of the South. Why else did the collapse of the socialist regimes in eastern and Central Europe have such an immense impact on Africa?

With the end of the Cold War, there is a tendency among some governments in Europe and North America to wish to democratise the Third World. Development aid is made dependent on democratic reforms, and dictators in the South have to put up with external pressure as well as lectures on democracy from the North. Even the World Bank, although in a somewhat guarded manner and often concealed behind the concept of good governance, has discovered democratisation of the Third World. Under President Reagan, the US government proclaimed a 'crusade for democracy' that has now been revived by the Clinton administration. At the beginning of the 1990s, the European Union made development aid dependent on

1

democratisation. Theorists have discovered a new 'wave of democracy' that is enveloping the Third World and Eastern Europe.[1] According to Marc F. Plattner, democracy is not only ideologically more attractive than its alternatives, it is also economically and militarily stronger. It is his view that '… we may at least be entering a sustained period of peaceful democratic hegemony – a kind of "Pax Democratica"'.[2]

This zealous optimism is also to be found in the countries of the South, where one-time Marxist liberation movements discuss the value of free elections and the advantages of *civil society*,[3] previous military dictators prescribe new versions of democratisation, national conferences in Africa gently depose their dictators, and non-governmental organisations have become the new hope for a democratic awakening. The Organisation for African Unity proclaimed in 1990 the need 'to continue to democratise our societies and to consolidate democratic institutions'.[4] Almost every second-rate dictator routinely 'professes his faith' in democracy, while simultaneously banning parties, censoring the press and having opponents tortured in prison. This 'declaration of faith' in democracy, this soap-box democracy, often takes the place of democracy itself, and frequently occurs to the applause of Western politicians.

This general interest in democracy exists in a context in which the old political and ideological confrontation between the two antagonistic blocks has been overcome. The end of that division is reflected ideologically in, among other things, the broad unity that exists in the debate about democracy in the North and South, in the one-time East and West, among the social movements of the Third World and the governments of the industrialised countries. The increasing extension of this debate, however, has been achieved at some cost to depth and rigorousness. 'Democracy' doesn't mean the same for a non-governmental organisation in Mindanao as it does for the National Endowment for Democracy in Washington, nor is it the same for an unemployed youth in Algiers or for the World Bank. The fact that all the relevant actors today are in favour of democracy doesn't mean that they all have the same thing in mind.

The present article looks at the West's approach to democracy in the Third World and its strategy of democratisation. Any discussion of this subject has to begin from two historical premises: firstly, the highly contradictory policy of Western governments, up to the present, in their approach to democracy in the Third World and, secondly, the relation between Western ideology and Western interests where influence in the Third World is concerned. Neither of these points is particularly original, but they are systematically ignored in many writings and speeches on the subject.

Democratic and Anti-democratic Practices of the Past

Throughout the Cold War and afterwards, governments of the North have always expressed themselves clearly in favour of democracy in the Third World. This, in a different form, was also true of the Soviet Union. Democracy was always a positive concept, an openly declared goal. Behind the soap-box rhetoric, however, there was a long list of examples where democracy, free elections and human rights took second place when vested interests seemed threatened. The coups against democratic and elected governments in Iran (1953), Guatemala (1954), Brazil (1964) and Chile (1973), directed or massively supported by the CIA and other services, are just some of the best-known examples.[5] Such operations were publicly justified, as a rule, in terms of the Cold War and the Soviet threat. However, there were pragmatic reasons for intervention quite independent of the East-West conflict; for instance, oil interests in Iran were an essential element in the promotion of the overthrow there in 1953. The US Secretary of State at the time, John Foster Dulles, explained the link between interests and ideology in 1954 in the case of Guatemala. A democratically elected government in Guatemala had carried out a land reform that severely affected the interests of the US-owned United Fruit, which had massive banana plantations there as well as in other Central American countries.

> If the United Fruit matter was settled, if they gave a gold price for every banana, the problem would remain just as it is today as far as the presence of communist infiltration in Guatemala is concerned. This is the problem, not United Fruit.[6]

It is difficult to say whether Dulles wanted to provide an anti-Communist cover for a putsch that was mainly in the pursuit of economic interests, or whether these interests were really secondary. Both he and his brother, the CIA director, Allen Dulles, had economic links with United Fruit. The case of Guatemala was of particular interest because, even with a generous interpretation of events, no case could be made for Communist infiltration. The Guatemalan government was of a social-democratic, pragmatic-nationalist character and had been freely elected by a large majority of the population. In spite of this, the government was overthrown by the CIA's 'Operation Success' and was replaced by an unusually bloody dictatorship. The dictator was flown to the capital city to take over power in the US ambassador's aircraft.

There were a number of such extreme cases where democracy was directly destroyed by Western governments, but these were exceptions. Much more common were cases in which democracies were put under pressure, in which the military was strengthened in its opposition to civilian politicians, and in which influence was brought to bear secretly to prevent trade unions, left-wing parties or peasant associations from coming close to power. In addition, there were situations in which Western governments pushed for free elections but were unhappy with the outcome and then claimed irregularities; this happened in Nicaragua in 1984, despite numerous competent international observers declaring the election free and fair. There were also clearly invalid elections which Western governments were quick to declare democratic and correct. This had happened six months previously in Panama, where General Manuel Noriega had blatantly manipulated election results. Long after the facts had been made clear, officials of the US State Department declared that the elections 'appear to bring Panama into the democratic current that is moving so powerfully in this hemisphere'.[7]

In other cases, Western governments went even further and, in the name of democracy and freedom, supported, armed and financed anti-democratic groups, groups that abused human rights, even terrorist paramilitary groups. The best known example here are the Nicaraguan Contras, the activities of which were described by Admiral Stansfield Turner, who had been CIA boss under Carter, as 'state supported terrorism'.[8] The US government, however, defended the Contras as defenders of democracy. The Secretary of State for Defence at the time, Caspar Weinberger, told a congressional committee that the Contras 'were striving for democracy in their own country' while the Secretary of State, George Shultz, expressed the view that they were 'the product of a democratic revolt'. President Reagan described them as 'freedom fighters' who were 'fighting for democracy', and he compared them to the US founding fathers.[9] While support for UNITA in Angola or for Hekmatyar's Mujahidin in Afghanistan was not directed against democratic governments, the justification for Western support of these organisations, however, was equally absurd.

Interference, pressure, as well as economic, political or military intervention by the Northern powers in the Third World have occurred regularly. We should not forget, however, that these practices were not directed exclusively or mainly against democracy and their goal was not necessarily the weakening or destruction of democracy.

There was a similar number of equally massive interventions against states that had little or no democracy. Examples of the latter were US-supported coups and government changes in South Vietnam, the secret interventions against the pro-Soviet government of Afghanistan, operations against the Vietnamese-supported government of Kampuchea, as well as the (not very successful) military and intelligence measures against the governments of Libya and Cuba. These were also, in most cases, publicly justified in the context of the Cold War.

Western governments have also supported democratic developments. The massive financial support for democracy in Western Europe after the Second World War is the most important example, but there are quite a number of similar cases in the Third World. Examples include: President Kennedy's policy of supporting the 'democratic left' in Latin America; elements of President Carter's human rights policy; the demonstration of US political and military power in the Philippines that led to the fall of the Marcos dictatorship and contributed to the stability of the presidency of Corazon Aquino; US pressure on the military and the oligarchy in El Salvador to implement land reform and a series of elections; pressure on the Chilean dictatorship to introduce measures of democratisation; the violent military intervention in Panama and Grenada that brought about a return to parliamentarism. These policies were clearly contradictory and not always very successful. They may have been merely tactical. But even if they were not consistent or were not motivated by purely 'selfless' reasons, they nevertheless existed.

In spite of all the rhetoric, the North did not have, in the past, a firm policy either for or against democracy in the Third World. Sometimes it destroyed democracy, sometimes it was indifferent, and sometimes it provided massive support. The US expert on Latin America, Abraham F. Lowenthal, has come to a similar conclusion:

> From the turn of the century to the 1980s, the overall impact of US policy on Latin America's ability to achieve democratic politics was usually negligible, often counter-productive, and only occasionally positive. Although it is too soon to be sure, this general conclusion may hold true for the 1980s and 1990s as well.[10]

Ideology and Interests: A Historical View

Historically, Northern policy towards the Third World has been characterised by two apparently contradictory but in fact closely related features. Not surprisingly, the central concern was always the North's own economic, political, strategic or even ideological interests. Export markets, access to raw materials, the elimination of competitors, military bases, the settlement of one's own 'surplus' population, the security of sea routes – these and other similar factors have been the determinants of Northern policy towards the South. In the absence of such material interests, colonialism and indirect forms of imperial control would have had no attraction.

But colonialism and imperial domination were, at the same time, highly moral undertakings. Control of the Third World, however useful it might be (and the advantages were often overestimated), was often represented as altruistic. It was a civilising mission; barbarians were to be given all the blessings of Western culture. Imperialism and Northern control of the Third World were frequently understood to be beneficial. This missionary zeal often came cloaked as religion, in the form of Christianisation. Souls had to be saved, so the barbarians had first to be subdued and then Christianised. The Bible followed the sword, or vice versa, depending on the circumstances. The final act of subjugation of a foreign culture was to rescue it – by Westernising it.

The goal of the North was control of the South and the extension of Northern civilisation, whether for altruistic or imperialistic reasons. At the end of the twentieth century it is difficult to see what has changed in this basic structure. While Northern interests in the Third World are not the same as they were one or two hundred years ago, they have become stronger, not weaker. Today it is not spices or the slave trade, cotton, rubber plantations, or the sea route to India that are of interest to the North. The energy needs of the world (control of the Persian Gulf), the control of immigration (not the export of one's own population), the security of jobs in the export industries, the export of capital, the repayment of debts, the security of strategic raw materials, preventing the Third World from acquiring the same weapons of mass destruction to which the North has access – these are today the central interests of the North. With the end of the Cold War, control of the Third World is one of the basic principles of foreign policy of the Northern states. There is essentially nothing new in all this, nor is there in the linking of democracy and Northern domination of the South. Walden Bello has pointed out that the need to democratise (and, of course, to civilise) the Filipinos was one of the principal justifications for the 48 years of US colonial rule in the Philippines.[11]

The West as Driving Force

Why does the North now have an interest in the democratisation of the South? And why, precisely at this time, has this become such a major issue?

Now that the Cold War is over, support for democracy can't simply be dropped. After four decades of fighting the Cold War under the banner of democracy, this would be difficult to explain. In addition, the end of the competition between the two world systems means that the risks and uncertainties that would normally have accompanied democratisation in the Third World have been reduced. In the past, democratisation in the Third World often strengthened the positions of left-wing liberation movements and of the Soviet Union. Today, however, the extension of democracy brings no advantage to the Soviet Union. One of the preconditions for the recent emphasis on democracy is the fact that it has fewer risks attached. The scope for tolerance is greater today because a democratisation process that has got out of control, however unpleasant it might be, no longer offers advantage to some strategic opponent. Claude Aké has described how this new situation has affected Africa:

> The marginalisation of Africa gives the West more latitude to conduct its relations with Africa in a principled way. In the past, the West adopted a posture of indifference to issues of human rights and democracy in Africa in order to avoid jeopardizing its own economic and strategic interests and to facilitate its obsessive search for allies against communism. Now that these concerns have diminished, the West finds itself free to bring its African policies into greater harmony with its democratic principles.[12]

At the same time, the moral and political superiority of democracy, in relation to other forms of rule, remains unchallenged in the West. Its power of legitimation remains unbroken. The significance of this, however, is limited. Democracy is an attractive ideology and there is now greater scope for democratic experiments in the South. This may throw some light on the general political context but it doesn't really explain why Western governments are putting such emphasis on democracy in their actual policies. Not every political concept with some scope for implementation is given such prominence.

Why this democratic offensive by the West? Isn't there a real danger that this policy could lead to a loss of influence? Wouldn't a democratisation of the South lead to domestic interests being given greater priority than Western interests, and wouldn't this lead to the North having less control? Finally, could democratisation lead to the Third World getting 'out of control'? The indirect exercise of power through Westernised elites who share in the benefits of Northern control is, after all, simpler for the West than having to deal with elected representatives who have some obligation to their electors. Pakistan's nuclear program, for instance, is very popular among its people, and nobody believes that Pakistan could do without the atom bomb since India already has such a weapon. The more democratic the political process is in Pakistan, the more difficult it will be to prevent that country from acquiring nuclear weapons.

Since democratisation of the Third World could pose such problems for the West, how does one explain its demonstrative commitment to democratisation? Is this one of those exceptional cases where people are acting from moral motives, against their own interests? The so-called 'realist school' of political theory has often posed similar questions. Tony Smith poses such a problem, when he writes:

> Some, indeed, have felt it frankly dangerous to propagate democracy for others, arguing that it creates the illusion that anyone, anywhere, anytime might be democratic if only the United States showed them how.[13]

He adds the critical comment that this democratic policy is only 'democratic big talk', 'little more than patriotic flag waving' and 'not appropriate for the practical direction of American foreign policy'.[14]

This scepticism is often concealed behind a powerful impulse to bring democracy to the world. In fact, it is even seen as an historic duty. This feeling is expressed in the title of Gregory Fossedal's book: *The Democratic Imperative – Exporting the American Revolution*. This programmatic imperative is maintained in the text, as when the author writes:

> That higher purpose is a diplomacy of democracy, by democracy, for democracy: a foreign policy for securing the rights of man ... Either America will help secure the rights of man for all, everywhere, or America itself, as a free and democratic state, will perish.[15]

The policy of democratisation of the Third World is thus either criticised as empty rhetoric, or it is seen as central to all foreign policy (as a kind of Western fundamentalism). Both extremes are clearly unsatisfactory as a way of explaining Western policy. Democratic fundamentalism obviously has little to do with the real events of recent decades. There have been so many clear cases of anti-democratic policy that one can only be sceptical about the fundamentalist explanation. The view that the great powers would promote 'human rights everywhere and for everyone' is as romantic as it is unreal. On the other hand, if the Western policy of democratisation of the Third World were as unreal and idealistic as some of the 'realists' maintain, then how do we explain the fact that, in recent years, a large number of governments, quite aware of their own interests and their own power, have carried out such a policy? Should we simply categorise Presidents Carter, Reagan and Clinton as naive and idealistic because of their 'crusade for democracy'? Or could it be the case that there is indeed a 'realistic' policy behind these high-sounding and idealistic formulations?

The Creation of Western Self-identity

The ideological starting point of the Western crusade for democracy is relatively simple. During the Cold War, the West and Western politics were always legitimated by the fact that they were 'democratic' in both form and content. It was this that distinguished them from their Soviet opponent. 'Democracy versus Communism' was the fundamental slogan of the West during the Cold War. This was a foreign policy parole, an ideological weapon in the East-West conflict. To represent democracy against the principle of Communist dictatorship legitimated one's own existence, one's own policies, even one's own crimes. Support for repressive dictatorships in the Third World, or the organisation of coups against democratically elected governments were justified as long as they were part of the battle against anti-democratic Communism. The fine distinction between 'authoritarian' and 'totalitarian' dictatorships was introduced into the academic and political debate by Jeanne Kirkpatrick: 'authoritarian' dictatorships were supported by the West in the struggle against 'totalitarian' dictatorships.[16] The support for Pinochet or Mobutu, or the overthrow of governments in Guatemala or Iran, are just a few examples of this policy in action. The fact that such practices had little to do with Communism (and even less with democracy) but had, in fact, quite a lot to do with self-interest, didn't alter the mechanism, nor did the fact that the Soviet Union attempted to legitimate itself in a very similar manner.

Democracy was, at the same time, an important element of Western self-perception and identity. The East-West conflict was not just a matter of international politics but was also a factor that made it possible for political systems and for numerous individuals to adopt a very convenient and positive self-definition. The two elements of this self-definition were anti-Communism and democracy, each being a side of the same coin. This opposition allowed the West and its citizens to define themselves as good, and their opponents as bad. President Reagan's description of the Soviet Union as the 'evil empire' was plausible for many people only because of that country's undemocratic character.

With the disintegration of the Soviet Union and the disappearance of Communism as a credible threat, anti-Communism has become obsolete. It can no longer serve as a constituent element of self-definition for the West. Democracy, therefore, in spite of its loss of anti-Communist substance, has become even more important for the formation of positive self-identity since it has to fill the vacuum created by the loss of negative self-definition.

It should come as no surprise that the Northern states tend to identify democracy with themselves. This takes away some of the concept's indefiniteness, while adding to its charm. There are quite a few different though related reasons for this convenient equation. It is the product, first of all, of a rather abbreviated logic. The West (North) is democratic, as demonstrated by its struggle against Communism, and it respects, by and large, the rules of representative democracy and human rights. Western and democratic quickly become synonyms.

In the post-Cold War epoch, Western identity can no longer rely on the old schema. It's no accident that we are experiencing a boom in the search for new friend-foe images, that new identity definitions are in great demand. This is not just the case in the street culture of revived nationalism and racism; it is true also of the discourse of politicians and political scientists. Samuel Huntington had precisely this in mind when he wrote his essay, 'The Clash of Civilisations'. He postulates a struggle of 'the West against the rest', which is already a definition of identity, and identifies 'Western ideas' as the substance of Western political identity. Western ideas are, for him: 'Individualism, liberalism, constitutionality, human rights, rule of law, democracy, the free market, the separation of church and state.[17]

We don't have to deal here with some of the less significant flaws in Huntington's approach, for instance, the 'separation of *church* and state', which makes sense only in a Christian society. But, at a more serious level, by declaring these 'ideas' (is the 'free market' an idea? a value? a moral category?) to be *Western*, he is denying them to other cultures. For if these were *universal* values, then a 'clash of civilisations' would be meaningless. Freedom and democracy belong to the core of Western identity, and the people of the South are confronted intellectually with the false set of alternatives, either, if they support freedom and democracy, to consider themselves 'Western', or, if they don't want to be Western, to reject these values. This kind of intellectual imperialism would be funny were it not for the fact that so many take it seriously.

What is at stake, of course, is the structuring of Western identity after the end of the Cold War. We, the West, are firstly a unity (culturally); secondly, we are threatened from outside ('the West against the rest'); and, thirdly, we are morally and culturally superior (democracy and the other high values are, after all, 'Western' values). For people in the West who, with the loss of the enemy images of the Cold War, have also lost a part of their identity, such considerations may be comforting but, for the people of the South, they are rather a threat. A Western export of democracy, in this context, would not mean that the people of the South, so often oppressed by dictatorial regimes, would at last be able to rule themselves. As an export of Western ideology, as an ideological weapon against the 'rest of the world', such an export would in fact mean Westernisation. If democracy is essentially a Western value, then the export of democracy is ideological imperialism.

The link is frequently made between democracy and global Western supremacy after the Cold War. Marc Plattner has written: 'Thus we find ourselves living in the new post-Cold War world – a world with one dominant principle of political legitimacy, democracy, and only one Superpower, the United States'.[18] For most authors, the fact that both are closely linked is beyond doubt. Plattner's previously quoted phrase summarises the matter succinctly: 'peaceful political hegemony – a kind of Pax Democratica'. If democracy is Western, then a Pax Democratica (like the old Pax Americana) means Western rule, even if by means of 'peaceful political hegemony'.

In 1992, the American Enterprise Institute, a right-wing think tank, published a book by Joshua Muravchik, *Exporting Democracy – Fulfilling America's Destiny*. According to Muravchik, the USA should export democracy worldwide, but should concentrate principally on the two most important countries, China and the (then still existing) Soviet Union.

If we succeed, we will have forged a *Pax Americana* unlike any previous peace, one of harmony, not of conquest. Then the twenty-first century will be the American century by virtue of the triumph of the human idea born in the American experiment: all men are created equal and endowed with inalienable rights.[19]

Maybe the victory celebration after the collapse of the Soviet Union inspired some wishful thinking. This author writes regularly and with relish about the need for 'ideological combat', and he is perfectly aware that his notion of the export of democracy is basically the export of the American model. That is precisely his goal. The export of democracy and the export of the American model are identical since the West (in this case the USA) and democracy are two expressions for the same thing. Externally aggressive, internally creating consensus and identity – 'democratic' ideology can be a useful tool for policy.

Democratisation and the Foreign Policy Makers

It would be rash to automatically equate academic assumptions with the conceptions of foreign policy officials, even though the divide between universities, think tanks and politics is much narrower in the USA than it is in Germany, for example. Just as academics in North America often see their role as direct advisers to politicians, so also the politicians often feel under pressure to give their political practice an ideological gloss, and they look to whatever is the current intellectual fashion.

Anthony Lake is national security adviser to President Clinton and, with the Secretary of State, belongs to the inner circle of foreign policy decision making. In September 1993, Lake gave a talk at Johns Hopkins University on the fundamental principles of American foreign policy, in which he declared that democratisation of the world was one of the central tasks of the Clinton administration. Lake explicitly distanced himself from the 'clash of civilisations' concept and said that the desire for freedom was universal, not just Western. Lake gave the following summary of the US government's basic perspective:

> We see individuals as equally created with a God-given right to life, liberty and the pursuit of happiness. So we trust in the equal wisdom of free individuals to protect those rights: through democracy, as the process for best meeting shared needs in the face of competing desires; and through markets, as the process for best meeting the private needs in a way that expands opportunity.[20]

Lake recalled President Woodrow Wilson, who had 'understood that our security is influenced by the forms of government of other countries'. Building on this understanding, Lake formulated his overall conception of US foreign policy in the post-Cold War epoch:

> During the Cold War, even children understood America's security mission; as they looked at those maps on the schoolroom walls, they knew we were trying to contain the creeping expansion of the big, red blob. Today, at great risk of oversimplification, we might visualise our security mission as promoting the enlargement of the 'blue areas' of market democracies. The difference, of course, is that we do not seek to expand the reach of our institutions by force, subversion or repression.[21]

This then is the goal of US foreign and military policy, 'to extend the reach of our institutions', albeit by non-violent means. What is also remarkable about Lake's formulation is that the extension and export of democracy itself is not the goal, but rather the export of the particular variant, *market democracy*. This is because market democracies 'protect our interests and our security, at the same time reflecting values which are American and universal'. This policy of extending one's own reach and that of market democracies is thus both moral and guided by self-interest, and American moral values are represented as indistinguishable from universal values.

> Our strategy must be pragmatic. Our interests in democracy and markets do not stand alone. Other American interests will at times require us to befriend and even defend non-democratic states for mutually beneficial reasons. ... Beyond seeing to our base, the second imperative for our strategy must be to help democracy and markets expand and survive in places where we have the strongest security concern and where we can make the greatest difference. This is not a democratic crusade; it is a pragmatic commitment to see freedom take hold *where that will help us most*. Thus, we must target our efforts to assist states that affect our strategic interests, such as those with large economies, critical locations, nuclear weapons or the potential to generate refugee flows into our own nation or into key friends and allies.[22]

Lake is correct when he says that this really isn't a democratic crusade. In this strategy, there is a positive support for democracy; this is then linked with the market economy and both are fused in the concept of market democracy. These market democracies will then be supported where it is in the USA's interests to do so. Support for democracy turns out then to have two quite distinct dimensions: on the one hand, there is an abstract support for the concept and for the values associated with it and, on the other hand, it is to be instrumentalised for economic and strategic goals. This is the meaning of his key formulation, that the USA would move from *containment* to *enlargement*, in other words, from containment of the Soviet Union to the enlargement of its own strategic sphere of market democracies. With regard to the instruments of policy, the National Security Advisor disappointed those who had dreamed that, with the end of the Cold War, the United Nations or some other multi-national body could become the central instrument of international politics: 'We should act multilaterally where doing so advances our interests – and we should act unilaterally when that best serves our purpose. The simple question in each instance is this: what works best?'[23]

We have quoted Lake at length not just because of the fundamental and programmatic nature of his speech, but because its contents had been shared and approved by the US government. The Secretary of State, the US ambassador to the United Nations and President Clinton himself have all defended the positions represented by Lake. Clinton did so in his speech to the United Nations General Assembly in September 1993, when he spoke of the need 'to expand and strengthen the world's community of market-based democracies', not democracy itself.[24]

Three months after his speech to Johns Hopkins University, and with the full backing of President Clinton, Lake went a step further. He made clear the way in which, in his view, democracy and the market were linked. In a speech to the Council on Foreign Relations in New York, he explained his ideas on *enlargement*, on the expansion of market democracies:

And the benefits to America are clear. When old command economies turn to the market, they generate a huge appetite for American exports. Furthermore, free markets create middle classes. Middle classes favor the emergence of democratic governments that accommodate ethnic diversity, protect the rights of their citizens and enhance stability.[25]

The priority is now clear: apart from export possibilities, which are here of secondary importance, the starting point and the fundamental category is the market economy. The market creates the social actors that can, in turn, create democracy. Market and democracy are therefore not equal in importance; it is democracy that is the subordinate category, made possible, in the first place, by economic reforms. Democracy is the desired outcome of capitalism. In a speech on the strategy of enlargement in Latin America, a little later, he made clear that this is exactly what he meant. In Latin America, he said: 'a growing number of nations are striving to open their markets, privatise their economies and make their democracies work better through better governance'.[26] Here, once again, the major factors are the opening of the market (for the West, of course) and the privatisation of the economy; democracy is in third place. And what concerns him is the 'efficiency' of the democracies, not the substance of democracy itself. And the means of achieving this is 'good governance', a somewhat peculiar formulation having to do with higher levels of administrative competence. (On the meaning of this concept, see the contributions by Basker Vashee and Susan George in Chapters 10 and 11 of the present volume.)

In summary, one can say that the main goal of the democratisation offensive, as proclaimed and practised by the Clinton administration, is not to make it possible for the people of the Third World to determine their own destiny. It is aimed not at the marginalised poor majority of the population that is on the periphery of or outside the political process, but at the middle classes. Finally, democracy is here merely an instrument for the promotion and expansion of market economic reforms and will be supported only where it appears advantageous to US interests.

This is not meant to be a moral critique of US policy since it really isn't surprising that a major world power should pursue its own interests rather than the interests of marginalised populations in Third World countries. It is meant more as a caution, not to misunderstand, in an idealistic or naive manner, the policies, intentions and strategy of the USA and of Western governments in general. When governments speak of 'values' and proclaim a strategy of democratisation for the Third World, this should not be confused with some genuine desire to make the world a better place. What is involved is the pursuit of self-interest, and democratic reforms are of interest only as long as they contribute to this.

The Struggle Over the Concept

If the United States, or Western governments in general, are of the view that democracy is only a political expression of capitalism, and if they support democracy only if it can be instrumentalised for other goals, then this opens up two problems. Firstly, there is the question of the concept of democracy, its substance. How can 'democracy' be used in the South as an instrument of Northern control without draining the concept of democracy of meaning? What do Western governments understand by this concept? The second problem is a more practical one: how, in concrete terms, can democracy be used in the South as an instrument of Northern supremacy? Let us begin with the first problem.

The most common concept associated with 'democracy' and 'democratisation' is 'freedom'. Almost every political current and almost every political regime attempts to instrumentalise and claim this concept for itself. This doesn't mean that the concept is automatically meaningless or unusable. But it does demonstrate two things: firstly, the need to elucidate how and for what purpose the concept is used and, secondly, the fact that what is generally at stake here are not analytic categories but battle concepts. The concept of democracy is itself a battlefield.

Whoever can successfully and credibly lay claim to the democratic concept and define it (in his own way) has created for himself an invaluable political advantage. Likewise, the one that can successfully characterise an opponent as 'undemocratic' has already half won the battle. Almost nobody would voluntarily accept such a characterisation and almost all political forces would fight to take possession of the democratic concept for themselves. Pluralist liberal governments of Western Europe and North America, Stalinist 'democratic centralists', numerous dictatorial or authoritarian regimes in the Third World, all want to be 'democratic' or to embody the model of a true democracy.[27]

Democracy was always a battle cry in the attempt to seize or hold on to power. It is the lack of clarity in the concept itself that makes this situation possible. It doesn't really help very much, to define democracy as 'the rule of the people', an undoubtedly appropriate but still unclear definition. What exactly can or should 'rule' mean? Does it mean the assumption of government office or of total power? Can or should this rule be limited by juridical or other means, or would this be a limitation of popular rule? Is a dictatorship of the majority possible, and could this manifest itself in the dictatorship of a party? Does 'rule by the people' automatically mean party pluralism? And, last but not least, who are the 'people'? Is this an ethnic national category or does it simply refer to the inhabitants of a geographical unit? When do immigrants become part of the 'people'? What about national, linguistic, religious or political minorities? When do they belong to the 'people' that rule, and when not? Most of these questions are anything but new but they are still unresolved. Liisa

Laakso, in Chapter 12 of the present volume, points to the differences between an instrumental and a substantial use of the concept of democracy.

One of the reasons why the concept of 'rule by the people' is so unclear is the fact that every political force and every individual can themselves define what is meant by 'rule' and by 'people'. Anthony Lake seems to limit the subject of democracy to the middle classes and the actors in the free market, and is obviously not disturbed by the marginalisation of whole layers of people. Alternatively, one can see it as the political and economic self-determination of really existing people and groups, or one can sacrifice these really existing people to an abstract concept of popular rule that could only be enforced against the resistance or the interests of many individuals. This Rousseau-style concept may have found its fulfilment in fascism and Stalinism, but it is not alien to democratic modernisation: when the middle classes, by means of the free market, come to power and construct democratic institutions for and on behalf of the people, this is in the service of the 'people', even when the majority of them are impoverished by the same free market. To ask the majority their opinion or, what's more, to let them decide, would only be a hindrance to this kind of democratisation.

In this situation, to believe that a mere 'declaration of faith in democracy' is adequate is either to indulge in illusions or to be involved in attracting others to one's own particular interpretation. Democracy is not something that we can or should simply profess belief in; it is rather a very uncertain category, the definition of which is a matter of political controversy. Whoever wants to limit the option to 'democracy – yes or no', and avoid the conflict over the character, limits and preconditions of democracy, may be suspected of wanting to instrumentalise this concept for their own purposes. 'Democracy – yes or no' is often a demagogic mechanism, an attempt to conceal a friend-foe setup behind the veil of an unassailable concept. The demagogy consists in identifying democracy with oneself, its opposite with one's opponent and, on this basis, to demand a 'declaration of faith' in democracy. This is, to a great extent, the political core of the democratisation offensive of Western governments. The victors in the Cold War have claimed the concept for themselves, endowed it with their own particular meaning, and turned it into an instrument of ideological dominance. Who, after all, could deny to the United States, the 'cradle of democracy' (ancient Greece is too distant), the authority to claim this concept for itself?

In the current discourse of Western elites, 'democracy' is identified with 'freedom', and the latter is identified with *economic* freedom, which in turn is equated with 'free-market economy'. Democracy and the free market economy thus become synonymous. Democracy becomes the political form of capitalism. This is the basic thesis behind the Clinton administration's support for 'market-oriented democracies'. Since, after the end of the Cold War, there is no relevant alternative to capitalism, the notion of democracy has been narrowed politically to conform to the Western conception, in which it is seen merely as the liberal political organisational form of a market economy, with a minimum of rules pertaining to electoral mechanisms and political rights. According to this conception, there can be no democracy without a market economy because, in the absence of the latter, the citizen would lack economic freedom. Democracy, within this discourse, is the organisation of political freedom, while capitalism is the corresponding organisational form of economic freedom. Democracy, in this way of thinking, is nothing but the application of the capitalist, free-market form to politics: parties and politicians are the providers of services who have to compete for customers (voters); votes are money and voting is buying. The democratisation offensive of Western governments is essentially the ideological component of an offensive on the part of capitalism that wants to reap the benefits of its victory in the Cold War. The last pockets of resistance on the map of globally victorious capitalism can now be overcome.

What is at issue here is the global imposition of the Western economic and development model. This doesn't mean that all Third World countries could or should follow the Western path. It doesn't imply that all countries of the South could acquire carbon copies of the North American or Western European political system, nor does it suggest that all these countries could adopt Germany's 'social market economy' or the USA's economic and social order. The preconditions for this simply don't exist and this is not, in any case, the real goal. The goal is the imposition of the Western model in the sense that the Western states acquire access to the markets of all countries, to their economic and political structures, that Western dominance is secured on a global scale. The Pax Democratica is actually a new Pax Americana, a new Western (or North American) century.

Warren Christopher, the current (1995) US Secretary of State, has repeatedly stated the USA's claim to leadership of the world, a position continued from the Reagan and Bush administration and with which President Clinton is fully in agreement. To quote just one example: 'America must lead. And the need for American leadership is undiminished. We are a blessed and a powerful nation.

We shoulder the responsibility for world leadership.'[28] Shortly after this statement, Christopher claimed that 'the need for American leadership is one of the fundamental tenets of the Clinton administration'. He went so far as to say that the US leadership of the world was a central element of a 'Clinton doctrine'.[29]

The democratisation offensive of the US government doesn't contradict this; it is merely an expression of it. The Western democratisation offensive is an element of the Western dominance of world politics following the end of the Cold War.

Democracy as a Technique for Domination of the South

Although, from a governmental perspective (not from the perspective of non-governmental organisations, human rights groups and the like), the export of democracy is meant to be an element in the politics of domination, this doesn't automatically make it happen. The question still has to be asked: is this merely an ideological offensive or are Western governments actually succeeding in using democratisation, in a practical and concrete manner, as an instrument of domination in the Third World? There are two levels of interest here: democratisation as an element in the strategy of low-intensity warfare, in the sruggle to suppress or prevent popular resistance, and democratisation in connection with World Bank programmes for structural adjustment.

Dealing With Resistance Movements

Military planners agree that fighting resistance movements is not a purely military operation; social, economic and political measures are essential. This is not the place to go into detail about the concept of low-intensity warfare and other forms of military struggle against resistance movements, but some remarks are necessary.[30] Since the purely military suppression of guerrilla movements is generally not possible (because of the way that guerrillas are part of the civilian population), a combination of military and civil measures is essential to success. The goal is not so much military victory as control over the population. This can be achieved by force but, in the longer term, some positive incentive is necessary. An overly repressive policy will only drive the population into the arms of the guerrilla movement. The population, therefore, has to be at least neutralised or, better still, won over positively, and this can only be achieved if they are given the feeling that their situation can be improved within the framework of the existing order. In the final analysis, they have to be given the *hope* that they have a better future without armed resistance and they have to be convinced that it is the guerrillas, and not the government or the army, that is the main obstacle to an improvement in their situation. Propaganda alone cannot achieve that; reforms are needed. Improvements in human rights, land reform and democratic changes are standard elements of such a strategy. The problem consists in implementing reforms that are not mere window dressing, that are genuine enough to give real hope, but are not such that would fundamentally alter the power structures of the country. The point in defeating the resistance movement is precisely to stabilise the power structures (reformed if necessary). Any serious disturbance in the balance of power could destabilise the country even more and undermine the anti-guerrilla war.

Our interest, in the present essay, is focused on the element of democratisation, and there are two decisive elements here. The first of these is dealing with the problem of dictatorship. Repressive dictators can have a mobilising effect on people; they unite the resistance and can make the conflict a much more intense one. The pacification of the Philippines in the mid-1980s required the overthrow of the Marcos dictatorship, otherwise the mass mobilisation would have escalated and become more radical. 'Democratisation', in the sense of overthrowing a hated dictator, is a way of preventing political radicalisation, at least where this can be successfully achieved in a controlled manner. What is decisive here, of course, is that the dynamic that is set off brings 'moderate' forces to power, and not the radical opposition. The second element is the need, after the necessary cleansing process, to institutionalise elections that are credible. They can't be patently falsified and they have to satisfy certain minimum standards. They cannot, however, lead to an electoral victory by the forces that one wants to keep from power. The whole plan would be pointless if elections gave power to a guerrilla movement.[31]

Standard procedures for the organisation of such elections include: the division of the opposition into, on one side, cooperative ('moderate') groups and, on the other, militant groups that will be excluded, in principle or in practice, from participating in the election; the creation of conditions for participation in the electoral process (such as the handing over of weapons by the opposition while government forces retain theirs, or the formal acceptance by the opposition of the legitimacy of the existing government); the kidnapping, 'disappearance' or political murder of opposition leaders, to make it difficult or impossible for the opposition to wage an

election campaign; limitations on media reporting of opposition activities; the non-registration of refugees or of inhabitants of particular regions; an election law that favours the governing party or those areas under government control. If necessary, the risks of an election can be reduced through a manipulation of the count as long as this isn't too blatant or on too massive a scale. Such restrictions are aimed not at the middle layers but at the poorer and more marginalised sections of the population and their organisations. Peasant farmers, agricultural workers, the unemployed and squatters are intimidated by a massive military presence in their electoral regions or on polling day itself, while the more educated and better-off sections of the population are offered the smoothest poll possible. In this way, not only is the opposition split (between those that vote and those that boycott the poll), but a social line is also drawn between the lower sections of society and the potential leading elements from the middle layer.

As a rule, these measures will be effective enough to weaken the opposition without giving them a sufficient reason for withdrawing from the polls. If the opposition does withdraw, then they are attacked as 'undemocratic', or it is claimed that their withdrawal was motivated by the certainty of losing.[32] Some of these restrictions are political, coming from the government, others are administrative, for instance, deriving from the regulations of an electoral commission, while others come from groups that are not officially linked with the government – death squads, militias, police or army officers operating unofficially, or hired groups from that sector of society that one used to describe as 'lumpenproletariat'.

The result of all these measures can be that the weakened and divided opposition loses the election (to the extent they didn't boycott it). Observers may criticise numerous individual points about the election but, in the end, they will confirm that, technically, the election was run properly. And if there are many citizens that still have their doubts about the propriety of the process, they can be consoled by the fact that democracy has at least made a beginning.

A central goal of such an electoral process is the alienation of the middle layers from the hard core of the opposition and their social demobilisation. The degree of mobilisation and the level of political participation of the poorer sectors of the population has to be reduced and political behaviour has to be limited to the act of voting. If this goal is achieved, then the ruling elites have achieved an important victory; the smaller the degree of social mobilisation, the more secure they can feel. And once this democracy has been established, it is much more difficult than before to justify militant resistance because this resistance is now directed against an elected government, no matter how 'imperfect' that election may have been.

Structural Adjustment

A possibly even more important level at which democratisation is used as an instrument of domination by Northern governments and domestic elites is that of economic structural adjustment, under the direction of the International Monetary Fund and the World Bank.

These institutions, which are controlled by the major industrial countries, grant credits to the highly indebted countries of the Third World, credits that are conditionally linked to the implementation of a so-called structural adjustment program. I don't want to describe in detail the function of these programs.[33] It can be briefly summarised as follows:

- devaluation of the national currency and a limiting of domestic and external debt; liberalisation of foreign trade;
- imposing positive interest rates, improving prices for manufacturers, changing the price system to the advantage of direct producers;
- reduction in state budget expenditure, especially in subsidies;
- reduction in the role of the state by means of the privatisation or closure of state-owned enterprises;
- a restrictive wages policy;
- cutting personnel and subsidies in the public sector.

In the recent period, this catalogue of requirements has been expanded. Stefan Mair gives us the following summary of the demands placed on Kenya at the end of 1991 by the Paris Club of donor countries: 'The reforms demanded included deregulation of the economy, a reduction in the budget deficit, strong measures against corruption, political democratisation and liberalisation.'[34] This catalogue of measures imposed on the indebted countries are part of what the US national security adviser, Anthony Lake, describes as 'opening of markets'. The liberalisation of foreign trade is only another description of the same goal. The policy of structural adjustment is really a way of forcing a market orientation on the Third World, both internally and in its external trade. Let us recall that it is precisely the 'market democracies' that the democratisation offensive is meant to support and extend. This is the material essence of the democratisation offensive. For the Third World, this means a new internal political order: economic liberalisation, privatisation, opening to the world market, access to internal markets for the big international corporations, reduction and weakening of the state sector. These policy decisions are not taken by the countries themselves but are imposed from outside by the IMF and the World Bank. A complete market orientation is the obvious goal of this packet of measures and it is therefore completely in keeping with the demands from Washington, Bonn and London.

But how does democracy fit into all of this? For the official ideology, it is quite simple; the market and democracy are twins and a strengthening of the market will lead, via the advancement of the middle layers, directly or indirectly to a strengthening of democracy, although this may take a little longer to achieve. The reality is unfortunately different. The structural adjustment programme aims at reducing and weakening the state apparatus in the Third World.[35] This doesn't mean a sensible de-bureaucratisation, a reduction in the overblown and incompetent state apparatus. There could be no argument against that. But the state apparatuses of the Third World, in Africa for instance, are not being made more effective or more efficient by means of sensible reductions. What is happening, in reality, is that important functions are being taken away from them. Basker Vashee has described the effects of such policies:

In many countries of the Third World, especially in the poorer countries, the state is important for the survival of millions of people. There is no other institution there that looks after the needs of the people, that helps to improve the general living standard, in such things as education, subsidising incomes, food production. If the state doesn't spend money on these things, then the people have no other alternative. Debt repayment by governments in the Third World means that these governments have less money to spend on their own people. The results are declining levels of nutrition and the absence of health care. People have to pay for their children's education and they can't afford it. The children have to leave school and join the ranks of the unemployed. The general level of poverty rises significantly as soon as the state cuts its spending on social programs.[36]

When international financial institutions, behind which the real decision makers are the USA, Western Europe and Japan, impose cutbacks on Third World governments, the effects are felt not just in areas of social spending but also in the functioning of the state itself. The IMF and the World Bank, for ideological reasons, are dismantling the state and removing from it some of its most important classical functions. Numerous state economic functions are being privatised, transferred to the private sector in the Third World or to international corporations. Other functions, particularly in the fields of economic and fiscal policy, that have such a big influence on politics and social policies, are being internationalised, in other words, are being exercised, directly or indirectly, in Washington or London. The central economic variables in the impoverished and indebted states of the Third World are often being negotiated today directly between their finance ministers and the World Bank/IMF, the latter with their centre in Washington, and it is always the Third World finance minister who has the least clout. Third World parliaments, and even prime ministers, are often excluded from the decision-making process and quite often don't even have access to the necessary information. Even domestic state budgets are often decided by bureaucrats of the IMF and the World Bank who have never been directly elected and are not responsible to anyone. In many regions of the Third World, the state is being gutted. A country that doesn't have sovereignty over its own national budget has no chance of determining its own destiny. In addition, international financial institutions intervene directly in these countries, determining interest rates, deciding on the value, especially the devaluation, of the national currency and dictating food and energy prices through cutbacks in state subsidies. Weak and poorly functioning state apparatuses are not made more efficient but are in fact made devoid of any function whatever. In these poorer countries, the privatisation and internationalisation of so many state functions leaves just an empty hull of a state, something no Northern state would tolerate in spite of all their enthusiasm for the ideology of privatisation and free markets. What the state is left with in so many Third World countries are the police, the army and the secret service: the instruments of repression. By their nature, these can't be privatised or transferred to the North.

In this way, state structures are created with an undeniable 'market orientation'. A 'democratisation' of these structures is then purely a matter of form, with no risks involved. Having taken away their most important functions, the North then 'democratises' the empty hull that remains. Elections can be organised, possibly even ones that are free and fair. But they are largely irrelevant since the elected representatives no longer have the power to organise and structure their own country's policies. Claude Aké has aptly described this as a 'democratisation of disempowerment'. Democracy is reduced to the administration of a situation that essentially cannot be improved: democracy becomes meaningless. This also answers the question why the North needs to have no fear of democratisation in the South: in the context of structural adjustment, it is only the empty shell of democracy.

One result of this is that the citizens in the South become disillusioned with their 'democracy' and with their own state, and indeed they must become disillusioned since the governments and politicians elected by them do not solve, and are incapable of solving, the most fundamental problems confronting them. Disillusionment leads to a turn away from democracy, to apathy or to pointless rebellion.

Jorge Dominguez has described this problem in the English-speaking Caribbean:

> At issue is the need to recognise that liberal democracy cannot survive if all the pillars on which it was built are destroyed without replacing them with new foundations. The society's habits of resistance to dictatorship could turn against the liberal democratic order.[37]

In Chapter 6 of the present volume, Niala Maharaj deals with precisely this problem with respect to Trinidad.

The 'national state', in many cases still in its infancy, is becoming discredited and other forms of identity, ethnic or ethnic-religious, become more important. The democratisation offensive of the North has been effective but it has not enabled the people of the Third World to determine their own destiny. In the wake of its 'enlargement' policy, the dominance of market-oriented democracies has been increased, the influence of the North has been strengthened and the people of the North have the good feelings that come from seeing themselves as global democrats. But the possibilities of Third World people determining their own fate have decreased even further. In spite of all the democratic mechanisms, in spite of the regular and, to a certain extent, free elections, little exists in the South of a real 'rule by the people'.

Democratisation of the South

Some critics use strong words to describe this situation. Cyrus Bina has written, in a different context: 'American global hegemony has taken precedence over the cause of liberty and the pursuit of happiness.' He accuses the USA of 'crying for democracy and preventing it simultaneously.'[38]

That isn't entirely true. The West does *promote* democracy in the Third World. But it does this in a very specific way, which serves its own interests. As long as its own interests are not damaged, it prefers free and fair elections to dictatorship. This is for both material and ideological reasons: elected governments have greater legitimacy and can be a basis for greater stability. Elected government can also demand more from their populations than illegitimate dictators. Why then should the West be against democracy?

The problem is not that Western governments are against democracy in the Third World. The problem is that, apart from a general ideological sympathy for democracy, they take for granted that, in the South, democracy is subordinate to their own economic and strategic interests, and they try to shape democracy in such a way that it becomes a mere form of free-market management. For Western governments, democracy is a real problem, but it is a problem of management. For the people of the South, however, it presents quite a different problem, namely, how to determine their own destiny and not to be ruled by either local dictators or foreign or international financial officials. The question is not 'democracy – yes or no'. The question is: 'should democracy be the fundamental category of self-determination and control over one's own destiny, or should it be a technique of rule that guarantees international hegemony and rule by native elites?'

For progressive or even not so progressive movements in the Third World, the situation is a difficult and complex one. Quite frequently, they find themselves in a situation where dictatorial or oligarchic systems are weakened or overthrown and elections are held; but the purpose of this process is not infrequently to marginalise them. Democracy becomes market economy, of some relevance to the social elites and the middle layers, but to which the majority of the population remain mere spectators. It is difficult for them to fight against this because they could easily go back to the old forces of dictatorship and repression. But they can't be satisfied with this development because it is directed precisely against themselves. There is a strong temptation to withdraw from the struggle for state power and to give this some positive gloss as a strengthening of civil society. But this would be to play into the hands of those who instrumentalise democracy as a technique of domination.

Whatever the importance of an active civil society, democracy has much to do with the state. The problem today is not just who controls the state, although that continues to be important. There is also the problem of what vision of the state progressive movements, non-governmental organisations and civil society are able to develop. The struggle must revolve around the state, around the influence and

participation of the poor and marginalised sectors in the state apparatus. This cannot be left to the elites and the middle layers. It isn't just a matter of justice. Rueschemeyer, Stephens and Stephens concluded, in their extensive study, that: 'The dominant classes accommodated to democracy only as long as the party system effectively protected their interests'.[40]

While the majority of the population, and especially the lower social classes, need democracy in order to have any kind of influence on society, for the power elites democracy is only one option among several.

But the goal of this struggle around the state must be its strengthening, the restoration of its ability to function effectively. In many countries of the Third World, the task is to make the state, for the first time, into an effective instrument of social policy. Elections have no point if the state is not capable of fulfilling its functions. The Northern policy of weakening the state in the Third World is aimed at weakening the one institution that might have some minimal prospect of resisting Northern domination. It also increases the atomisation of the Third World, which then confronts the dominant powers of the North only as an object, not as an active, self-defending or autonomous subject.

There are two aspects of democratisation that are important. It cannot be denied that certain *forms* of democracy are indispensable and valuable achievements. Free and fair elections[41], civil and human rights, and the accompanying processes and legal concepts should not and can not be relinquished or devalued simply because they have been instrumentalised in a particular political context to serve the interests of Northern domination (and the stabilisation of Southern elites). To respond to the North's democratisation offensive by opposing free elections and other democratic forms, as some Islamic currents and some authoritarian rulers in Asia are now doing, would be fatal. What is important is that these often merely 'formal' elements of democracy should be strengthened, defended and developed further.

But that isn't enough. If democracy is to be something more than a collection of useful techniques for changing governments, if it is to be understood and fought for as an organisational form in which people and societies can determine their own destiny, then we have to be concerned about the second important aspect, its social substance. Beyond formal or juridical equality, beyond the notion that all citizens have equal rights before the law and in the election booth, it is essential to fight, not just for the principle, but for the *real possibility* of democratic participation by the whole population. The decisive question is therefore 'Democracy for whom?'. Will it be for the educated and well-off minority who will play an active part in the structuring of their own society, or will the large majority of the people in the Third World, people who are now on the periphery or totally outside the global market economy, be able to participate in a real and practical way? Will women, landless day-workers, marginalised ethnic minorities, the illiterate, workers and the unemployed have a real chance, for the first time, to be part of the political process in their own countries and to exercise real power?

Edelberto Torres-Rivas gives us the following description of the situation in Central America:

> In Guatemala, El Salvador, Honduras and Nicaragua, democracy is practised at the centre, (the capital cities, small towns) and is weaker in the (rural) periphery. The upper classes make use of it, now enjoying direct participation; for the peasants, there is still just the politics of clientship, the merely formal exercise of the vote, and repression.[42]

The export version of Western democracy undercuts the participation of the majority of the people. The practical combination of democratic formalities with the exclusion of the effective participation of the majority of the people is what 'market democracy' is all about. Those who drop out of the market, who are unable to compete, have practically no influence, even though theoretically and legally they may have the same rights.

Economic marginalisation leads to political marginalisation. People on the border of or below the subsistence minimum cannot really exercise their democratic rights, even if they were allowed to. A democratic development which involves the broad majority of the people is made even more difficult by the privatisation of education, which excludes from the education system those that are unable to pay. Those people who want to organise societies by giving unlimited freedom to market forces, according to Social Darwinist principles, can expect no real political equality, whatever the democratic forms and processes.

The basic social and economic structures, especially the free market, reinforce the power of social elites and favour a version of democracy in which a change of government is merely a change within different sections of the elite. The poor majority has no choice but to accept its marginalisation, to limit its participation to the occasional act of voting, or, by organising and mobilising, to make itself into a factor of power that attempts to put its stamp on civil society. But this dualism is only a semi-democracy: the elites have power and civil society groups may criticise them. This is better than nothing but it is not the structure of a genuine democratically organised society. The social substance of democracy will only be achieved when civil society is not outside the structure of power but actually imprints its stamp on it.

This, however would be democracy, not market democracy, and it would have some negative effect on the political and economic interests of the North.

Notes

1   See Samuel P. Huntington, *The Third Wave; Democratization in the Late Twentieth Century*, (Norman, Oklahoma: University of Oklahoma Press, 1991).

2   Marc F. Plattner, 'The Democratic Moment', in Larry Diamond and Marc F. Plattner (eds), *The Global Resurgence of Democracy* (Baltimore: Johns Hopkins University Press, 1993) p. 32.

3   See Jochen Hippler, *Pax Americana?: Hegemony and Decline* (London: Pluto Press, 1994) pp. 105–10.

4   Quoted from Heather Deegan, *The Middle East and Problems of Democracy* (Buckingham: Open University Press, 1993) p. 132.

5   See David P. Forsythe, 'Democracy, War, and Covert Action', *Journal of Peace Research*, vol. 29, no. 4 (1992) pp. 385–95.

6   Quoted from Richard H. Zimmerman, 'Guatemala as Cold War History', *Political Science Quarterly*, vol. 95, no. 4 (1980–81) p. 639.

7   Elliot Abrams, in a speech on Panama, 30 May 1987.

8   In a statement before a Congressional Committee: 'US Support for the Contras – Hearing Before the Subcommittee on Western Hemispheric Affairs, US House of Representatives', 16–18 April 1985, p. 9.

9   'Weinberger: Aid to UNO "Vital" to Democracy, US Defence', *USIS, US Policy – Information and Texts* (6 March 1986) p. 23; 'Shulz Urges Support for Aid to Nicaraguan Resistance', *USIS* (28 February 1986) p. 16; 'Reagan Urges Congress to Pass Contra Aid Package', *USIS* (6 March 1986) p. 18.

10 Abraham F. Lowenthal, 'The United States and Latin American Democracy: Learning From History', in Abraham F. Lowenthal (ed), *Exporting Democracy; The United States and Latin America* (Baltimore: Johns Hopkins University Press, 1991) p. 261.

11   Walden Bello, *People and Power in the Pacific; The Struggle for the Post-Cold War Order* (London: Pluto Press, 1992) pp. 30ff.

12   Claude Aké, 'Rethinking African Democracy', in Diamond and Plattner (eds), *The Global Resurgence*, p. 71.

13   Tony Smith, 'Making the World Safe for Democracy', *Washington Quarterly*, vol. 16, no. 4, p. 200.

14   ibid.

15   Gregory Fossedal, *The Democratic Imperative; Exporting the American Revolution* (New York: Basic Books, 1989) pp. 238–9.

16   Jeanne Kirkpatrick, 'Dictatorships and Double Standards', *Commentary* (November 1979) pp. 34–45.

17   Samuel P. Huntington, 'The Clash of Civilizations', *Foreign Affairs*, vol. 72, no. 3 (Summer 1993) p. 40.

18   Marc F. Plattner, 'The Democratic Moment', in Diamond and Plattner (eds), *Global Resurgence*, p. 28.

19   Joshua Muravchik, *Exporting Democracy; Fulfilling America's Destiny* (Washington: AEI Press, 1992) p. 227.

20   'Lake Says US Interests Compel Engagement Abroad', *USIS* (23 September 1993) p. 7.

21   ibid., p. 8.

22   ibid., pp. 8–9.

23   ibid., p. 11.

24   'Clinton Warns of Peril Ahead Despite Cold War's End, Address to UN General Assembly', *USIS* (29 September 1993) p. 4.

25   Anthony Lake, 'Effective Enlargement in a Changing World', *USIS* (20 December 1993) p. 21.

26   ibid., p. 23.

27   Saddam Hussein's Iraq is an unusual exception. As an Iraqi diplomat said in a conversation with the author: 'Of course, Iraq is not a democracy, but a dictatorship. But, for our country, that is the only possible way to solve our problems.' In numerous conversations with members of the government in Baghdad, nobody claimed that Iraq was a democracy.

28   Warren Christopher, June 1993. Quoted in Jochen Hippler, *Pax Americana?: Hegemony and Decline* (London: Pluto Press, 1994) p. 91.

29   Quoted from Hippler, *Pax Americana*, p. 91.

30   See Jochen Hippler, 'Low-Intensity Warfare – Key Strategy for the Third World Theatre', *MERIP Middle East Report* (New York/Washington) vol. 17, no. 1 (January/February 1987) pp. 32–8.

31   On the problem of elections, see Edward S. Herman and Frank Brodhead, *Demonstration Elections – US Staged Elections in the*

Dominican Republic, Vietnam and El Salvador (Boston: South End Press, 1984). In spite of occasional rhetorical overkills, this book contains interesting material.

32   Classic examples of this were the elections in El Salvador in 1982 and 1984. For security and other reasons, the opposition boycotted the election. See Jochen Hippler, *Menschenrechte und 'Politik der Stärke' – USA und Lateinamerika seit 1977* (Duisburg: Trikont, 1984) pp. 157–67.

33   See the various books on the debt crisis and the World Bank by Susan George, for example: *A Fate Worse Than Debt* (Harmondsworth: Penguin, 1987).

34   Stefan Mair, 'Kenias Weg in die Mehrparteiendemokratie', SWP –S387 (Ebenhausen, July 1993) p. 41.

35   These remarks do not apply to all regions of the Third World. The successful economies of South East Asia are not affected because, not having large debts, they don't undergo structural adjustment. The Central Asian states of the former Soviet Union receive better treatment, for political reasons. I am grateful to Welmoed Koekebakker (Amsterdam) who pointed this out to me.

36   From the transcript of a recording.

37   Jorge I. Dominguez, 'The Caribbean Question: Why has Liberal Democracy (surprisingly) Flourished?', in Jorge I. Dominguez, Robert A. Pastor and R. Delisle Worrell, *Democracy in the Caribbean; Political, Economic and Social Perspectives* (Baltimore: Johns Hopkins University Press, 1993) p. 25.

38   Cyrus Bina, 'The Rhetoric of Oil and the Dilemma of War and American Hegemony', *Arab Studies Quarterly*, vol. 15, no. 3 (Summer 1993) p. 14.

39   A very useful distinction between four types of present-day transition to democracy is made by Georg Sorensen, *Democracy and Democratization* (Boulder: Westview Press, 1993) pp. 47ff.

40   Dietrich Rueschemeyer, Evelyn Huber Stephens and John D. Stephens, *Capitalist Development and Democracy* (Chicago: University of Chicago Press, 1992) p. 287.

41   Interesting case studies of elections in Central America can be found in John A. Booth and Mitchell A. Seligson (eds), *Elections and Democracy in Central America* (Chapel Hill: University of North Carolina Press, 1989).

42   Edelberto Torres-Rivas, 'Democracy and the Peasants', in Kees Biekart and Martin Jelsma (eds), *Peasants Beyond Protest in Latin America* (Amsterdam: Transnational Institute, 1994) p. 54.

2

Social Movements and Democratisation in the Philippines

Joel Rocamora

By intention the most democratic organisations in the South are progressive political parties and a wide variety of social movements. Their main source of power is the mobilisation of quiescent sectors of the population into political activity. Their political banners – justice, equality, fraternity – lie at the core of the democratic idea. But these movements' experience of 'democracy', the way the term has been used in their countries' history, has generated ambiguity.

In most of the countries of the South gross economic inequalities, political control by small minorities and often outright repression exist under governments that call themselves democracies. Representative institutions are playgrounds of the rich and powerful; elections circuses in reverse where freaks buy and terrorise their audience. Even dictators such as Somoza in Nicaragua, Marcos in the Philippines and Mobutu in Zaire cloaked themselves in the mantle of democracy. In these and many other countries in the South scepticism of democracy is the understandable result.

The very fact that Western countries push 'democratisation' in the South is another source of scepticism. Memories of a colonial past under the same Western countries as (hardly democratic) colonial masters remain. After nominal independence former colonial masters and other defenders of the 'free world' frequently intervened, often in favour of antidemocratic oligarchs. Societies shaped by these colonial and neocolonial dispensations display grossly undemocratic distribution of economic power that makes a mockery of formal democratic institutions.

Still another source of scepticism about democracy derives from the Marxist tradition common to a majority of the progressive political parties and social movements of the South. The Marxist critique of capitalism and identification of egalitarian socialism as an alternative is the main reason for its popularity among progressives in the South. But key elements in the twentieth-century manifestations of Marxism, especially as practised by communist

32

parties following the precepts of Lenin and Stalin, also introduced antidemocratic tendencies among progressives in the South.

In the Marxist framework the state is the institutionalisation of the 'dictatorship of the ruling class/classes'. Thus, the 'dictatorship of the bourgeoisie' under capitalism will give way to the 'dictatorship of the proletariat' under socialism. Lenin later introduced the idea of the 'vanguard' – the communist party, a conspiratorial party tightly organised around the principle of 'democratic centralism'. As interpreted by Stalin, if socialism is organised as a 'dictatorship of the proletariat' then the party of the proletariat, the communist party, logically becomes the ruling party. The first socialist state, the USSR, became a one-party state, a model followed by all subsequent communist states.

For most of this century many progressives in the South believed that Marxism provided the best critique of capitalism, that the Leninist communist party was the best instrument for fighting capitalists and the Stalinist state the most effective way to organise rapid 'socialist construction'. Attacks on the communist model as antidemocratic and totalitarian were brushed aside as self-serving capitalist propaganda. Communist countries were defended not just because they represented the socialist future but, equally importantly, these countries provided substantial material and political support to progressive movements in the South.

Soviet intervention in Hungary and Czechoslovakia, Khrushchev's attacks on Stalin and the Sino-Soviet dispute slowly eroded this consensus. Popular movements in Eastern Europe and the Soviet Union slowly revealed the anti-democratic core of communist regimes. The communist model had been discredited enough by the time the FSLN won in Nicaragua in 1979 and the ZANU/ZAPU in Zimbabwe a year later, that their Marxist leaders avoided using the model. Gorbachev's reform movement and the subsequent collapse of communist regimes in Eastern Europe and the Soviet Union provided the final nail that sealed the coffin of Stalinist socialism in the South.

The collapse of the Marxist-Leninist paradigm has led to profound disillusionment and disorientation among progressives in the South. But it has also freed these movements from ideological blinkers that blocked their path to growth. Without these blinkers they will be better able to assess their past and face the challenge of the future. One key challenge is facing up to the often antidemocratic structure of Marxist political parties and their relations with popular organisations. Another is the continuing ideological offensive of the advanced capitalist countries, an offensive couched in the powerful language of democracy.

Low Intensity Democracy

Democracy has always been a key instrument in the ideological arsenal of the advanced capitalist countries. This does not mean that these countries have always supported democracy in the South.

More often than not dictators and authoritarian regimes of various stripes were supported. Anti-communism and its catch phrases provided a thin ideological veneer for supporting dictators against their democratic opponents. On other occasions, however, Western countries have undermined authoritarian regimes and helped to establish formal democracies. To understand the current post-Cold War drive towards 'democratisation', its immediate Cold War predecessor during the Reagan era of the 1980s will provide illustrative contrast.

In 1982, US President Reagan announced a 'Crusade for Democracy' in a speech to the British Parliament in London. From then on the USA, long a staunch supporter of anti-communist authoritarianism in the South, adopted a more positive attitude to facilitating democracy. From the mid-1980s, the USA found itself increasingly forced to take sides against political clients in their moments of crisis: Marcos in the Philippines, Chun Doo-Hwan in South Korea, Duvalier in Haiti, Pinochet in Chile and Stroessner in Paraguay. This policy reversed an earlier policy of selective support for authoritarian regimes based on a distinction between 'totalitarianism' and capitalist dictatorship, a doctrine associated with former US Ambassador to the UN Jeanne Kirkpatrick.[1]

The overthrow of these authoritarian regimes was first and foremost the result of popular impetus. Except in a few isolated cases, the US did not actively push against authoritarian regimes and for democracy until the authoritarian regime was already in the midst of domestic crisis, usually brought on by its failure to resolve deep economic and political problems or stem the rapid development of popular anti-dictatorship forces. In most cases, the US response was based on the realisation that authoritarianism could not sustain itself indefinitely and that democratisation was inevitable in the long term. Therefore, it was preferable for the USA to gain a guiding influence in the process of democratisation before it developed along lines out of US control, as had occurred in the latter part of the 1970s in the Iranian and Nicaraguan revolutions.

By the early 1980s, the USA realised that conditions were favourable for an 'apertura', a democratic opening, in many countries of the South, given that years of military rule had greatly reduced the organisational power of the Left labour and other popular forces. The USA wanted stable and viable 'democratic' regimes that could preempt more radical change by incorporating broad popular forces in electoral participation yet which guaranteed continuity with the anti-communist and anti-reformist traditions of their military or civilian authoritarian predecessors. Democracy as defined by the US was in fact a component of low intensity conflict, an instrument of intervention – 'low intensity democracy'.

The Philippines provides a perfect example. By the mid-1980s, the Marcos dictatorship was deep in crisis. The collapse of the Philippine financial system in 1982 combined with the international debt crisis of that year to produce a depression which saw the Philippine gross national product decline by more than 15 per cent in a span of three years. The murder of opposition leader Benigno Aquino in 1983 added a political dimension to the regime's economic crisis. Aquino's murder by government soldiers mobilised urban middle-class groups and divided the upper classes into pro- and anti-Marcos factions.

Through most of the period of the dictatorship, starting with Marcos' declaration of martial law in 1972, the underground National Democratic Front (NDF) led the anti-Marcos struggle. Starting with armed guerrillas in the countryside, the NDF spread to urban areas mobilising hundreds of thousands of workers, urban poor and student youth. Despite their anti-communist ideological bias, newly mobilised middle-class groups were forced to work with the NDF which was better organised for mass actions – for what at the time was called the 'parliament of the streets'.

The US had supported the Marcos dictatorship with massive amounts of economic aid loans and military assistance. As late as 1981 at Marcos' inauguration after a rigged presidential election, then US Vice President George Bush extolled Marcos' 'adherence to democratic principles'. Marcos' 15-year monopoly of power had badly divided the upper classes. Large sections of the middle-class had been won over to the NDF or were in uneasy alliance with it. NDF mass organisations and its guerrilla army were growing by leaps and bounds. To head off these dangerous developments, the US at first tried to get Marcos to share power with some of his upper-class opponents. When Marcos proved recalcitrant, the US began to manoeuvre to replace him.

Because popular opinion was universally anti-dictatorship, the US had to find a replacement with good democratic credentials. This was difficult to do because even upper-class anti-Marcos people such as Aquino's widow Corazon were allied to the open organisations of the Left. The US encouraged Aquino and other middle-class anti-Marcos people to break with the Left. Fortunately for the US, hardliners in the Left leadership helped out by breaking up the anti-dictatorship front in May 1985. Soon afterwards US pressure forced Marcos to schedule early elections in February 1986, then assisted opposition candidate Aquino in her bid to unseat Marcos. When Marcos used fraud and violence to win the elections, the US denounced the election. When a combined military rebellion and popular uprising broke out, the US warned Marcos against using his troops and later when he decided to leave provided the helicopter that brought him and his family to exile in the US.

The US continued to intervene throughout Aquino's term to head off reform on the one hand and to defend Aquino against a series of coup attempts on the other. When Aquino attempted land reform and negotiations with the guerrillas in her first year in office, the US held back military and economic assistance and worked with big business and the military to get Aquino to abandon reform and fire the more liberal members of her cabinet. After Aquino capitulated to US pressure, the US then defended her against military rebels by threatening to cut off military aid in the event of a successful coup and during the 1990 coup attempt threatening coup forces with air power from the US airbase near Manila.

Democratisation and the New World Order

In the past, the Western push for democracy in the South was almost always pitched in anti-communist terms. The collapse of Reagan's 'evil empire' has generated a new dynamic. Anti-communism has suddenly disappeared as the all-purpose ideological instrument to be used against all kinds of real and perceived enemies of the advanced capitalist countries in the South. The political forms existing in the world are being restructured to reflect and accommodate the present realities of the global political economy. In the ideal New World Order as conceived by present hegemonic power-holders all states will be capitalist and incorporated in the capitalist world economy to a greater or lesser degree. All states will also be 'democratic'.

In this crusade, democracy is given specific meanings that exclude other meanings. Samir Amin points to one distinct trend occurring at the same time as the push for democracy:

> ... a generalised offensive for the liberation of 'market forces' aimed at the ideological rehabilitation of the absolute superiority

of private property, legitimation of social inequality and anti-statism of all kinds ... The coincidence of these two trends makes ours an era of intense confusion ... The 'market' – a euphemism for capitalism – is regarded as the central axis of any 'development' and such development is seen as part of an 'ineluctable worldwide expansion'. The desirability of total openness to the forces governing worldwide evolution and simultaneous adoption of an internal system based on the 'market' are taken to be self-evident. Democratisation is considered the necessary and natural product of submission to the rationality of the worldwide market.[2]

The imposition of this logic is accompanied by a bias in many Western studies of politics in the South – a conviction that external factors do not play a significant causal role in the political and economic development of these countries. The seeming lack of congruence here with what Amin pointed to is explained away by seeing the economic intervention of for example the IMF as part of the natural processes of the global marketplace. The IMF does not impose policies, it is merely correcting 'market distortions' generated by the local economy. The reality is that IMF strictures determine overall economic policy in many countries in the South which are under IMF agreements. Fiscal and monetary parameters set by the IMF determine foreign exchange rates, interest rates, budget deficits, rates of inflation and as a result overall rates of economic growth. Structural Adjustment Policies pushed by the IMF, the World Bank, regional banks and by bilateral ODA donors mandate deeper economic changes in key sectors of the economy.

The political implications of these economic policies are massive. The political component of IMF economic conditionalities is weak government – limits on state licensing and regulatory functions, the privatisation of government corporations, cutbacks in subsidies to disadvantaged economic groups and in social spending in general. Underlying these demands is an assumption common to mainstream democratic theory, the separation of economic and political power. Democratic political theory mandates explicit limits on what citizens can do through bills of rights and extensive legal systems. Government is supposed to 'represent' public interest, to work for the public good. In the economic sphere, the 'market' is supposed to perform all these functions, including imposing limits on what economic units, individuals or corporations can do in relations with each other. Unless absolutely necessary, under the IMF regime, the political sphere should be kept out of the economic sphere.

In the South, this framework is used to justify the yawning gap between claims of 'democracy' in the political sphere and concentration of power in the economic sphere. The obvious way in which economic power is used to win elections and gain position in battles in legislatures and bureaucracies is supposed to be part of the 'normal' workings of democracy. While giving leeway to the political action of oligarchies, Western democratic theory limits popular participation to elections. As Fernando Rojas puts it:

> Political struggles being fought in arenas other than electoral politics are either ignored, condemned or forced to follow the channels of electoral politics. Necessary spaces for conflictive and/or challenging expressions of civil society are thereby reduced or silenced by the monopolisation of politics at the state level and the privileged legitimation granted to the electoral process.[3]

The ideological framework of 'democratisation' therefore works at several levels to limit participation. The denial of international intervention, especially in economic policy, removes a key arena of struggle. Fiscal and monetary policy in many countries of the South are negotiated by finance ministers and central bank governors with the IMF with little input from legislatures or the public. Preference for a weak state inhibits political action in the economic sphere, not only to regulate the 'market' but also to organise social reform. Finally, popular political participation is limited to elections, to selecting among candidates determined by political parties which are often only coalitions of upper-class fractions.

Progressive Democracy

The progressive response to the 'democratisation' offensive of the West is conditioned by several things. Firstly, by the exclusion of most Left groups from the state and state power and the Left's preference for accumulation of power through organising lower classes. Secondly, by the interplay of its own ideological traditions, theoretical lessons from its history and the components of the Western 'democratisation' framework. The Left's position in society challenging oligarchic centres of power from the vantage point of the powerless provides a strongly democratic core to Left political action. In the past, the Left tended to shy away from the debate on democracy because it was an ideological arena dominated by the capitalist West and its allies in the South. Lessons drawn from the collapse of 'actually existing socialism' and from its own history of struggle and the opportunities opened by the continuing crisis of political rule in the South have pushed the Left to pay more attention to democracy. In the third of a series of conferences of progressive Latin American organisations held in Managua in July 1992, delegates affirmed that:

> Revolution and democracy are indivisible. Democracy refers both to the internal life of leftist organisations and to the democratic political and social organisation of society. The latter includes formal representative democracy (elections, the rule of law, traditional civil and political liberties etc.) as well as social justice, economic democracy, grassroots participation and empowerment and democratisation of the state ... The history of Eastern Europe made it crystal clear that absolute power is an error and that people do not live on bread alone', affirms FMLN's Joaquin Villalobos. 'There is no democracy without revolution and no revolution without democracy'.[4]

There is continuing opposition to the West's push for 'democratisation', partly because of the West's history of support for antidemocratic regimes in the past and because specific prescriptions are perceived as limiting democracy to the ideological justification of ruling oligarchies. Considerable attention is also devoted to the antidemocratic impact of Western pressure on economic policy-making. The role of the IMF and the World Bank in shaping macro-economic policy removes the most important arena of policy-making from the elected representatives of the people. These policies, moreover, are designed specifically to increase the economic power of local elites and to limit the role of government in social reform in the process exacerbating the antidemocratic distribution of economic power.

At the same time, there is increasing recognition of the still-evolving changes resulting from the end of the Cold War and the ongoing reorganisation of power in international capitalism. Without the ideological blinkers of anti-communism there may be certain situations where Western countries may support progressive elements in the South. The continuing erosion of American hegemony in international capitalism which has led to the evolution of competing trade and investment blocs is likely to spill over into competing political thrusts which will provide openings for progressives in the South. While the situation in Haiti remains unresolved, American support for the progressive President Jean-Bertrand Aristide is considerably different from support for a Cory Aquino, a Duarte or a

Cerezo. This has blunted the usual no-questions-asked opposition to American intervention.

There are also situations such as in the Philippines where oligarchs stand in the way of further capitalist development and reform elements can work with the IMF and the World Bank for the dismantling of oligarchies. Progressive economists in the Philippines have developed a position in support of selective dismantling of protectionist policies and are working slowly to educate the popular movement about the need to move away from traditional Left opposition to import liberalisation. But while increasing attention is being devoted to more imaginative progressive economic policy positions on a range of issues, there is continuing opposition to IMF austerity policies – to the narrow fiscal and monetary parameters imposed by the IMF. Apart from specific economic policy arguments, this position is premised on opposition to Western arguments for a limited and weak state.

Progressives in the South are in the process of sorting out contradictory elements in its approach to the nature of the state. On the one hand, in reaction to the concentration of power in the state and the deliberate emasculation of mass organisations in former socialist states, progressives in the South are more open to the idea of limiting state power. On the other hand, they believe that organising social reform and economic development requires a strong state that is capable of blunting the economic power of oligarchies. They also believe that a strong state is necessary for negotiating with international capitalism, whether it is with the IMF and other multinational financial institutions or with private transnational corporations.

Coming to terms with the antidemocratic results of socialist one-party states has also led to serious rethinking of strategies for progressive change. Armed struggle as the main revolutionary strategy is being reconsidered not just because the possibility of victory has receded with the demise of socialist states as sources of weapons, but because of the way preoccupation with armed struggle has distorted relations between political parties running armed struggles and mass movements which support them. The requirements of clandestinity in an armed struggle has generated pressure for revolutionary political parties to impose the kind of control on mass organisations that many now see as antidemocratic.

Revolutionary projects may unfold in the context of political and social pluralism, and civic and electoral competition. Far from arguing that the 'new world order' has rendered popular struggles and revolutionary aspirations obsolete, the new Left is proposing that recent developments have opened the possibility for social confrontation to take place on the political terrain without a military dimension and that meaningful social change can be achieved through battles waged within the realm of civil societies liberated from military influence.[5]

The growth of autonomous social movements has generated a lot of discussion about 'civil society' and its relation to the state. There is considerable confusion about the meaning of 'civil society' – the phrase is alternately used in its Gramscian, Eastern European and Latin American meanings. The most pervasive meaning given to the term, one closest to its Latin American usage, focuses on relations between political parties and social movements and on the need to maintain the dynamism of these movements after victory. The rapid growth of development NGOs which play key roles in organising, especially in the countryside, has also contributed to 'civil society' discussions. NGO activists are particularly careful about their relations with Left political parties and see their role as continuing even after the victory of revolutionary movements.

Using the Nicaraguan experience for inspiration, new Left theorists say that revolutionary movements can win only if they give full play to the potential of mass organisations and social movements. Seizing state power remains important. Having seized state power, revolutionary parties should change the balance of economic power in order to bring about economic as well as political democracy. Government institutions, especially the military and police, should be reoriented away from their repressive functions. If revolutionary governments are to take democracy seriously, however, they must also take elections seriously. Doing that requires the establishment of a multi-party system and acceptance of the possibility that ruling revolutionary parties can lose elections. Even if they lose an election, as the FSLN did in Nicaragua, these parties can increase their chances of returning to power in later elections if they do not demobilise mass organisations – if they maintain the vitality of organisations in civil society. The state in this framework becomes a neutral arbiter of electoral battle, moving it away from the Marxist analysis that the state is always a 'dictatorship of the ruling classes'.

The increasing importance given to democracy in the theory and practice of progressive organisations in the South is only marginally the result of Western countries' push for democratisation. While open to the limited possibilities of this campaign, these movements are by and large critical of Western countries' push for democracy in their countries. The more important influences derive from these movements' reading of the lessons from the collapse of socialist states in Eastern Europe and the Soviet Union, ideas drawn from progressive groups in the West and from their own revolutionary practice. As such this development has a firm base and is likely to continue into the future.

Whether or not these movements succeed in their struggle for their version of democracy in their countries is difficult to predict. Leaders of these movements are fully aware that international conditions are not conducive to the success of their struggles. When Brazilian Workers Party presidential candidate Lula looked like he had a good chance of winning in 1990, party activists worried about whether the progressive movement would be best served by his victory. These activists were afraid that the international and local bourgeoisie might sabotage a victorious Lula and force him to impose anti-popular economic policies. Whether or not these fears are justified is a matter of great debate among left activists all over the South.

Increasing attention to elections as an element in overall strategy is more than the result of decreasing hopes for the success of armed struggle. It forms part of the continuing dynamism of social movements, especially those based in rural and urban lower classes. Ideas on direct democracy as a necessary complement to representative democracy have taken shape in a growing movement to participate actively in local governments. Although more advanced in Latin America, participation in local governments is also growing in the Philippines in the aftermath of the collapse of the NDF and the passage of a Local Government Code in 1992. Progressive groups are also active in pushing for a shift from presidential to parliamentary forms of national government.

Revolutionary movements used to use ideologies that promised quasi-religious certainty as a way to make it possible for militants to make the difficult sacrifices of revolutionary struggle. Recent history has made it impossible to continue to believe in those certainties. Those who persist in revolutionary struggle understand that the kind of ideological certainty demanded in the past is not only impossible under current conditions but also sets the ideological basis for authoritarianism.

The increasing importance given to democracy introduces another element of uncertainty because democratic processes cannot be organised neatly. But the commitment to progressive participatory democracy is already deeply embedded in movements in the South. Democracy with all of its uncertainties will continue to be central to progressive struggles.

Notes

1 These sections are taken from an article on 'Low Intensity Democracy' that Barry Gills and I published in the *Third World Quarterly*, vol. 13, no. 3 (1992).

2 Quoted in Rocamora and Gills, 'Low Intensity Democracy', p. 503.

3 Fernando Rojas, 'Political Transition in Latin America: The Unchallenged Imposition of Formal Democracy', *CEDLA Lectures* (October–November 1989), p. 3.

4 William Robinson, 'The Sao Paulo Forum and Post-Cold War Thinking in Latin America', *Monthly Review*, vol. 44, no. 7 (December 1992).

5 Robinson, 'The Sao Paulo Forum', p. 7.

3

Political Elites and the Process of Democratisation in Africa

Peter J. Schraeder[1]

Introduction

Dozens of countries in Africa, Asia, Latin America and Eastern and Southern Europe made transitions from authoritarian to democratic forms of governance from 1974 to 1994, prompting American proponents of democracy, such as Samuel P. Huntington, to speak of democracy's 'third wave' of expansion in world history (the first two waves began in the 1820s and the 1940s).[2] In the case of Africa, this third wave – often referred to as Africa's 'second independence' – largely began in 1989 and was sparked by the end of the Cold War and the downfall of communist regimes in Eastern Europe and the former Soviet Union.[3] Although one should not downplay the important impact of international factors on democratisation in Africa, the primary impetus for this process was a variety of internal trends that prompted African ruling elites to negotiate with pro-democracy movements, such as severe economic stagnation and decline, the so-called 'crisis' of the state, and popular demonstrations against rising human rights abuses and political repression.[4]

Africanists initially viewed the democratisation process in highly optimistic terms. 'The prospects for democracy in Africa are now unquestionably brighter than they were three decades ago', explained Michael Clough, Senior Fellow for Africa at the New York Council on Foreign Relations, 'if for no other reason than that Africans now know all too well the costs of failure of democracy'.[5] Adopting a more sanguine viewpoint, René Lemarchand warned of 'compelling reasons to fear that the movement toward democracy may contain within itself the seeds of its own undoing', including the continued ability of authoritarian ruling elites to manipulate the democratisation process for personal gain at the expense of the welfare of their respective political systems; the inability of opposition forces to rally around a credible alternative due to the religious, ethnic and regional divisions evident within most African societies; and the crushing socioeconomic impact of internal economic decline and externally enforced structural adjustment programs (SAPs).[6] Indeed, according to Claude Aké, the director of the Centre for Advanced Social Science at Port Harcourt, Nigeria, what one is witnessing in Africa is the 'democratisation of disempowerment' – a process whereby newly installed multi-party systems merely allow rotating and competing portions of ruling elites to exploit the vast majority of Africa's largely rural populations who continue to remain disempowered from their respective political systems.[7] Yet regardless of whether they are optimistic or pessimistic, very few (if any) Africanists reject the normative value of a process that replaces authoritarian, single-party systems with more democratic forms of governance.

Differences of opinion over the strength and future viability of democracy in Africa are matched by an ongoing debate over the proper roles of external powers in facilitating the democratisation process. According to Huntington, for example, the United States and the West in general should be in the forefront of ensuring that the 'global democratic revolution' reaches 'virtually every country in the world', including those on the African continent.[8] Scholars operating from a more critical perspective seriously question the implications of external pressures for reform. Africanist Timothy M. Shaw emphasises that Western pressures for what in essence constitutes the 'Westernisation' of Africa and the other regions of the Third World literally amounts to a form of 'neocolonialism'.[9] Several Africanists have even begun to speak of the 'recolonisation' or the 'second scramble' for Africa (the 'first scramble' was formalised in 1884–85 when the colonial powers divided up the African continent at the Berlin Conference in Germany).

The primary focus of this chapter is the internal dimension of the democratisation process in Africa, most notably the varied roles of ruling elites as facilitators and impediments to change. For the purposes of our analysis, the ruling elite is defined as the small, privileged leadership sector of African societies that controls the reigns of government and sets the rules of the political system. This ruling elite historically assumed power through either civilian-based independence movements or military-based *coups d'état* (and, to a lesser degree, guerrilla insurgencies) and often finds itself in conflict with other elite groups seeking change within their respective societies. Among those elites seeking change include opposition political leaders, lower-ranking military officers, elders, the heads of women's organisations, ethnic and religious leaders, labour and student activists and powerful financial and business interests.[10] After briefly outlining the authoritarian (that is antidemocratic) tendencies of

African ruling elites from the 1950s to the 1980s, including a discussion of official rationales for the creation of single-party political systems, the majority of this chapter focuses on the responses of these elites to popular demands for democratisation beginning in 1989.

The First Generation of African Ruling Elites and the Movement toward Authoritarianism (1960–89)

The first generation of African ruling elites was confronted by two major paradoxes during the heady independence period of the 1960s. First, although they were raised and politically socialised within highly authoritarian, colonial political cultures, these leaders achieved independence at the head of hastily constructed, untested and ill-suited 'democratic' political systems left behind by the retreating European powers. The colonial powers sought to establish a system of 'checks-and-balances' in which newly created, independent offices of the president, legislatures and judiciaries would 'balance' each other's power and 'check' the rise of authoritarian leaders. For example, whereas the relatively decentralised Westminster model of parliamentary governance was grafted onto the authoritarian structures of colonial rule in the former British colonies, the more centralised French formula of ensuring a strong executive – the Élysee model – was similarly introduced into the former Francophone colonies.[11] This state of affairs contributed to an 'authoritarian-democratic' paradox in which ruling elites trained within an authoritarian tradition were expected to abide by the constraints and 'rules of the game' of Western democratic society.

The first generation of ruling elites also faced what can be termed the 'great expectations–minimal capabilities' paradox. Newly elected political elites were confronted by popular expectations that the fruits of independence – most notably higher wages and better living conditions – would be quickly and widely shared after the departure of the former colonial powers. In almost every case, the African 'state' (that is the institutions of governance and power within a country) as constructed just prior to independence simply did not have the capabilities required by ruling elites to satisfy public demands.[12] In addition to remaining heavily dependent on the former colonial power (or new surrogates such as the US or the former Soviet Union) for trade, investment and even personnel to staff key governmental ministries, the capabilities of the state often were constrained by mono-crop and mono-mineral-based economies, low levels of education among the general population and perverse infrastructural development favouring the maintenance of external links as opposed to internal development.[13]

In almost every case, the contradictions associated with the above-noted paradoxes of independence prompted the first generation of ruling elites to systematically dismantle the ill-suited 'democratic' political systems left behind by the former colonial powers and replace them with more authoritarian forms of governance based on centralisation of power and personal rule.[14] It is important to note, however, that ruling elites were not exclusively interested in acquiring power for power's sake, but often shared many high-minded principles (for example, quick development to satisfy popular demands) that, at least in their eyes, made the suspension of democratic practices an undesirable necessity.

Yet what originally were envisioned as 'temporary' suspensions of democratic procedures, in practice usually became long term in nature. Even the most principled of African leaders, such as Julius Nyerere of Tanzania, Kenneth Kaunda of Zambia and Félix Houphouët-Boigny of the Ivory Coast, invariably turned to a variety of authoritarian measures to enhance their powers and ensure political survival at the expense of other elite groups within society. Among those actions taken were the stacking of enlarged bureaucracies, militaries and police forces with members of the leader's ethnic or clan groups (as well as with members of their primary ethnic or clan allies); the rejection of 'federalist' principles (such as constitutional amendments) that guaranteed autonomy for ethnic, linguistic and religious minorities; the emasculation and, in many cases, the disbanding of independent parliaments and judiciaries that at best became 'rubber stamp' organisations incapable of serving as a check on the powers of the executive; the imprisonment or exile of vocal critics from a variety of competitive elite groups, including labour unions and student organisations; and the outlawing of rival political parties and the disbanding of multi-party political systems in favour of the creation of single-party systems.[15]

The creation of single-party regimes constituted the most important authoritarian trend undertaken by African presidents during the post-colonial era.[16] These parties ranged from Chama Cha Mapinduzi (CCM), a mass mobilising party created by Julius Nyerere (the former socialist president of Tanzania), to the Workers Party of Ethiopia (WPE), a vanguard party created by Mengistu Haile Mariam, the former Marxist president of Ethiopia, and the Kenya African National Union (KANU), the sole ruling party of capitalist-oriented Kenya that was created by former President Jomo Kenyatta and strengthened by his successor, Daniel arap Moi. In short, regardless of their political ideology, nearly all ruling elites exhibited authoritarian tendencies that inevitably resulted in the creation of single-party political systems during the post-colonial era.[17]

Ruling elites offered numerous rationales to justify what in essence constituted the establishment of political monopolies over their respective political systems.[18] The first justification was that single-party regimes were reflective of traditional African political systems as they existed prior to the imposition of direct colonial rule.[19] According to this argument, the single-party system was not to be perceived as a 'temporary aberration' from a universal norm of multi-party democracy, but rather as a 'modern adaptation of traditional African political behaviour'.[20] Unlike the divisive nature of Western multi-party systems (that is one party emerges dominant and the others are marginalised) the concept of single-party democracy was heralded as conducive to promoting traditional African norms of consensus and inclusivity of the entire community. It is for this reason that Tanzanian President Nyerere chose *ujamaa* (the Kiswahili term for 'brotherhood') as the symbolic guiding principle of the CCM and his country's 'return' to traditional African socialism.[21]

The necessity of overcoming existing and potential 'crises' constituted the second rationale for the creation of single-party systems. For example, crises of development ('How best to quickly develop our society?'), crises of administration ('How do we quickly educate the required leaders?') and, most important, crises of governance ('How do we quickly satisfy rising popular demands for the fruits of independence?') led ruling elites to argue against 'frittering away' scarce resources on competitive politics.[22] Just as unity was crucial to the attainment of independence from colonial rule, argued the ruling elites who in most cases led the independence struggles during the 1950s and the 1960s, so too was unity important once that independence had been achieved. Equally important, ruling elites feared that multi-party systems would lead to the fragmentation of ethnically, religiously and regionally divided African societies and therefore perceived the single-party system as one of the most important tools for transforming artificial, colonially inspired states into true nations.

Finally, numerous ruling elites, most notably those from the African-Marxist tradition, justified the creation of single-party systems in terms of the 'vanguard' role that single parties were expected to play. Drawing upon the Leninist concept that the 'masses' of individual African societies needed to be led by an 'enlightened elite', the single party was envisioned as serving in the vanguard (that is in the 'forefront') of promoting and protecting socialist revolutions on the

African continent.[23] The single party was oriented toward the future evolution of African societies, particularly in terms of ensuring industrial development and the promotion of basic human needs such as guaranteed access to adequate food, shelter and health care.

Regardless of the rationales offered by its political proponents, the nearly 30-year experiment with single-party systems is regarded by academics from all points of the ideological spectrum as, at worst, a complete failure and at best, as achieving few if any results that would make such a system preferable to other forms of democracy.[24] To be sure, single-party systems have differed in terms of governance and their general treatment of their respective populations. As explained by Samuel Decalo:

> The single party system has been the means to govern society relatively benevolently – by Julius Nyerere, Kenneth Kaunda and Félix Houphouët-Boigny in Tanzania, Zambia and Ivory Coast respectively; more harshly but still responsibly – by Kamuzu Banda and Thomas Sankara in Malawi and Burkina Faso; to venally plunder it – as have Mobutu Sese Seko and Samuel Doe in Zaire and Liberia; or as a camouflage for personal or class tyranny – as under Jean-Bedel Bokassa, Mengistu Haile Mariam or Macias Nguema in the Central African Republic, Ethiopia and Equatorial Guinea.[25]

However, even in the most benevolent of examples, such as Nyerere's *ujamaa* experiment in Tanzania, the country made significant strides promoting mass literacy and the provision of basic human needs only at the expense of a failed overall economy that witnessed an annual average decline of 7 per cent in agricultural output. One of the primary reasons for this failure was that the initially 'voluntary' villagisation program – the centrepiece of the *ujamaa* ideology in which peasants would be grouped together in new communal villages – ultimately became coercive in nature. Specifically, many peasants were forced off of their traditional (and productive) lands to villagisation projects chosen by party bureaucrats that were either poorly conceived or simply inappropriate for farming practices. If the state inevitably became coercive (and therefore counterproductive to the goal of development) in the most benevolent of single-party systems, one has only to imagine its impact on the development of the most tyrannical single-party systems such as that of Mengistu's Ethiopia.

The most notable problem associated with the single-party experiment of Tanzania and its contemporaries was that it led to a 'stagnation of ideas'. For example, although legislative candidates were allowed to run against each other under the unified banner of the CCM, they were not permitted to question either the socialist domestic ideology or the foreign policy of the Nyerere regime. Candidates could debate the instrumental aspects of carrying out party-approved policies, but were unable to offer alternatives even in the face of obviously misguided policies. In this and other cases, ruling elites who felt they 'knew best' restricted the range of political debate to such a degree that the single party ultimately became a means for maintaining control rather than a dynamic tool for promoting change and development.

The growing stagnation of single-party rule from the 1950s to the end of the 1980s was matched by the growing power and influence of African militaries and military elites.[26] Specifically, a veritable explosion of military *coups d'état* led to the replacement of entrenched civilian elites with their military counterparts. Such coups became the primary form of regime change in African politics during the post-colonial era. From 1956 to 1986, for example, 60 out of 131 attempted *coups d'état* resulted in the overthrow of the civilian regime of an African country.[27] (If one includes reported 'plots' against an established government, the number of potential episodes of military involvement equals 257.)[28] Only three African countries – Botswana, Cape Verde and Djibouti – have not experienced some form of extra-legal involvement by their military forces within the political arena. Most important, the emergence of military elites as power brokers within African executive mansions and parliaments did not usher in a new period of democracy and prosperity. Rather, it soon became clear that military *coups d'état* usually led to new forms of military-led authoritarianism as bad as, if not worse than, their civilian counterparts.[29]

The Democratisation Process and the Second Generation of African Elites (1989–)

The combination of a variety of international and domestic trends beginning in 1989 ushered in a period of democratic transition previously unknown in African history. First, the downfall of single-party communist systems throughout Eastern Europe and the former Soviet Union – the intellectual heartland of single-party rule – sent shock waves throughout the African continent. Ruling elites who had depended on the Eastern bloc nations for economic and military assistance, such as Mengistu in Ethiopia, suddenly found themselves abandoned by their former allies. Most important, once single-party systems had become almost completely discredited throughout the former Eastern bloc (except in the People's Republic of China, North Korea and Cuba), the rationales that ruling elites offered for the maintenance of single-party systems throughout Africa became especially hollow.

Cold War-inspired international factors were reinforced by a host of domestic trends at the end of the 1980s. First, growing levels of political repression and human rights abuses throughout the African continent increasingly were being countered by popular resistance and demands for political reform.[30] Second, the majority of African economies were in crisis due to internal economic decline and the tremendous burden of structural adjustment programs (SAPs) imposed by the International Monetary Fund (IMF) and the World Bank. Economic decline was hastened by bloated, corrupt and inefficient bureaucracies – the so-called 'crisis of the state' – that increasingly were incapable of responding to the day-to-day needs of their respective populations.[31] In short, the combination of domestic and international trends fostered the rise of democratisation movements seeking the replacement of single-party systems with more inclusive forms of democracy.

As succinctly indicated in the July–August 1993 edition of *Africa Demos*, a quarterly publication of the African Governance Program of the Carter Centre in Atlanta, Georgia, out of a total of 54 African countries for which data are compiled, 15 (roughly 28 per cent) are described as either maintaining or having ensured a successful transition to 'democratic' forms of governance – defined as 'wide competition between organised groups, numerous opportunities for popular participation in government and elections that are regularly and fairly conducted'. This stood in sharp contrast to the smaller number of only five democracies (roughly 9 per cent of the total) that existed as late as 1990. Another 24 countries (roughly 44 per cent) are described as 'in transition' as of 1993 from various types of authoritarian rule to potentially more democratic forms of governance.[32] In short, the vast majority of African regimes (72 per cent) seemingly either have become democratic or are embodying a transition process potentially leading to more democratic forms of governance.

Despite high expectations, Africanists are quick to underscore that the new democracies of Africa are extremely fragile, lack political cultures supportive of democratic principles and, most important, are not immune to setbacks by either civilian or military ruling elites more interested in personal power than in the principles of democratic practice.[33] In the case of Burundi, for example, which was praised by the Clinton administration as holding 'exemplary presidential elections' in June 1993, the newly elected democratic government was overthrown in a successful military *coup d'état* in October 1993. Similarly, a number of the transitions to democracy have either stalled, are being co-opted, or have been completely derailed by ruling elites intent upon maintaining themselves in power. Simply put, the democratic *process* – which should not be equated with democratic *outcomes* – is extremely fluid and anything but irreversible.

In order to provide a tentative assessment of the strength of African democratisation movements, especially in terms of the varied roles of ruling elites as facilitators or impediments to change, one must distinguish between the various types of transition processes currently unfolding on the African continent. Toward this end, an analysis of the impact of ruling elites is divided according to six types of democratic transition that builds upon a typology originally proposed by Guy Martin.[34] These six types are:

1   regime change via multi-party elections;
2   regime change via the national conference;
3   co-opted transitions;
4   guided democratisation;
5   authoritarian reaction;
6   civil war and contested sovereignty.

Regime Change via Multi-party Elections

Fifteen African countries have carried out at least one set of multi-party elections in which there has occurred a relatively peaceful transfer of power from one ruling elite to another. The shifts in power that were formalised by these elections ranged from the transformation of Benin (1991) from the African-Marxist dictatorship of Mathieu Kerekou to the pro-Western presidency of Nicephore Soglo, the independence of Namibia from South Africa in 1990 under the elected leadership of Sam Nujoma, to the election in 1980 of Botswana President Quett Masire after his predecessor, Sir Seretse Khama, died in a plane crash during that same year. In this final case, elections fostered a change in 'government' (as opposed to a change in regime) in that both Masire and Khama were elected under the party sponsorship of the ruling Botswana Democratic Party.

It is important to note, however, that the successful holding of multi-party elections does not ensure that democratic practices have become institutionalised in countries still marked by democratic fragility.[35] 'The frequency of democratic breakdowns in this century – and the difficulties of consolidating new democracies – must give serious pause to those who would argue teleologically for the inevitability of global democracy', explains Larry Diamond, a Senior Research Fellow at the Hoover Institution.[36] 'As a result, those concerned about how countries can move "beyond authoritarianism and totalitarianism" must also ponder the conditions that permit such movement to endure', concludes Diamond. 'To rid a country of an authoritarian regime or dictator is not necessarily to move it fundamentally beyond authoritarianism.'[37]

The concept of democratic fragility is captured by an eight-point scale of democracy ranging from the lowest rating of 'democratic decay' (one point on the scale) in which the government 'loses its ability to manage basic aspects of its agenda, such as personal security and economic welfare', to the highest rating of 'democratic consolidation' (eight points on the scale) in which a secure political culture fosters 'widespread respect for fundamental constitutional provisions, especially the rules governing succession in office.'[38] According to this scale of democracy, none of the above-noted 15 African countries categorised under the democratic category in 1993 received the highest ranking of democratic consolidation.[39]

Two examples highlight the caution that one must adopt when analysing regime change via multi-party elections and especially the role of ruling elites in either facilitating or impeding that process. First, scholars rightfully have described Botswana as Africa's oldest surviving multi-party democracy (presidential and legislative elections have been held six times since independence in 1966) and have suggested that it potentially can serve as a model for more recently emerging democracies on the African continent.[40] However, when one closely examines the results of presidential and legislative elections, it soon becomes clear that, despite the outward appearance of a vibrant multi-party democracy, Botswana can be characterised as constituting a de facto single-party system. Specifically, although Botswana's post-independence era has witnessed a proliferation of political parties, ranging from the labour-oriented Botswana Liberal Party (BLP) to the socialist-inspired Botswana National Front (BNF), the ruling Botswana Democratic Party (BDP) has dominated the political system.[41] In every election since independence in 1966, the BDP not only has won the presidency, but it has never failed to win less than 77 per cent of all seats within the National Assembly and consolidated its hold over national politics by winning 91 per cent of all legislative seats in the latest elections in 1989.[42]

The primary reason for the BDP's success is a strong presidential system that heavily favours the incumbent president and his ruling party.[43] Although the opposition is able to freely organise and compete in national elections, it is nearly impossible to break the monopoly of the ruling party which controls both executive and legislative branches of government. Commenting on the overwhelming victory of the BNP in the 1989 national elections, for example, Bojosi Otlhogile, a Lecturer in Law at the University of Botswana, succinctly noted that 'any determined government with such parliamentary strength [91 per cent of all seats] can easily pass any legislation effecting any changes it so wishes'.[44] Moreover, the ruling party combines government control of the most significant media outlets with the president's unique vested powers to co-opt any rising opposition elite groups. 'Conflict over key issues occurs inside the BDP and is sometimes continued in the National Assembly', explains Kenneth Good, 'but after a backbencher, critical of the Government's urban housing policy, was actually ejected in 1974 over the issue, he became an assistant minister [to the president]'.[45]

The potential impediments posed by ruling elites to the consolidation of multi-party democracy are also demonstrated by events in Zambia, a country which in 1991 made a successful transition from the single-party system headed by President Kenneth Kaunda (who ruled since independence in 1964) to a multi-party political system under the elected leadership of President Frederik Chiluba, the candidate of the Movement for Multi-party Democracy (MMD).[46] Eighteen months after achieving victory, Chiluba reinstated a 'state of emergency' that had existed throughout Kaunda's rule and arrested and detained without charges at least 14 members of the official opposition, the United National Independence Party (UNIP).[47] One of the reasons offered for Chiluba's actions was a desire to preempt what he and his cabinet perceived as UNIP's intentions to destabilise the government as outlined in a leaked UNIP document published in the *Times of Zambia*.[48]

Critics of the government's actions drew parallels between Kaunda's use of the state of emergency to silence political opponents and Chiluba's desire to stem rising criticism of his regime's inability to resolve Zambia's pressing economic problems. Most important, critics noted that the domination of Zambia's parliament by Chiluba's ruling MMD party (125 out of 150 seats) in reality called into question the independence of this branch of government from the executive, especially after Chiluba was successful in acquiring legislative approval for his harsh measures. 'It did not take much to silence enough back-benchers with promises of senior positions in the next cabinet reshuffle for the government to win a comfortable majority of 114 to 23', explained one observer of events in Zambia. 'Only three back-benchers voted against the motion, although several registered protest by not showing up.'[49] In short, even a democratically elected president in control of party structures can use that party to thwart the opposition and suppress dissent.

Regime Change via the National Conference

A second important vehicle of the democratisation process that particularly has taken root in Francophone Africa is the so-called 'national conference'.[50] In this scenario, a broad coalition of individuals from all major elite groups – including elders and the heads of women's organisations, ethnic and religious leaders, labour and student activists, and ruling and opposition political leaders – holds an extended 'national' conference or gathering that serves as the basis for debating the outlines of a new democratic political order. In its ideal form, such a conference builds upon the traditional African concept of 'consensus' building in which every participant has the right to voice his/her opinion, and decisions are made only when agreed upon by all members present (as opposed to the more Western-centric concept of majority rule).

The democratisation process under the guidance of the national conference generally follows five major steps.[51] First, a broad coalition of opposition elite groups responds to a growing crisis of governance in the country by convening a national conference in the capital city. The guiding principle of this body is its self-appointed 'sovereignty' (that is independence) from either the existing constitutional framework or any interference on the part of the ruling regime. Second, the national conference appoints a transitional government that initially seeks a dialogue with the ruling elite. Over time, however, a weakened president is either gradually robbed of his executive powers or is simply declared an illegitimate authority who no longer has the authority to lead. In either case, the president is usually reduced to a figurehead. Fourth, the national conference transforms itself into a transitional legislative body (often referred to as the High Council) that, in turn, formally elects a prime minister who manages the transition process. Finally, the transitional government adopts a new constitution and holds legislative and presidential elections, subsequently dissolving itself upon the inauguration of the new democratically elected regime.

The strong appeal of the national conference approach to democratisation – demanded in some shape or form by pro-democracy movements in almost every non-democratic African country – lies in the dramatic success achieved in its first application to Benin and subsequent initial successes in other African countries such as the Congo, Gabon, Mali and Niger.[52] In the case of Benin, more than 18 years of authoritarian rule under the African-Marxist dictatorship of President Kerekou were peacefully overcome by a 488-member national conference that lasted ten days. Between 19 and 28 February 1990, the national conference declared its sovereignty, provided Kerekou with political amnesty while at the same time stripping him of his official powers and drafted a timetable that ultimately led to the successful holding of multi-party elections in 1991. The critical element that contributed to the success of this democratisation process was Kerekou's peaceful acceptance of the national conference's self-declared right to take control of the political process. As observed by Jacques Mariel Nzouankeu, Director of the Centre for Study and Research on Plural Democracy in the Third World (CERDET), Kerekou still enjoyed the loyalty of the Beninois Armed Forces and presumably could have crushed the opposition with military force.[53] Moreover, the military elite constituted a potential threat to the national conference in that the transition to a civilian regime inevitably was expected to lead to a reduction in the political power of the military. Nonetheless, both Kerekou and the military elite inevitably accepted the popular legitimacy of the national conference and embraced its timetable for the introduction of multi-party politics to Benin.[54]

The critical importance of the ruling elite's ultimate response to the demands of a national conference is clearly demonstrated by the counter-example of Zaire.[55] In sharp contrast to the unfolding of events in Benin, Zairian President Mobutu Sese Seko skilfully has utilised a combination of political manoeuvring and repression to effectively forestall the efforts of a Zairian national conference convened by opposition parties. Utilising many of the classic tools of political survival that have enabled him to remain in power since leading a military *coup d'état* in 1965, Mobutu not only successfully stacked the national conference with hundreds of his own supporters (who subsequently have been able to delay, divert and water down the proceedings), but created and sponsored pro-government parties that, although legally independent, in essence serve as front organisations for the maintenance of single-party rule. Equally important, Mobutu effectively fomented divisions within the opposition forces by 'buying off' renegade members (several of whom have been provided with plum jobs within the government) and fostering ethnically based rivalries among delegates.[56]

Co-opted Transitions

A third scenario occurs when the ruling elite is able to 'co-opt' the transition process and maintains itself in power despite the holding of relatively free and fair elections. This co-optation of the democratic process usually follows three major steps.[57] First, unlike the successful cases of transition by national conference in which an embattled president is stripped of his powers, the president under this scenario is acutely aware of the precarious nature of his political rule and acts in a quick, albeit relatively peaceful manner to preempt the democratisation forces. The usual course of action is to quickly accede to opposition demands to dismantle the single-party system and to legalise all opposition parties within a new multi-party framework. Second, rather than giving the new opposition parties time to organise and therefore present a viable alternative to the voters capable of defeating the ruling regime, 'snap' elections (often to be held within months) are announced by the ruling party. In this case, the ruling party – which usually still commands a formidable organisational structure and supporters within every region of the country – ideally desires the proliferation of numerous new parties so as to divide the opposition vote. Finally, during the period immediately preceding the elections, the president uses his party's monopoly of the government-controlled print, radio and television media to dominate the political debate. The net result is a 'peaceful', albeit tainted, victory by the incumbent president and his party.

Multi-party elections held in Ivory Coast in October 1990 offer a classic example of a ruling elite's ability to peacefully co-opt the democratisation process.[58] Considered by many analysts as a 'master-tactician', President Félix Houphouët-Boigny 'completely outmanoeuvred' his country's pro-democracy movement by 'promptly legalising all political parties and acceding to their fullest demands – open presidential and legislative elections – rushing the democratic transformation before opposition leaders could expand or redefine their demands, sharpen their tactics or properly organise for electoral contests'.[59] 'When some requested a delay (so they could get organised) this was rejected on the grounds of their own recent demonstrations for instant national elections', explains Samuel Decalo, a noted observer of the democratisation process in Africa. 'Election funds were allocated to all parties so they could not claim being at a disadvantage (some parties took the funds and withdrew from the elections!) and the outcome was never in doubt'.[60] Deep divisions within an

unprepared opposition and government control of all the major
media outlets not only ensured President Houphouët-Boigny's victory
in presidential elections with approximately 81 per cent of the
popular vote, but his ruling party – the Democratic Party of Ivory
Coast-African Democratic Assembly (PDCI-RDA) – won 163 out of a
total of 175 seats in the National Assembly. In short, Houphouët-
Boigny's foresight and ability to act quickly and decisively enabled
him to co-opt the democratisation process peacefully under the
guise of free (but ultimately unfair) multi-party elections that left
opposition elites with little alternative but to accept the results and
set their sights on future electoral contests.

Guided Democratisation

Unlike the process of co-optation in which an incumbent ruling elite
is *forced* by events to quickly take action, the model of guided
democratisation is one in which the military elite maintains tight
control over the transition process. The hallmark of this process is
an extremely powerful military leader who, due to the lack of any major
competing centres of power, is capable of slowly instituting 'democratisation from above' according to his own timetable and preferences.

The Ghanaian military regime of Flight Lieutenant Jerry Rawlings
provides a clear-cut example of the process of guided democratisation.[61] Assuming power in a military *coup d'état* in June 1979, Rawlings
led the Ghanaian Armed Forces back to the barracks in September
1979 after Dr. Hilla Limann was elected president in democratic
elections. However, political corruption, economic stagnation and
popular discontent with the Limann regime prompted Rawlings to
once again assume the leadership of Ghana in a military *coup d'état*
in December 1981. Rather than returning to the barracks for a second
time, Rawlings remained in power at the head of the Provisional
National Defense Council (PNDC), a military-based revolutionary
organ that outlawed opposition political parties and enforced its vision
of economically restructuring the country. The unchallenged status
of the PNDC would only be altered in 1992 – nearly eleven years after
assuming power – when Rawlings decided that Ghana was ready for
another attempt at multi-party democracy.

Rawlings oversaw a deliberately slow and measured liberalisation
of the Ghanaian political system that ultimately included the writing
of a new constitution, the unbanning of political parties, the
emergence of a private press and the creation of independent national
human rights organisations.[62] In multi-party presidential elections
held in November 1992, a combination of popular support (especially
within the rural areas), careful planning and strong control exerted

by the ruling PNDC led to a Rawlings victory with 58.3 per cent of the popular vote. Claiming that Rawlings and the PNDC had exerted 'excessive control' over an inherently flawed election process, opposition elites boycotted the legislative elections held one month later, thereby ensuring a sweep of the National Legislature by pro-Rawlings parties.[63]

Despite the fact that electoral irregularities, most notably flawed voter registration lists reportedly favouring the ruling elite, marred the democratisation process, Rawlings nonetheless remains firmly in control of the Ghanaian political system. As is the case with other military leaders intent on promoting guided democracy from above, however, Rawlings' 'toughest test' will be that of 'shedding the image of the radical military dictator and becoming a democratic constitutional ruler able to create a climate of tolerance'.[64]

Authoritarian Reaction

In contrast to the previous examples, the scenario of 'authoritarian reaction' entails high levels of state-sponsored violence against proponents of democracy in order to preserve the existing status quo. In this case, the ruling elite conducts elections that are neither free nor fair with the intent of stealing them. One of the hallmarks of this authoritarian response is the promotion of ethnic fighting by the ruling elite in order to divide the opposition and intimidate the general population. After this elite 'wins' the elections, it uses 'victory' to silence the opposition through such varied means as imprisonment, exile and, in the extreme, execution.

The extent to which ruling elites are willing to maintain themselves in office through the use of authoritarian tactics is clearly demonstrated by the example of Cameroon.[65] In October 1992, President Paul Biya and his ruling Cameroon People's Democratic Movement (CPDM) declared victory in the country's first multi-party presidential elections with 39.9 per cent of the popular vote. During the two years preceding the elections, human rights groups estimate that at least 400 people associated with the democratisation movement were killed by the Biya regime and the elections themselves were fraught with gross violations of human rights and electoral procedures. 'Widespread irregularities during the election period, on election day, and in the tabulation of results seriously calls into question, for any fair observer, the validity of the outcome', explained a report of the US National Democratic Institute for International Affairs (NDI), one of the foreign groups that monitored the elections. 'It would not be an exaggeration to suggest that this election system was designed to fail.'[66]

Biya's self-proclaimed victory in the elections was followed by a wave of repression and arrests directed against opposition elites. For example, John Fru Ndi, the leader of the Social Democratic Front (SDF) who took second place in the presidential elections with 35.9 per cent of the popular vote, was placed under house arrest with 135 of his supporters. Another 200 opposition figures were also jailed and a state of emergency was declared in the province of Western Cameroon. 'The brutality of the forces of law and order, particularly during arrests, is very alarming', explains Solomon Nfor Gwei, the chairman of Cameroon's National Commission for Human Rights and Freedom. 'Many detainees are continuously being subjected to psychological and physical torture, some of whom we saw in great pain, with swollen limbs and genitals, blisters and deep wounds and cracks on skulls.'[67] In short, the facade of victory actually serves to embolden authoritarian ruling elites to unleash waves of repression that are designed to maintain the status quo at any cost.

Civil War and Contested Sovereignty

In the extreme, the authoritarian response of the incumbent elite can lead to civil war and the complete breakdown of the state. The resulting state of affairs has been referred to as 'contested sovereignty'[68] due to the simple reality that no one group is capable of asserting its authority over the entire territory or constructing a government considered to be legitimate either domestically or internationally.

The most recent example of this extreme scenario is the bloody inter- and intra-clan warfare that erupted in Somalia after Somali dictator Mohammed Siad Barre was overthrown by a coalition of guerrilla forces in January 1991. Rather than abide by an 2 October 1990 accord in which the major guerrilla groups agreed to decide the shape of a post-Siad political system, the United Somali Congress (USC), by virtue of its control of the capital, unilaterally named a Hawiye, Ali Mahdi Mohammed, president of the country. This move heightened the already tense relations between the Isaak-dominated Somali National Movement (SNM), the Hawiye-dominated USC and the Ogadeni-dominated Somali Patriotic Movement (SPM) as well as among scores of other less-organised clan groupings.[69] In a move based on a strongly held Isaak belief that the north would continue to be victimised by a southern-dominated government, the SNM announced on 17 May 1991 that the former British Somaliland territory was seceding from the 1960 union and henceforth would be known as the Somaliland Republic. This event was followed by the intensification of clan conflict in the southern portion of the country between the USC and the SPM, which, in turn, was exacerbated by a regrouping of Siad's Darod clan groupings under the military banner of the Somali National Front (SNF). Moreover, a brutal intra-clan power struggle erupted in Mogadishu between USC forces loyal to interim President Mahdi, a member of the Abgal subclan of the Hawiye and those led by General Mohamed Farah Aidid, a member of the Habar Gedir subclan of the Hawiye. In short, once the common political enemy no longer existed, traditional clan differences, exacerbated by the dictatorial divide-and-rule practices of the Siad years, led to an intensification of clan conflict and famine throughout southern and central Somalia.

As of early 1995, however, no permanent political solution has been found and analysts and policy-makers are fearful that the departure of US and other Western military forces in 1994, and of the UN in 1995, will be followed by the re-emergence of clan conflict in Somalia. Indeed, the US-led military operation has underscored the difficulty of imposing solutions from abroad, but internal reconciliation processes have also faltered due to historically based clan enmities exacerbated by over 21 years of the 'divide-and-rule' policies of the Siad regime. Other African countries that have erupted in warfare and therefore represent varying degrees of contested sovereignty include ongoing civil wars in Angola, Liberia, Spanish Sahara (claimed by Morocco) and the Sudan.

Conclusion: Optimism or Pessimism?

The period of democratisation unfolding in Africa since 1989 has fostered both optimism and pessimism among Africanists. Optimism was particularly generated by a host of early successes, most notably the national conference experiment in Benin during 1990, that led to the successful transfer of power from authoritarian regimes to popularly elected multi-party democracies. Pessimism increasingly has been generated by the simple reality that, beginning in 1992, the democratisation process in Africa significantly stalled and in some cases such as Burundi it was reversed.[70]

Ruling elites have played the most critical role in this process, invariably serving as either facilitators or impediments to rising popular demands for democracy. In the case of Benin, for example, President Kerekou's willingness to cede power to the national conference (and therefore act in the end as a facilitator) was critical in avoiding the potential bloodbath that could have occurred if he had attempted to suppress the democratisation process with the support of the military.

NEED OF
STRUCTURAL CHANGE.

The willingness to accede to opposition demands seemingly has diminished as ruling elites have 'learned the lessons' of democratisation movements in neighbouring countries – most notably that the failure to act quickly and decisively almost always ensures their departure from office. In the case of Zaire, this meant a very proactive stance on the part of Mobutu to derail the national conference. In Ivory Coast, Houphouët-Boigny quickly embraced the central demands of the democratisation movement and held national elections before the opposition could mount an effective challenge. In the case of Ghana, Rawlings also pre-empted the opposition by implementing a tightly monitored reform process made possible by his control of the military and popular support in the countryside. Finally, Biya of Cameroon literally stole the elections and turned to more authoritarian tactics in their aftermath to silence opposition voices. The net result of these cases is that all four leaders were able to manipulate the democratisation process to maintain their elite coalitions in power. It is precisely these types of responses, as opposed to the earlier, more accommodating stances that appear to be most likely at least in the short-term future.

Yet even in those cases in which African countries have made a successful transition to more democratic forms of governance, their newly elected regimes are extremely fragile and thus have not achieved levels of consolidation enjoyed within the industrialised West. As was the case with the inherited democratic systems of the 1950s and the 1960s, the newly formed democracies of the 1980s and the 1990s face the 'great expectations–minimal capabilities' paradox that led to the creation of single-party political systems. In the case of Zambia, for example, a significant portion of the Zambian people seemingly believed that the overthrow of single-party rule and the ushering in of a multi-party system would somehow serve as a panacea for the country's economic problems. However, the combination of the minimal capabilities of the Zambian state and the constraints imposed on executive action by the democratic system have led to little success within the economic realm, followed by growing public weariness and disenchantment with the Chiluba regime.

The net result of Chiluba's declining popularity has been the necessity of coming to grips with the 'authoritarian–democratic' paradox faced by ruling elites during the independence era. Although largely socialised and trained within an authoritarian tradition like his predecessors, Chiluba is expected to abide by the 'rules of the game' of the newly inaugurated multi-party political system. Strict adherence to those rules, however, could effectively seal Chiluba's fate at the hands of new opposition movements who increasingly criticise his lack of leadership. Unfortunately, some of Chiluba's responses to the growing economic and political crisis, most notably the imposition of a state of emergency, harken back to the authoritarian excesses of his predecessors and could severely undermine the very democratic political system he sought to create.

These paradoxes are not unique to Chiluba's situation in Zambia, but are instead applicable to all the democratisation movements in Africa. Similar to the decisions adopted by newly elected elites during the late 1950s and early 1960s which led to approximately 30 years of single-party rule on the African continent, the way in which current elites resolve these paradoxes during the 1990s may establish the outlines of a new form of political rule in Africa that will continue to exist well into the beginning of the twenty-first century. Although it is still too early to make a definitive assessment as to what shape or form that political rule will take, it does appear that, at least for the short term, ruling elites more often than not will continue to act as impediments to the democratisation process in order to maintain themselves in office.

The most important conclusion suggested by the preceding analysis, however, is that neither ruling elites nor their replacements in the cases of successful democratisation have allowed the contest for governance to slip beyond their control. In other words, the contest over political ascendency in Africa still largely takes place among the same group of contestants: a very small elite (whether civilian or military) that generally favours political self-preservation over policies and political structures truly designed to benefit the disempowered majorities of most African countries. In case after case, ruling elites continue to impede the process of sharing political and economic power more broadly.

As suggested by our six-fold typology, however, the process of democratisation in Africa and other regions of the world is extremely complex and cannot be reduced to simple dichotomies of democratic and non-democratic outcomes. Different processes yield different outcomes, which in turn have different implications for the future evolution of African experiments with democracy.[71] For example, countries currently employing relatively effective (albeit still flawed) democratic systems (such as Zambia and Botswana) are building the basis for effective links between civil society and newly reformulated state structures and therefore deserve the support of foreign governments and institutions. In other more authoritarian cases, such as Cameroon and Kenya, foreign observers must resist the urge to reward superficial changes and instead seriously consider coercive measures (such as economic sanctions) to strengthen the position of opposition movements relative to entrenched authoritarian elites. Yet as demonstrated in the case of UN-sponsored and US-led military intervention in Somalia, the use of military force is incapable of imposing a solution from abroad and may instead further intensify existing ethnic, clan or religious animosities within a given country.

Notes

1 The author appreciates the comments of Patrick Boyle and Guy Martin on earlier drafts of this chapter and the research support provided by Bruce Taylor and Gary Gordon.

2 See Samuel P. Huntington, *The Third Wave. Democratisation in the Late Twentieth Century* (Oklahoma: University of Oklahoma Press, 1991).

3 See Jeffrey Herbst, 'The Fall of Afro-Marxism', *Journal of Democracy*, vol. 1, no. 3 (1990) pp. 92–101; and Gilbert M. Khadiagala, 'Thoughts on Africa and the New World Order', *The Round Table*, vol. 324 (1992) pp. 431–50.

4 See, for example, Michael Bratton and Nicolas van de Walle, 'Toward Governance in Africa. Popular Demands and State Responses', in Goran Hyden and Michael Bratton (ed), *Governance and Politics in Africa* (Boulder: Lynne Rienner, 1992) pp. 27-56. See also Richard Sandbrook, *The Politics of Africa's Economic Recovery* (Cambridge: Cambridge University Press, 1993) pp. 21–55.

5 Quoted in Guy Martin, 'Preface. Democratic Transition in Africa', *Issue: A Journal of Opinion*, vol. 21, no. 1–2 (1993) p. 3.

6 See René Lemarchand, 'Africa's Troubled Transitions', *Journal of Democracy*, vol. 3, no. 4 (October 1992) pp. 98–109.

7 This was the thesis of Aké's presentation at a conference sponsored by the Transnational Institute, 'Democracy as Crusade: How Western Governments and Third World Elites are Trying to Use "Democracy" as a Tool of Controlling the Third World', Cologne, Germany (13 November 1993).

8 See Samuel P. Huntington, 'Democracy's Third Wave', *Journal of Democracy*, vol. 2, no. 2 (1991) p. 12. See also Graham T. Allison Jr and Robert P. Beschel, Jr, 'Can the United States Promote Democracy?', *Political Science Quarterly*, vol. 107, no. 1 (1992) pp. 81–98.

9 Timothy M. Shaw, 'Reformism, Revisionism and Radicalism in African Political Economy during the 1990s', *Journal of Modern African Studies*, vol. 29, no. 2 (1991) pp. 91–212.

10 For a brief discussion of elite conflicts, see Naomi Chazan, Robert Mortimer, John Ravenhill and Donald Rothchild, *Politics and Society in Contemporary Africa* (Boulder: Lynne Rienner, 1992) pp. 190–93.

11 See, for example, Donald Rothchild, 'On the Application of the Westminster Model to Ghana', *Centennial Review*, vol. 4, no. 4 (Fall 1960); Barry Munslow, 'Why has the Westminster Model Failed in Africa?', *Parliamentary Affairs*, no. 36 (1983) pp. 218–28.

12 For an introduction to the evolving debates over the nature of the African state, see Robert H. Jackson and Carl G. Rosberg, 'Why Africa's Weak States Persist. The Empirical and the Juridical in Statehood', *World Politics*, no. 27 (1982) pp. 1–29; Frank M. Stark, 'Theories of Contemporary State Formation in Africa. A Reassessment', *Journal of Modern African Studies*, vol. 24, no. 2 (1986) pp. 335–47; Robert Fatton Jr, 'The State of African Studies and Studies of the African State. The Theoretical Softness of the "Soft State"', *Journal of Asian and African Studies*, vol. 24, no. 3–4 (1989) pp. 170–87; Martin Doornbos, 'The African State in Academic Debate. Retrospect and Prospect', *Journal of Modern African Studies*, vol. 28, no. 2 (1990) pp. 179–98.

13 See Claude Aké, *A Political Economy of Africa* (Harlow: Longman, 1981).

14 See Robert H. Jackson and Carl G. Rosberg, *Personal Rule in Black Africa* (Berkeley: University of California Press, 1982).

15 For discussion, see Naomi Chazan, Robert Mortimer, John Ravenhill and Donald Rothchild, *Politics and Society in Contemporary Africa* (Boulder: Lynne Rienner, 1992) pp. 37–72.

16 For a good overview of this trend, see Ruth Berins Collier, *Regimes in Tropical Africa: Changing Forms of Supremacy, 1945–75* (Berkeley: University of California Press, 1982).

17 For an early analysis, see Martin Kilson, 'Authoritarian and Single-Party Tendencies in African Politics', *World Politics*, vol. 25, no. 2 (1963) pp. 262–94. See also Lanciné Sylla, *Tribalisme et Parti Unique en Afrique Noire* (Paris: Presses de la Fondation Nationale des Sciences Politiques, 1977).

18 For a good overview from which this discussion is drawn, see J. Gus Liebenow, *African Politics: Crises and Challenges* (Bloomington: Indiana University Press, 1986) pp. 225–29.

19 For a critique of this argument, see John Lonsdale, 'African Pasts in African Futures', *Canadian Journal of African Studies*, vol. 23, no. 1 (1989) pp. 126–46.

20 Lonsdale, 'African Pasts', p. 226.

21 See Julius Nyerere, *Freedom and Socialism: Uhuru and Ujumaa* (Dar es Salaam: Oxford University Press, 1968).

22 Liebenow, *African Politics*, p. 225.
23 Liebenow, *African Politics*, pp. 228–29.
24 For example, compare the assessments provided by Peter Anyang' Nyong'o, 'Africa. The Failure of One-Party Rule', *Journal of Democracy*, vol. 3, no. 1 (1992) pp. 90–96; and Samuel Decalo, 'The Process, Prospects and Constraints of Democratisation in Africa', *African Affairs*, no. 91 (1992) pp. 7–35.
25 Decalo, 'The Process, Prospects and Constraints', p. 11.
26 For a good overview, see Samuel Decalo, *Coups and Army Rule in Africa. Motivations and Constraints* (New Haven: Yale University Press, 1990).
27 There have been six more successful *coups* during the 1987–93 period.
28 See Pat McGowan and Thomas H. Johnson, 'African Military Coups d'État and Underdevelopment. A Quantitative Historical Analysis', *Journal of Modern African Studies*, vol. 22, no. 4 (1984) pp. 633–66. See also Pat McGowan and Thomas Johnson, 'Sixty Coups in Thirty Years. Further Evidence Regarding African Military Coups d'État', *Journal of Modern African Studies*, vol. 24, no. 3 (1986) pp. 539–46.
29 For a comparison of military versus civilian rule, see Liebenow, *African Politics*, pp. 237–66.
30 For example, see Bratton and Van de Walle, 'Toward Governance'.
31 See Richard Sandbrook, *The Politics of Africa's Economic Recovery* (Cambridge: Cambridge University Press, 1993).
32 The remaining countries are described as falling under one of three categories: 'authoritarian' rule (7 per cent), 'contested sovereignty' (7 per cent) and 'directed democracy' (13 per cent).
33 For empirically based analyses of the problems associated with the transition process in 26 Third World countries, see the multi-volume study by Larry Diamond, Juan J. Linz and Seymour Martin Lipset (ed), *Democracy in Developing Countries* (Boulder: Lynne Rienner, 1988–1989). For a summary of the results, see Diamond, Linz and Lipset, 'Building and Sustaining Democratic Government in Developing Countries. Some Tentative Findings', *World Affairs*, vol. 150, no. 1 (1987) pp. 5–19. See also Juan J. Linz, *The Breakdown of Democratic Regimes: Crisis, Breakdown and Reequilibration* (Baltimore: The Johns Hopkins University Press, 1978); and G. Bingham Powell Jr, *Contemporary Democracies. Participation, Stability and Violence* (Cambridge: Harvard University Press, 1982).
34 Martin, 'Preface', pp. 6–7.

35 For a good summary, see Tom Young, 'Introduction. Elections and Electoral Politics in Africa', *Africa: Journal of the International African Institute*, vol. 63, no. 3 (1993) pp. 299–312.

36 Larry Diamond, 'Beyond Authoritarianism and Totalitarianism. Strategies for Democratisation', *Washington Quarterly* (Winter 1989) p. 142.

37 Diamond, 'Beyond Authoritarianism'.

38 See any issue of *Africa Demos*, a quarterly publication of the Carter Center in Atlanta, Georgia.

39 For a more extended discussion of this concept, see Guillermo O'Donnell and Philippe C. Schmitter, *Transitions From Authoritarian Rule: Tentative Conclusions About Uncertain Democracies* (Baltimore: The Johns Hopkins University Press, 1986).

40 For an introduction to the Botswana's multi-party political system, see John A. Wiseman, 'Multi-Partyism in Africa. The Case of Botswana', *African Affairs*, vol. 76, no. 302 (1977) pp. 70–79; and James H. Polhemus, 'Botswana Votes. Parties and Elections in an African Democracy', *Journal of Modern African Studies*, vol. 21, no. 3 (1983) pp. 397–430.

41 Other parties include the Botswana Independence Party (BIP), the Botswana People's Party (BPP) and the Bostwana Progressive Union (BPU).

42 For a good overview of election results for every election held between 1965 and 1989, see Mpho G. Molomo, 'The Political Process. Does Multi-Partyism Persist Due to the Lack of a Strong Opposition?', *Southern Africa: Political and Economic Monthly*, vol. 3, no. 7 (1990) pp. 6–7. See also Roger Charlton, 'The Politics of Elections in Botswana', *Africa: Journal of the International African Institute*, vol. 63, no. 3 (1993) pp. 330–71.

43 See Patrick P. Molutsi and John D. Holm, 'Developing Democracy When Civil Society is Weak. The Case of Botswana', *African Affairs*, vol. 89, no. 356 (1990) pp. 323–40.

44 See Bojosi Otlhogile, 'How Free and How Fair? The Role of the State', *Southern Africa: Political and Economic Monthly*, vol. 3, no. 7 (1990) p. 10.

45 See Kenneth Good, 'Interpreting the Exceptionality of Botswana', *Journal of Modern African Studies*, vol. 30, no. 1 (1992) p. 88.

46 For an overview, see Eric Bjornlund, Michael Bratton and Clark Gibson, 'Observing Multi-party Elections in Africa. Lessons From Zambia', *African Affairs* no. 91 (1992) pp. 405–31.

47 See Melinda Ham, 'Zambia. History Repeats Itself', *Africa Report*, vol. 38, no. 3 (May–June 1993) pp. 13–16.

48 Ham, 'Zambia'.

49 Ham, 'Zambia'.

50 For an introduction, see Ebusi Boulaga, *Les Conférences Nationales* (Paris: Karthala, 1993). See also Guy Martin (ed), *Democratic Transition in Francophone Africa* (Boulder: Westview, forthcoming).

51 See Martin, 'Preface', p. 6.

52 For discussion, see Jacques Mariel Nzouankeu, 'The Role of the National Conference in the Transition to Democracy in Africa. The Cases of Benin and Mali', *Issue*, vol. 21, no. 1–2 (1993) pp. 44–50; and John R. Heilbrunn, 'Social Origins of National Conferences in Benin and Togo', *Journal of Modern African Studies*, vol. 31, no. 2 (1993) pp. 277–99.

53 Nzouankeu, 'Role of the National Conference', p. 45.

54 Nzouankeu, 'Role of the National Conference'.

55 See René Lemarchand, *Mobutu and the National Conference. The Arts of Political Survival*, paper presented at a US State Department conference on Zaire, Washington, DC, 12–13 March 1992.

56 See Lemarchand, 'Africa's Troubled Transitions', p. 105.

57 Lemarchand, 'Africa's Troubled Transitions'.

58 For a summary, see Jennifer A. Widner, 'The 1990 Elections in Côte d'Ivoire', *Issue*, no. 201 (1991) pp. 31–40. See also Yves Fauré, 'Democracy and Realism. Reflections on the Case of Côte d'Ivoire', *Africa: Journal of the International African Institute*, vol. 63, no. 3 (1993) pp. 313–29.

59 Decalo, 'The Process, Prospects and Constraints', p. 27.

60 Decalo, 'The Process, Prospects and Constraints'.

61 See Naomi Chazan, 'Planning Democracy in Africa. A Comparative Perspective on Nigeria and Ghana', *Policy Sciences*, no. 22 (1989) pp. 325–57.

62 See Ruby Ofori, 'Ghana. The Elections Controversy', *Africa Report*, vol. 38, no. 4 (July–August 1993) pp. 33–35.

63 Richard Joseph, 'Ghana. A Winning Formula', *Africa Report*, vol. 38, no. 1 (January–February 1993) pp. 45–46.

64 Ofori, 'Ghana', p. 35.

65 For discussion, see Mark Hubbard, 'Cameroon. A Flawed Victory', *Africa Report*, vol. 38, no. 1 (January–February 1993) pp. 41–44.

66 Hubbard, 'Cameroon', p. 42.

67 Hubbard, 'Cameroon'.

68 See any issue of *Africa Demos*, a quarterly publication of the Carter Center in Atlanta, Georgia.

69 For an overview of the origins and evolution of these guerrilla groups, see Daniel Compagnon, 'The Somali Opposition Fronts.

Some Comments and Questions', *Horn of Africa*, vol. 13, no. 1–2 (1990).

70 For a preliminary quantitative analysis of successes and setbacks between 1988 and 1992, see Bratton, 'Political Liberalisation', pp. 58–61.

71 See, for example, Michael Bratton and Nicolas van de Walle, *Neopatrimonial Regimes and Political Transitions in Africa*, MSU Working Paper no. 1 on Political Reform in Africa, May 1993.

4

The Democratisation of Disempowerment in Africa

Claude Aké

The democratisation of Africa appears to have been largely a matter of form rather than content. But the ascendancy of form over content results in a significant blockage to democratisation. For the people of Africa, instead of emancipating them, democratisation is becoming a legitimation of their disempowerment. They are effectively worse off than they were before democratisation, for their alienation from power and their oppression are no longer visible as problems inviting solution.

In the general enthusiasm for democratisation worldwide, it seemed as if the old question of whether democratisation is relevant to African conditions of endemic high poverty and illiteracy and the struggle for subsistence, had faded into the background. But as the tragic effects of the economic regression in Africa come into clearer relief, the question is being raised again, notably by the new French government, which is breaking away from the Euro-American commitment to supporting democracy in Africa and reverting to the old argument that what Africa needs is political stability and development. This is a dangerous misjudgment and one bound to be fuelled by the inevitable disillusion with African democratisation. That is why I must begin by pointing out that it is politics, especially the lack of democratic politics, rather than development, which is at the root of the African crisis.

We do not generally understand the need for the transformation of the state because we tend to think of democratisation as a process of extending access to political participation, civil liberties, basic rights, the prerogative of consenting to governance. But for most of post-colonial Africa, democratisation is not really about access. Freedom of speech and of the press are not very useful to the peasants of rural Africa. Nor does the right to run for public office or to vote help them very much, given their total absorption in the daily struggle for survival and the futility of exercising choice in ignorance. Even access to equality before the law and due process does not help them

70

very much, for they have neither the confidence nor the resources to seek justice in a judicial system which is prohibitively expensive, utterly intimidating and totally alien to their culture. Access will only be meaningful and relevant if its provision entails the removal of these obstacles. The first task is to create an enabling environment.

Language and Subordination

Formal access to democratic participation does little for people in rural Africa, because domination is constituted in such a way that they cannot take advantage of such access. A key (though not the major) obstacle is language. Adoption of the colonisers' language was part of the structure of colonial domination. Mastery of it was required for political competition and debate and for manoeuvring through the minefields of competing claims for the appropriation of meaning and values. Language thus created a power hierarchy in which those who did not understand the dominant language of politics were effectively disenfranchised. The elite, who spoke the dominant language, formed the dominant political community, to which everyone else was subordinate.

This problem of subordination has been compounded by heterogeneity. The subordinate stratum is divided by language into a host of localised 'interpretative communities' defined by their common understanding of speech markers and the memory of language which are isolated from each other politically, because linguistically, and are thus uncompetitive, manipulable and controllable. Meanwhile, the 'common' language, that of the dominant group, while ostensibly a major instrument of national and political integration, in fact facilitates dispersion, isolation and domination.

Interpretative communities also share values and meanings with regard to goals, modalities, perception of reality, sense of efficacy and so on: a kind of grammar of politics. This grammar is central to the solidarity and identity of the political community and can thus be an instrument either of inclusion and unity or of exclusion and fragmentation. The political linguistic paradigm defines political experience, committing those who use it to a view of how the world is, how it ought to be and how it might be. It speaks not to objectivity but to commitment and by insisting on commitment, the grammar of politics homogenises its adherents. People are socialised or talked into accepting the world as the grammar represents it. It is difficult to sustain dissent against the tide of the linguistic paradigm. To attain status and to appropriate values, including power, one needs to speak the language of politics. But just as it homogenises the interpretative community, the grammar of politics separates the community from others.

It is one of the problems of the state-building project in the multi-national societies of Africa that in seeking to integrate it has instead produced disintegration. It has relied too much on violence, it has cared too little about the subjects and has helped to create a multi-plicity of interpretative communities which, despite their subordination to a central power, remain sharply and consciously differentiated by their cognitive maps, political practice and political morality. The polity is so fragmented that it is all but impossible to produce the basic consensus which democracy presupposes. The introduction of democratic processes such as elections is meaning-less if the radical social transformation that will enable these processes to take root are not effected.

The Politics of Power

We have seen the African crisis broadly as a crisis of development and more specifically as an economic crisis, because of the compelling presence of its economic dimensions the relentless falls in real incomes, share of world investment and trade, commodity prices and food production; growing malnutrition, decaying cities and collapsing infrastructure. But the crisis is, to my mind, primarily a crisis of politics, from which the economic crisis derives. We do not see it as such because we have always regarded development as an autonomous process not significantly mediated by cultural or political factors; we do not show much interest in the social context in which develop-ment takes place. We assumed all too easily that development was being pursued even if unsuccessfully simply because we were repeatedly told so; we did not ask whether development had ever really been on the agenda, or whether social and political conditions were conducive to the launching of a development project.

But development cannot always be assumed to be desirable and it does not take place independently of specific values, political and social conditions and struggles, or a determinate state. Development always occurs in the context of a state system and a political leadership committed to development. As a rule, the highest priority for the political class in power is its own survival. This interest may be compatible with development; it may even be advanced by the pursuit of development. On the other hand, it may not. A political class is unlikely to be interested in pursuing development which threatens the perpetuation of its hegemony. But then it is surprising that we so readily believe claims by African states and their political leaderships to be interested in development. In fact, there are serious reasons for assuming a lack of convergence between the pursuit of development and the priorities of the prevailing political system.

Following the Weberian tradition and political liberalism, we tend to regard the state as an objective public force: we dissociate it from politics, regarding it as an ensemble of public institutions related to politics only insofar as the political process selects those who manage the state in the public interest. Implicit in this is the autonomy of the state. The state cannot be impartial or embody the rule of law if it is captive to a particular class or particular interests. While it can and must be susceptible to pressures and influence from political society, it must nonetheless be substantially independent of every group in that society.

The distinguishing characteristic of the state in Africa, however, is that it has little autonomy. This is a legacy of colonialism, in which African states were used by the colonisers merely as the instrument for their colonial mission. Colonial politics was not about good governance but about the resolution of two exclusive claims to rulership; it was a struggle to capture the state and press it into the service of the captor. Not surprisingly, the postcolonial period saw little change in this pattern, as the African nationalists who took over at the end of the anticolonial struggle also regarded the state as the instrument of their will and still use it as such. The state is in effect privatised: it remains an enormous force but no longer a public force; no longer a reassuring presence guaranteeing the rule of law but a formidable threat to all except the few who control it, actually encouraging lawlessness and with little capacity to mediate conflicts in society.

Politics in Africa has been shaped by this character of the African state. It is mainly about access to state power and the goals of political struggle are the capture of an all-powerful state, which the winner can use as he or she pleases. The spoils, and the losses, are total. African politics thus puts a very high premium on power. Because power is overvalued, the struggle for it is intense and tinged with lawlessness. The rule of law is weak, to begin with, and the lure of power is so compelling that competitors will do whatever is necessary, legal or not, to get it. The stakes are high: elites have more to lose in a situation where power tends to be coextensive with rights, including the right of property. In this type of politics, violence and instability are endemic, with anarchy lurking just below the surface. Despite the enormous power of the state, a political order does not emerge.

Immersed in the anarchy of power-seeking, a political class is unable to crystallise, nor is the transition from power to hegemony effected. From time to time a faction of the fragmented political class gains ascendancy and may even accumulate enough power to repress or exterminate some of its opponents. But this ascendancy depends purely on force: the triumphant faction hangs on, with a siege mentality, until it is overthrown, usually by violence or systemic breakdown and the cycle of repression and struggle begins again. In this state of flux the political class has a rather fuzzy sense of its own identity and cannot establish hegemony, let alone formulate or execute a national development project.

Statism – a Brake on Economic Development

Not only unable to launch a national project, the African political class constrains capitalist development, partly through statism. The current elite came to power through the nationalist movement. It was not a bourgeoisie but a salaried class and African capitalism has hardly developed sufficiently to make it into a bourgeoisie. Thus the political class is forced to rely on state power for its material base and it therefore encourages the economic growth of state power, putting as much of the economy as possible under state control. Indeed, the one thing that has grown amidst the general stagnation in Africa is the state. But the expansion of the public sector has largely been dysfunctional from the point of view of economic development, however it may have been rationalised in terms either of national-interest socialism or of development needs. The rising tide of statism, proliferating bureaucratic apparatuses, large numbers of inefficient parastatals and a parasitical class feeding off a meagre surplus has guaranteed the persistence of underdevelopment.

The economic burden of statism goes beyond mere inefficiency and parasitism. By using state power for surplus appropriation, the political class has interposed force into the labour process, hampering the operation of the law of value. Also, it discourages capitalist accumulation. Ascendant political factions need to use state power for accumulation, because of their weak material base and their alienation from productive processes; they also choose to do so because it is easier and less risky than relying on entrepreneurial activity. Other factions of the political class fear that putting energy into entrepreneurial activity will be futile, since the economic sphere has so little autonomy and since, in the power-obsessed political struggle, losers tend to be incapacitated or even liquidated, while winners, once they have political power, no longer see the need for entrepreneurial activity. The power struggle always comes first.

Authoritarianism and Development

One reason why it has been so difficult to discern the political under-pinnings of underdevelopment in Africa is that African postcolonial regimes tend to be authoritarian or even despotic, qualities not generally associated with economic backwardness. Indeed, the development literature has tended to regard a political 'strong hand' as an asset rather than an obstacle to economic development, ensuring the political stability seen as a prerequisite to development, maintaining discipline among workers and curbing demands for redistribution. The protagonists of the system – Jomo Kenyatta, Julius Nyerere, Sakou Toure, Milton Obote, Kenneth Kaunda and Kwame Nkrumah – argued that development requires broad consensus which would suffer from the confusions of pluralist politics. They found implicit support for this argument from development economists, institutions and donor countries.

This thinking virtually became orthodoxy, with scholars and agents of development citing Japan, South Korea, Thailand, Singapore, Taiwan, Hong Kong, Malaysia and China as proof. Moreover, it was difficult to find instances of development occurring in the context of democratic politics. The Lipset theory of the social and political correlates of capitalist development was ignored as applying only to advanced capitalist development. Unfortunately, this misleading comparison has continued to influence development thinking in Africa, contributing to the persistence of political conditions unfavourable to the takeoff of the development project. It was also clearly a factor in the reluctance of the multilateral development institutions to apply political conditionality and the discomfort and laxity with which they apply it. Those who have difficulty seeing the close links between democracy and development and those who still prioritise development over democracy continue to draw on it.

What is wrong with the comparison is that it fails to differentiate political authoritarianism according to historical context. We need to know a lot more than the simple fact that an African country is authoritarian to understand its prospects for development or the lack of them. The particular ways in which African countries are authoritarian and the social and cultural context of their authoritarianism are determinant. As I have outlined above, these factors include:

1   A dynamic of political competition which prevents the crys-
    tallisation of the political class and makes it all but impossible
    to devise, let alone implement, a national development project;
2   The colonial legacy of a national leadership which is a salariat
    rather than a bourgeoisie;
3   The use of state power by those to have access to it for the accu-
    mulation of wealth, with the result that energies that might
    otherwise have gone into capitalist accumulation are diverted into
    the struggle for control of state power.

The result is a deformed capitalism which encourages parasitism
rather than profit-driven productivity and an alienation of states and
leaders from their people, who are consequently not available to be
mobilised for development.

The New Drive for Democratisation

We have made a great deal of the failure of the development project
in Africa: a failure brought home to us repeatedly by the now familiar
statistics of economic regression and social tragedy. But can we
properly speak of the failure of a non-event? Contrary to appearances,
development was never really attempted in Africa, for the political
conditions were not present. The present democracy movement in
Africa holds out the prospect of supplying the missing political
conditions. That is what makes it so important.

The struggle for democracy in Africa is not new. Africa's history
has been one long struggle for emancipation from Portuguese and
Arab slave traders, overzealous Christian missionaries, French and
British colonisers, homegrown dictators, Cold War ideologues, development bureaucracies and underdevelopment itself.

Unfortunately, it has seldom been assumed that democracy was
an issue. Africa's struggles were hardly ever treated by the outside
world – especially by those who had appropriated democratic
legitimacy – as emancipatory projects and none was ever accorded
the status of 'democratic'. If democracy was mentioned at all, it was
only to question its relevance so as to dismiss it as impossible.

Powerful forces conspired against even the admission that
democracy was possible in Africa. The colonial powers could only
justify their rule with the fiction that Africans were less than human
and not entitled to such amenities of civilised existence as democracy.
Political discourse excluded not only democracy but even the idea
of good government. This legacy continued after independence: by

deciding to take over the colonial system instead of transforming it in accordance with popular nationalist aspirations, most African leaders found themselves on a collision course with their people. Faced with pressures for structural transformation and redistribution, they claimed that the overriding priority must be development; the cake had to be baked before it could be shared. To discourage opposition and perpetuate their power, they argued that achieving development demanded complete unity of purpose and action, justifying on these grounds the criminalisation of political dissent and the inexorable march towards authoritarianism.

The rest of the world heartily encouraged these tendencies, fostering in the West a climate of opinion hostile to democracy in Africa. The former colonial masters, anxious for leverage with the new leaders, embraced the idea of partnership in development and gave indulgent support. The great powers ignored human rights violations and sought clients wherever possible. From time to time (for example, during the Carter administration) human rights abuse in Africa became an issue, but democracy never did. Even human rights organisations appeared not to connect human rights and democracy, nor understand that the ultimate – perhaps the only – guarantee of respect for human rights lies in democracy.

The development community added its own arguments against democracy. Some development economists implied that authoritarianism was good for development by emphasising the need for societal discipline, control of wage demands and encouragement of higher savings and investment, aspects which were taken to be incompatible with equitable income distribution and liberal politics. International agencies, translating their views into grim strategies of economic austerity, called for 'political will' – a euphemism for authoritarian imposition of the remedies proposed by the experts. Against all these forces, democracy had little chance of flourishing.

Now, all that has changed. Prospects for democracy now dominate the world's interest in Africa. But this is not because Africans have suddenly gained an interest in democracy; it is because the world is at last recognising Africa's long striving for democracy for what it is and what it has been all along. This change in perception has been prompted by the changes in Eastern Europe, which seemed to offer a dramatic vindication of Western values and the Western model of society. The West is now convinced of the feasibility of democracy all over the world, a development which will consummate its hegemony. That is why the West now regards democracy as an important item on the African agenda and Western media are increasingly preoccupied with African democratisation.

All these circumstances have given new impetus to the drive for democracy in Africa. But while it is at last receiving attention, it does so amidst considerable confusion about what it is, how it is engendered, and what it signifies. An important source of this confusion is the profusion of support for African democratisation coming from people whose concepts of democracy and whose motives for supporting it are widely divergent. Elites who have been kept out of power by dictators welcome democratisation as their one chance to compete for power. For most of them, democracy is merely a strategic instrument for getting power, as is clear in Nigeria, where civilians trying to displace the military rulers have displayed utter contempt for democracy in the conduct of their own political parties; or in Ghana, Kenya, Cameroon or Burkina Faso, where military rulers who had initially resisted democratisation supported multi-party competition, exploiting democracy as a way of remaining in power instead of continuing to resist it with increasingly uncertain prospects. Even human rights organisations have embraced democratisation simplistically, apparently regarding it merely as an extension of human rights.

Democracy Trivialised

Just over five years ago, Africa was still predominantly a continent of military, personal or single-party rule. But the unprecedented surge of democratisation has made these types of regime now the exception rather than the rule. Apart from a few redoubts, notably Sudan, Libya, Djibouti, Sierra Leone, Zaire, Swaziland and Equatorial Guinea, and some countries at war, such as Western Sahara and Somalia, every African country has moved significantly towards multi-party systems and elections. The tide of democratisation appears irresistible and may well prove irreversible. But the *quality* of democratisation in Africa is in question. It would appear that the process of democratisation in Africa is not a process of emancipation. On the contrary, it is legitimising the disempowerment of the people of Africa, leaving them possibly worse off than before by concealing their disempowerment so that it no longer appears problematic.

The paradox of democratising disempowerment cannot be understood by looking at what is happening in Africa alone. We must cast the net wider and look at how democracy is being trivialised worldwide.

In the aftermath of the Cold War there is no legitimate alternative to democracy and it does not seem likely that the surge of democracy can be resisted anywhere in the world or so it appears. The reality may be more complicated, however. Are we witnessing the universalisation of democracy or its final demise? In the West, the bastion of democracy, democracy has been under unrelenting pressure for centuries: pressure to reconstruct the meaning and practice of democracy in consonance with the rejection of popular sovereignty and an increasingly trivial notion of popular participation. The apparent universalisation of democracy is the consummation of this process. Democracy has been trivialised to the point where it is no longer threatening to power elites. Elites are now delighted to proclaim their democratic commitment, knowing that it demands very little of them. Democracy has been universalised in a highly devalued form which is largely irrelevant to the new political realities of the West, except as an ideological representation, but which is very dangerous to African and other Third World countries, which are obliged to take it seriously.

The end result is not really democracy. Democracy has been displaced by something else which has assumed its name while largely dispensing with its content. Liberal democracy has atrophied in a long process of devaluation and political reaction in which it has lost its redeeming democratic elements. In most countries of the West, the bastion of liberal democracy, 'liberal' is now a term of abuse, to be avoided by anyone who wants to win an election. Such are the standards of democratisation which Africa must meet, ignore or surpass.

Democracy in the African Democracy Movement

What kind of democracy is the democracy movement in Africa trying to make a reality? The answer to this question will determine the depth and viability of African democracy; the interface between democratisation, on the one hand, and political stability and economic development, on the other; and the emancipation of the peoples of Africa.

But it is a difficult question. First, what we call rather loosely the 'democracy movement' in Africa is really a complex, heterogeneous movement with numerous regional specificities. In each country the 'democracy movement' is usually a loose coalition of groups united by vague and sometimes misconceived notions of common interest, sometimes working at cross purposes. Different groups may have different motivations, interpretations and expectations of what they will get out of democratisation. The international support for the movement in each country makes the movement more disparate still. The nature of the democracy finally emerging from Africa will be a distillation of the dynamics of these diverse groups.

The following groups are salient in the democracy movements:

1   The international community, especially Western governments and the multilateral development institutions, notably the IMF and the World Bank;
2   Entrepreneurs who oppose statism, corruption and lawlessness as serious impediments to business;
3   Political elites with potential access to power but denied it by military rule, incumbent dictators, ethnic exclusion or some other form of discrimination;
4   Pro-democracy and human rights activists (intellectuals, lawyers and other professionals, trade unions, students, women's groups, minority rights movements and other mass organisations);
5   Workers and peasants.

International Influences
The first of these groups, the international community, supports the democratisation of Africa as part of its hegemonic project, in which Africa is instrumental. There is no doubt that the West is still 'mopping up' after the Cold War, redefining relations between itself as winner and the rest. Fighting the Cold War was itself a hegemonic project, of course, but it was also construed by its protagonists as a defensive war, a matter of material and cultural survival; these aspects obscured the hegemonic project. Now, however, that project, together with the cherished idea of universalising capitalism, democracy and the Western way of life, is paramount. The supremacy of these values, already established, is now being conflated with their desirability, without any reticence or concern about tailoring them to the requirements of different historical settings. No patience or tolerance is shown towards those who hesitate to accept Western values or are fussy about which version they accept; in this heady triumphalism, hesitation looks subversive and threatens to put the Western way on trial again.

The multilateral development institutions, principally the IMF and the World Bank, have gained a virtual monopoly of Western multilateralism in Africa and are also the main implementing agents of political conditionality. The Fund and the Bank together exert the most decisive influence on the development of Africa; so, by extension, their political posture is important in shaping the course of African democratisation.

Predictably, the multilaterals are putting their enormous influence into steering African democratisation in the direction of the minimalist brand of liberal democracy prevailing in the West today. But their vision of liberal democracy is even more minimalist and their support more perfunctory than those of the Western governments which underwrite them. Like all banks, the IMF and the World Bank have a predilection for apoliticism. For a long time they took the view that development was politically neutral; it was partly because they had run out of ideas to explain their ineffectiveness in Africa that they finally admitted the relevance of political factors, in *Sub-Saharan Africa: from crisis to sustainable development*. When the idea of political conditionality was first floated, the Bank and the Fund thought it misguided and repeatedly invoked the legal instruments forbidding them to take political action. In the face of Western governments' commitment to conditionality, they gave in reluctantly, but only after depoliticising democracy, first by reducing it to governance and then by reducing governance to technical political conditions important for the success of adjustment programmes: the rule of law, transparency and accountability – linchpins of bureaucratic organisation, and efficiency. The Bank thinks that these criteria will take care simultaneously of the pressing problems of polity and economy, making the one less corrupt and arbitrary, the other more efficient and both more pluralistic.

However, the multilaterals were not keen to enforce political conditionality even on these terms. They were absolutely convinced that structural adjustment programmes (SAPs) were the only way to get out of the African crisis, which they construed as essentially economic. And for them, getting out of the crisis was the only item on the African agenda. They welcomed every African leader willing to submit to adjustment, even military dictators like Jerry Rawlings and Ibrahim Babangida, turning a blind eye to their poor human rights performance and opposition to democratisation. Western countries also gave priority to the adoption of SAPs, but without the studied apoliticism of the IMF/World Bank. African leaders soon found they could trade SAPs for democratisation with the assistance of the multilateral development institutions and many tried to do so (for example Kenya, Houphouët-Boigny in the Ivory Coast, Paul Biya in Cameroon) with limited success, however, for public opinion in the West, sensitised by the human rights organisations, had grown impatient with African dictatorships.

In fact, what the IMF/World Bank have been supporting is economic liberalisation rather than democracy, convinced that economic liberalisation is the best way to promote democracy in Africa. Despite their aversion to political conditionality, they remain a major influence on the course of democratisation in Africa. But by depoliticising even the minimalist liberal democracy promoted by Western governments and by effectively redefining democratisation as economic liberalisation, they compound the problems of true democratisation in Africa, making it alienating and oppressive for ordinary Africans.

The Business Sector

There is apparently not a strong business lobby for democratisation in Africa. First, as noted above, the business class is very small because of the rudimentary development of capitalism, the prevalence of statism and the heavy dependence of wealth accumulation on state power. However, pockets of development of a real bourgeoisie exist in, for instance, Ivory Coast, Ghana, Senegal, Egypt, Nigeria, Tunisia, Morocco and South Africa. Those sectors of the business community which are relatively independent of state patronage (for example the Manufacturers' Association of Nigeria and the Nigerian Employment Association) tend to be very critical of government, especially state monopolies and their inefficiencies, state intervention in the labour process and governmental constraints on the market which hamper efficiency and development. They criticise the mismanagement which led to structural adjustment as well as the SAPs themselves, on the grounds that they cause inflation, reduce demand and capacity utilisation and expose local producers to unfair international competition. However, they concur with the multilateral agencies in supporting the rule of law, transparency and accountability. They support economic liberalisation, but mainly in the domestic sphere. Thus their influence on the democracy movement, like that of the multilaterals, leans in the direction of minimalist liberal democracy with an economistic tinge.

Some entrepreneurs are concerned that democratisation may redistribute political power broadly enough to embolden the masses to demand further redistribution and greater investment in the social sector. This fear surfaced in Nigeria when, in preparation for the return to civilian rule in 1979, the Federal Military Government set up a political bureau to recommend what type of government Nigeria should have. To everyone's surprise, the bureau recommended socialism, causing consternation in conservative, and especially business, circles. The business community intervened strongly in the transition politics, contributing to extensive political corruption, a presidential system with enormously concentrated power, supposedly to instil discipline, and a set of electoral rules which effectively restricted eligibility for public office to the relatively affluent self-employed.

Counter-elites

Counter-elites are among the most enthusiastic supporters of democratisation, but it is not always clear that they are supporting democracy. There is a dialectical unity between most of those holding office in Africa today and many of the leaders of the democracy movement challenging them. They come from the same elite; some previously belonged to the same factions and shared state power in the past. In Kenya, for instance, the leading proponents of multi-party rule are all prominent members of the political class. Some have held ministerial positions contentedly for years under the single-party system. Some, especially the powerful Kikuyu leadership, oppose the shift in the ethnic power base under Moi to the minority Kalinjini group. Others, such as Oginga Odinga, president of the Forum for The Restoration of Democracy, have reacted to the ethnocentrism of the Moi regime, which is extreme even by Kenyan standards. In the Central African Republic some of those who led the movement for pluralism which has now ended the 12-year rule of Andre Kolingba were people who had served under him or previous dictators. Similarly, the United Democratic Front in Malawi, the major group in opposition to the single-party rule of Kamuzu Banda and his Malawi Congress Party, is led by several of Banda's deposed former ministers.

Indeed, the former public officials who are so conspicuous in the leadership of the democracy movement generally have no previous history of commitment to democracy. It is, of course, entirely possible that some of them are new and genuine converts to the cause of democracy; but the indications are that their commitment springs from specific, frequently personal grievances such as their downgrading in the political hierarchy, diminishing access to government officials, personal disagreement with colleagues in power, perceived marginalisation of their own regional, ethnic or religious group, or simply frustrated ambition. Many who have been denied access to power under monolithic political systems see the resurgence of pluralism as a welcome opportunity to make a bid for power.

For these groups, support for democratisation is thus highly instrumental, and they may find themselves supporting democracy without much idea of what it entails or what obligations it enjoins. Sometimes they may even act against the interests of democracy, for they always give highest priority to the goals for which they espoused democratisation. Thus the leaders of the Kenyan democracy movement were so focused on acquiring power that they neutralised themselves and allowed Moi to prevail.

For similar reasons, these supporters of democracy refuse to accept the discipline of democracy and invariably subvert it in the end. In seeking office they are just as likely to violate the rule of law as the dictators they oppose. In Nigeria's transition to democracy in 1990–93, party nominations for public office at the primaries went to the highest bidder, votes were purchased openly, thugs were hired to destroy unfavourable results and get rid of the militants of opposing parties and potential opposition voters were denied electoral registration facilities.

The influence of the political class, especially opposition politicians, on the democracy movement is not salutary. They are committed to democracy only as a strategic route to power. This inclines them to a trivialised version of liberal democracy in which democracy is merely the institutionalisation of multi-party elections which are only significant as allocations of power rather than an exercise of the popular will.

We may conclude, then, that Western governments, the multilateral development institutions and the African business and political classes all have essentially the same vision of democracy in Africa. They tend to limit democratisation to the establishment of the rule of law and multi-party electoral competition. These powerful groups have had a decisive influence on the democracy movement. Even a cursory reading of the press shows clearly that the issue of democratisation in every African country eventually boils down to the transition from political monolithism to pluralism and the derivation of the mandate to govern from multi-party elections.

Let us now look at the two remaining groups important for the democracy movement. Their perspective is quite different from those we have been considering.

The Democracy Lobby Movement

The democracy lobby movement proper consists of two strands. The first consists of organisations like the Civil Liberties Organisation (CLO) in Nigeria, founded on a firm belief in human rights and democracy. Because these values have been so neglected in postcolonial Africa, members of such organisations have always been regarded as outsiders or radicals and have often been severely persecuted. Examples are Gani Fawhimi, Femi Falana and Ransome-Kuti, perpetual prisoners of Nigerian military regimes.

The second type of movement in this political formation are minority rights movements and mass organisations of various kinds. Examples are the Congress of South African Trade Unions and the Zambia Congress of Trade Unions. These organisations embrace democracy not out of abstract principle but because their social location and interests compel them to do so. Less articulate about the principles and modalities of democracy, they are better attuned to its substantive benefits, such as political participation, participative development and concrete economic and social rights such as the rights to education, work and shelter.

In common with elite pro-democracy groups this group supports the principles of liberal democracy (multi-party elections, accountability and the rule of law). But it supports them as part of a practical project of securing rights, overcoming economic and political marginalisation and exploitation, empowerment of vulnerable sectors and making public policy responsive to social needs. The democracy this group supports is qualitatively different.

Workers and Peasants
In this final group, those who are politically aware also have a deeper concept of democracy. However, they approach it somewhat differently, from the dialectics of economic and political oppression and the struggle for survival on the margins. Democratisation is their call for a *second independence*. The first independence, from the colonial masters, has clearly not worked. With few exceptions the nationalists who came to power have merely inherited, not transformed, the colonial state. Having betrayed the democratic aspirations of the nationalist movement, they have had constantly to fend off popular resentment and are caught in a vicious circle of resentment, alienation and repression. Totally preoccupied with their own survival, such leaders are clearly unable to elicit the cooperation of the populace in a development project or even to design one. Cut off from their base, leaderships have drifted into ever greater dependence, reproducing some of the very relations that generated underdevelopment.

But, all over Africa, ordinary people are in revolt against a leadership whose performance has become life-threatening. They are convinced that their economic plight will not improve until politics change and until they empower themselves to intervene in public life for the improvement of their own lives. So they are calling for a second independence from their own leaders, asserting the need for the colonial revolution to be followed by a democratic revolution. Clearly they will not be demanding a minimalist liberal democracy.

However, between the leadership and the social base of the democracy movement, there is a clear lack of fit. The leadership, basically urban and consisting of elements of the political and business classes and the intelligentsia and supported by Western NGOs, governments and development institutions, currently dominates the movement and has watered down its democratic content. But the actual base of the movement is the urban and rural masses, who are insisting on democratic incorporation in order to address the economic crisis threatening their lives. These are the people who form the historical social force of the movement: in country after country they have put their lives on the line in demonstrations against corrupt and incompetent dictatorships and have faced bullets to bring down rulers. Their social positioning and strategic interests demand a form of democracy radically different from the democracy the current leaders of the movement. The final resolution of the contradiction between leadership and base will determine the future of democracy in Africa.

Can the African State be made Democratic?

Looking at the postcolonial African state, we have seen that it must be transformed to make democracy possible. We have seen that electoral contests for the control of this state are not really exercises in democracy, for they merely determine who will run an inherently undemocratic political system. If Africa settles for a type of democratisation defined merely as multi-party electoral competitions, there will be no democracy, because elections will simply be a choice between oppressors. Recent democratic transitions make this clear. In Cameroon, Kenya, Burkina Faso, Nigeria, Ghana, Central African Republic and Ivory Coast, even the democratic opposition did not make an issue of the nature of the state or of the highly authoritarian character of national constitutions. Kenya, Cameroon, Zambia and Ivory Coast moved from one-party to multi-party electoral systems with constitutions that maintained or reproduced the state structure and authoritarianism of the single-party system. Nigeria, Burkina Faso and Ghana, making the transition from military rule, did so with constitutions which reproduced the concentration of power and the command structure of the military regimes. Particularly important in all of these cases is the overriding concentration of power in the presidency.

There are striking echoes of the colonial power structure here. In the colonial system power was concentrated at each level in the village chief (who was the agent of the colonial government at the grass roots), the district officer, the resident and the governor. At village level, for instance, the chief arranged the supply of labour for colonial officials and settlers, assessed, levied and collected taxes, adjudicated disputes and other cases, imposed sentences and carried them out.

With minor exceptions, this pattern is repeated in postcolonial Africa. The form and content of the colonial state have persisted, reproduced in personal rule, the single-party state and the military regime. The concentrated power of the president is reproduced at each level of the state, right down to the community chief or traditional ruler. This is a form of state which by its nature cannot be bent to the service of democracy. The power structure this state engenders does not allow democratic processes to work. It creates a dichotomy of exclusion and inclusion in the political community which means that the rewards and burdens of citizenship are not shared with equity. The state belongs to some but not to all; the rights of some people are not respected. The state therefore lacks legitimacy in the eyes of the excluded; power does not become authority but tends rather to be taken as coextensive with right. That leaves us with something akin to the prepolitical state of nature described by the social contract theorists, a condition in which democracy is not only impossible but irrelevant.

African Culture and the Imposed State

Those who compare Africa with the economically successful East Asian countries fail to see how uneasily political autocracy rests on certain major aspects of African culture, which was in some respects, albeit not straightforwardly, very democratic. This is important, because it touches not only on the problems of defining African authoritarianism but also on why the current trend towards democratisation is alienating to ordinary Africans. The particular way in which Africa is being democratised is problematic because it attempts to superimpose the modern state on African tradition and culture. This process has met with some resistance and the clash has thrown up some anomalies which stand in the way of political viability and the current version of democratisation.

The modern state presupposes a socially atomised society which, by virtue of the generalisation of commodity production and exchange, is already a market; the reduction of interests to private interests, whose conflicts have to be negotiated and adjudicated by laws; the emergence of the legal subject, who is essentially an abstract person; a bundle of rights and obligations; and, finally, a political community sufficiently homogenised to constitute a public. The single public hinges on the development of commodity relations to the point of constituting society as a market, the solidarity of exchange relations and a common interest in proprietorship, liberty and freedom. Liberal democracy is ideally for a society which has a public in this sense.

In many indigenous African cultures there are tendencies, still strong today, which impede the transformation of society into social atoms and people into legal subjects, the privatisation of interests and the reduction of qualitative differences to quantitative ones. The homogeneity which makes the civic polity a public does not really exist. The development of the public and the state is still rudimentary in Africa, at the most ecumenical level of the nation-state. But something akin to a public exists at subnational level, in the strong sense of cultural identity and a homogeneity that is not abstract but concrete, deriving from kinship, shared culture and experience. These identities, constituted by ethnic, national and subnational groups, we may call primordial publics, as opposed to the modern public of the market society which is the basis of the state.

Membership of the modern, general public is still very small in African societies, consisting of urban people who have broken out of precapitalist social relations of production and are involved in the networks of exchange and reciprocities. Many of them know the colonial language of power. However, even these members of the public are ambivalent about their membership. A civil servant in the city may also be a chief in his village; urban workers often cultivate farms in the countryside to supplement low wages. The elite which controls state power also has an ambiguous membership of the general public. They belong not only to this general public but also to the primordial public in their communities of origin. Often their attitudes towards the modern public are opportunistic and their loyalty is focused on the local public, suggesting that this is their substantive public. In these contexts the modern public often looks like a fiction and the public arena of the postcolonial state is like a battleground where interest groups with no sense of common identity go to struggle to appropriate values.

In writing off African political systems as authoritarian we also write off the rule of law, in two senses. The obvious sense is that Africa's civilian autocrats and military dictators do not respect the rule of law. But in a deeper sense we are saying that the basis of the rule of law does not even exist, insofar as the person has not emerged as a social atom and a legal subject in a social area of private interests and their real or potential collisions.

But a more stringent rule of law exists in many traditional African cultures. The kind of lawless governance we see in many postcolonial African states goes against the cultural grain and does great violence to the society and its members. In the communal societies of rural Africa, it is more useful to speak not of laws but of rules of conduct, rules which encompass value, norms, customs, precedence and taboos. They encapsulate the society's total experience – ontological, religious, epistemological, moral and ideological. They are not rules of convenience, but the articulation of the order of things. They apply not to abstract persons but to real human beings.

In the end, the logic of Africa's communal tradition and values is one for which the modern state is simply incompatible. It is a logic which accepts hierarchy while vehemently rejecting the possibility of political domination by the fusion of economy and polity and the subsuming of polity into society. African traditional political systems are not easily understood or interpreted by using the received concepts of civil society, state, rule of law, legal subject, polity, authoritarianism. It is unfortunate that we have not tried very hard to distinguish between not being democratic and being autocratic or authoritarian. This conflation has made it all too easy to gloss over the contradictions engendered by the different political autocracies of the colonialists and the indigenous postcolonial regimes. In fact, the autocracy of the postcolonial era did not sit well on African societies; the emergence of political authoritarianism has caused grotesque political distortions, disorientation, tension and conflict; very few African countries have been able to rise above these liabilities and carry forward a national development project.

Can the political dualism be resolved? If so, how? If the recent history of the former Soviet empire is anything to go by, it seems unlikely that African countries, increasingly becoming economic satellites of the West, can successfully resist the imposition of Western political models. Nevertheless, given the bleak prospects of accelerated capitalist development, African culture may well continue its fierce resistance. The contradictions may simply remain, or may spawn new, hybrid formations. Even in the prosperous West, the domination of the state may come under attack, as people's apparent freedom, expressed in an ever-expanding power to choose as consumers, is revealed as illusory in the face of the modern state's increasingly rigorous, ubiquitous and (what is worse) automatic control over its citizens, made possible by its mushrooming scientific and technological capabilities. It is by no means clear that anyone will settle for this decivilising state.

5

Problems and Chances of Democracy in Central America

Xabier Gorostiaga

Democracy is a complex, difficult and ambiguous topic. Complex and difficult because, in the case of Central America, it encompasses historical, ethnic, social and cultural roots within a specific geopolitical space; that is to say, the possibility of democracy in the 'backyard' of the greatest power of the century – the USA. Ambiguous because, although democracy now has the support of all Central American political actors and tendencies and the approval of the international community, it does not have the minimal material foundation needed to guarantee survival for the vast majority of the population, who are suffering even greater poverty and unemployment and a dramatic deterioration in living standards.

Following the greatest crisis in the region's history, the prospects for democracy in Central America are bound up with peace and an improvement in standards of living. These expectations of democracy have not been met. Although peace processes have advanced in Nicaragua and El Salvador, progress has not been made in Guatemala. Meanwhile, poverty and extreme poverty have reached levels higher than those which sparked the social explosion at the end of the 1970s.

This paper attempts to analyse the potential for democracy in Central America and the threats to it in the 1990s.

Central America has Never Experienced Democracy

Central America has been dominated, since the late nineteenth century, by a *triple alliance* composed of the oligarchic powers – the minority large landowners and agroexporters and the military who serve them – with the United States embassies playing an interventionist role. During the past 100 years, the region has experienced possibly more military interventions by foreign troops than any other region in the world – interventions carried out to consolidate

this triple power alliance or to redefine new US geostrategic interests. Democratisation of this regional power elite has now been initiated, after two decades of struggle and the emergence of civil society, but with differing results in each country.

Costa Rica is a special case. Nonetheless, its experience provides evidence that if democracy is not extended to the economic, social and cultural spaces of the majority of the population, as Don 'Pepe' Figueres began to do in Costa Rica in 1948 (in a temporary conservative/social-democratic coalition which laid the foundation for four decades of social-democratic government), democratic processes such as those begun recently in the other countries will be unsustainable.

This process requires its own time and pace, in order that the simple holding of elections may set in motion the democratic process of transforming an exclusive and excluding power into a participatory, that is to say democratic, power.

Democracy Requires its Own Political Space

The *Esquipulas process* (1987) made it possible to begin opening a regional space for the negotiation of armed conflicts. It initiated the process of creating a culture of negotiation and of concerted agreements. The Esquipulas agreements made it possible to end the war in Nicaragua; to carry out free elections with the most extensive international observation to date; and for the Sandinista Front (FSLN) to recognise their electoral defeat in 1990 and negotiate a Transition Agreement with the new government of Violeta Barrios de Chamorro. These were important accomplishments. The unexpected defeat of the ruling party, the FSLN, after eleven years in power and its acceptance of defeat despite winning 41 per cent of the vote and maintaining hegemonic control of the armed forces, set an historic precedent for the construction of democracy in Latin America. The peaceful transition negotiated between the new government and the FSLN in March 1990 seemed to indicate that the country would quickly embark on economic reactivation and the consolidation of democracy.

However, five years after the elections, Nicaragua is still sunk in deep economic crisis and social polarisation, putting democracy in threat. Widespread poverty and unemployment (affecting 60 per cent of the population); the serious weakening of the constitutional state arising from the conflict between the Executive and the National Assembly; the corruption and incoherence of the government; the disintegration of the governing coalition UNO, a ragbag of politically diverse parties artificially put together in 1989 by Washington to oppose the FSLN; the ethical crisis of the FSLN and the loss of its grassroots leadership – all these cry out for a national pact against poverty and unemployment and in defence of the constitutional state. Such a national pact is possible and is desired by the great majority of groups in the country as the only way of overcoming polarisation and restoring governability to manageable levels. The formation, in late 1993, of a Group for National Stability within the National Assembly[1] holds out the possibility of overcoming the legislative stalemate in the Assembly and finally addressing the question of economic stagnation.

In El Salvador, negotiations began by breaking the 'military impasse' between the government of Alfredo Cristiani and the Farabundo Martí National Liberation Front (FMLN), with international support, UN observation and verification and the mediation of the Group of Friendly Countries (Mexico, Spain, Venezuela and Colombia). Although the Cristiani government proved insufficiently willing to comply fully with the Peace Accords signed on 16 January 1992, and purge civilian and military officers identified by the Truth Commission as responsible for major human rights violations, or to undertake urgent judicial reforms, significant progress was made and, for the first time in its history, the political climate of El Salvador offered the possibility of free elections in March–April 1994. Although the right-wing ARENA party continues in government, the new president Calderón Sol has already promised to improve compliance with the Peace Accords and has made gestures towards dialogue with the opposition, it is possible that making these promises a reality will remain contingent on continued international pressure.

Unfortunately, Guatemala has not implemented either the letter or the spirit of the Esquipulas agreements. The long armed struggle between government forces and the Guatemalan National Revolutionary Unity (URNG) is as yet unresolved. After frequent setbacks and stalemates, the negotiations between them seemed likely to revive when a framework for future peace talks, including UN mediation and verification, was agreed in January 1994. A human rights agreement, with provisions for international verification, was expected to be signed in March, but has not yet appeared. In the meantime, heavy fighting continues. Washington does not exert substantial influence over the Guatemalan armed forces: they retain enormous political and economic autonomy. Optimistic expectations were aroused when human rights procurator Ramiro de León Carpio became president in June 1993, but they have not been fulfilled: serious human rights violations and military impunity continue almost unabated.

The designation of the Guatemalan indigenous leader Rigoberta Menchú as Nobel Peace Prize winner in 1992 points to the international recognition of the emergence of new social subjects in Latin America, particularly the indigenous movement. But the essential prerequisite for peace and genuine democracy is to overcome the 'democracy of terror' that still dominates this tormented nation, where indigenous people – more than 60 per cent of the inhabitants – are still not recognised as authentic citizens.[2]

Panama, which we include as part of Central America at the end of the twentieth century since it has taken advantage of the space opened by Esquipulas to join the regional integration process, does not enjoy true democracy either. Democracy cannot be imported or imposed, but comes from within and from below, springing from the reality of each civil society. The US invasion of Panama in 1989 got rid of a corrupt and authoritarian military leader but created a 'national trauma' which will make the consolidation of a genuine Panamanian democracy more difficult. The 1992 referendum on the abolition of the army demonstrated the people's rejection of a government that lacked both competence and legitimacy, but also of a process of demilitarisation that would leave the US Southern Command as the only military force in the country. Despite its high economic growth, Panama is not capable of meeting the needs of its population, 60 per cent of whom suffer serious levels of poverty.

The US Administration of President Bill Clinton could help consolidate the Central American process of democratisation by overcoming the polarisation created by the Bush administration's Cold War-style interventionist policies. But manipulation of foreign aid, such as the pressure exerted on Nicaragua ever since the Chamorro government took office to dismiss the chiefs of the police and the army leaves no room for manoeuvre for weak governments. Democracy cannot be consolidated when powerful, nearby foreign agents exacerbate and polarise domestic contradictions, especially during difficult transitions in countries which are inaugurating democracy for the first time.

Transcending the political status of 'backyard' and 'banana republic' is a prerequisite for the healthy initiation of a democratic process. Should the Clinton administration's greater interest in geoeconomics than in geopolitics make it possible for Washington to transcend its presumed hegemony over the region, this could be a fundamental factor in the consolidation of democracy in Central America.

The need for its own political space is a *sine qua non* for the consolidation of democracy. The political history of Central America possibly provides the most obvious case.

Democracy is Not Possible As Long As the Vast Majority Are Hungry, Unemployed, Excluded and Therefore Disempowered

Central America is not Somalia or sub-Saharan Africa. It is the region which had the world's highest sustained annual growth rates (6 per cent) for more than 20 years, from the late 1950s until 1978. It is a potentially wealthy region which has experienced rapid growth and is situated in a geostrategic and geoeconomic position and which could therefore achieve economic reactivation within the foreseeable future. Central Americans are well aware that hunger is a condition that can be overcome.

The social upheaval that exploded in the mid-1970s in Nicaragua, El Salvador and Guatemala and was stifled bloodily in Honduras was basically the result of two decades of political struggle for social rights and national space in the context of intense economic growth whose fruits had not been distributed throughout the population. According to the Economic Commission for Latin America (CEPAL), 60 per cent of the region's population was below the poverty line and 38 per cent below the extreme poverty line in 1980. In 1990, poverty engulfed 68 per cent and extreme poverty 46 per cent. That is to say, poverty:

> affects two out of every three persons ... Currently, more than 20 million Central Americans live in poverty: 14 million live in extreme poverty and are unable to meet their basic food needs. Nearly 7 million poor were added to the 14 million existing in 1980 and the outlook for the year 2000 indicates that more than 5 million additional persons could join them ... furthermore, even outstanding economic growth is not enough by itself to overcome the high levels of poverty.[3]

These are not favourable conditions for initiating or consolidating democracy. Yet the escalation of poverty, especially in Nicaragua, has been even more acute than CEPAL predicted in 1990. It is important to point out that today there is a clearer awareness of this phenomenon, which encompasses all of Latin America and is continuing to expand in nearly all countries, particularly Peru,

Ecuador, Venezuela and Brazil. Even those countries that were 'successful in their adjustment', such as Chile and Mexico, have undergone a deterioration in their socioeconomic indicators.

The outstanding 'discovery' of 1992 was the massive extent of poverty in the hemisphere and its public recognition by international organisations and governments. The 1991 and 1992 global *Human Development Reports* from the United Nations Development Programme (UNDP) and recent reports from CEPAL, the Inter-American Development Bank (IDB) and the World Bank itself, point to the dangers and threats posed by the growing poverty. At the Fourth General Conference of Latin American Bishops, held in Santo Domingo in October 1992, the Pope and the bishops were even more emphatic regarding the 'unbearable weight of poverty ... aggravated by the neoliberal model, which principally affects the poorest'. They went on to say, 'We cannot remain aloof at a time when no-one is protecting their interests ... we must make the cry of the poor our own cry'.

Indicative of the new awareness of the threat of escalating poverty are the statements of the Inter-American Dialogue (IAD), the Washington think-tank with perhaps the greatest influence on the Clinton administration. In its 1992 report, the IAD said:

The bitter truth is that, if democracy could come under siege in Venezuela, few governments in Latin America can feel secure ... The struggle for social justice is the most difficult challenge facing the Americas in the 1990s. Whatever progress Latin America has made in consolidating democratic politics, restoring economic dynamism and building towards an economically integrated hemisphere, is tarnished and jeopardised by the mass poverty and profound inequalities of income and wealth that plague most nations of the region. When all is said and done, democracy is incompatible with persistent and gross social inequities. Democracy and equality are intertwined concepts. It is hard to build and sustain democratic institutions in a society divided sharply by income and wealth. Confronting poverty and expanding opportunities for the poor, in short, are no less crucial for economic progress than investing in industry or controlling inflation. Reducing inequality is no less vital for democratic stability and advance than conducting fair elections or assuring civilian control over military forces ... Thus, our first recommendations: All countries in the Americas should give as much priority to alleviating poverty and reducing inequality as they do to promoting growth. These goals must go hand-in-hand.

These statements concur with those made by the Latin American finance ministers meeting in Washington with Secretary of the Treasury Brady in June 1992. They maintained that poverty is a threat to democracy, integration and economic growth itself.

This crisis is not just a socioeconomic problem. It presupposes a crisis of credibility and legitimacy in the democratic system, for the great majority of people, and implies a crisis of governability and a desperation at the absence of any vision of a better future. The expectations created by democracy have to a very large extent been frustrated.

The causes of the reproduction of poverty are systemic. They are not an error or an accident, but a logical consequence of a system of asymmetrical accumulation. The foreign debt, deteriorating terms of trade, increasing protectionism, the asymmetry in world trade between rich and poor nations, increasingly centralised control of technology, financial speculation, are well analysed in Chapter 4, entitled 'International Markets, Poor Nations and Poor People', of the UNDP's 1992 report. The inability – which some consider unwillingness – of the World Bank, the International Monetary Fund and, especially, the Group of Seven to address these kinds of problem as 'historically democratic' nations increases resentment – or at the very least perplexity – over the future of democracy in the current structural conditions of the international market.

The UNDP depicts those conditions graphically by using the image of a champagne glass to illustrate the international distribution of wealth, in which the poorest 20 per cent of the world's population receives 1.4 per cent of total world income, while the richest 20 per cent has 82.7 per cent. World economic growth rarely filters down from the rich to the poor. The strengthening of the free market intensifies this pattern and these conditions mean less democracy.

The recent history of Venezuela, Panama, Brazil, Peru, Colombia and Nicaragua reveals the serious crisis facing democratic processes that maintain poverty and unjust income distribution. Yet the will to defend and strengthen democracy persists, as was demonstrated in the broad-based, peaceful movement to impeach Brazilian President Collor de Mello in 1992. That is the democratic dilemma of today.

The Possible Democracy

The most serious obstacle to democracy in Central America and throughout most of Latin America, in this current phase of overcoming the historical barriers of authoritarian power, lies basically in the lack of an economic base capable of supporting democracy by satisfying people's basic needs and minimum democratic expectations. However, democracy is both possible and necessary in Central and Latin America, because the potential for development exists, but, as history has shown, without democracy it will never be attained.

What has not yet been established is *the definition of the character and social content of Latin American democracy*. The guidelines and models of Western democracy as it is practised by developed countries, and above all the United States, are still being imitated. In those countries, the character and benefits of democracy reach at least two-thirds of the population and marginalised groups have institutional rights that cover their survival needs. In Latin America, however, democracy does not reach more than one-third of the population and thus the majority of people are marginalised or excluded from the benefits of the democratic system by reason of poverty, unemployment and exclusion from the economic system. In most countries there are no social support systems to guarantee survival. This economic marginalisation and exclusion of the great majority provokes disillusionment with democracy or, at best, apathetic democracy. Both these attitudes can turn into vicious circles hindering economic development and the consolidation of democracy itself.

We have seen how in Central America the problem in the past has not been lack of capacity for economic growth. Rather it was accelerated growth, undemocratically distributed, which generated the political and economic crises of the last two decades. Numerous studies show the region's economic potential – for example, the 1989 report of the Sanford Commission on Central American recovery and development and the Kissinger report of 1984.[4] This potential is evident even for Nicaragua, the country in the worst economic shape. Even World Bank reports stress Nicaragua's economic potential.

These studies reveal the exhaustion of the old model of accumulation based on 'dessert economies' (bananas, sugar, cacao, coffee) and of the traditional export commodities (cotton, beef, fish and timber). This old model is capable of producing, perhaps, 50 per cent of the GDP required. But it must be complemented by regional self-sufficiency in food production, which entails the capacity for labour absorption and creation of an effective demand in the domestic market; agroindustrialisation of exports, yielding added value; the export of non-traditional products; and the creation of free trade zones and industrial assembly plants (*maquila*).

The new economic emphases come as a consequence of regional integration and ties to the hemispheric market. Central America risks losing the advantages it enjoyed from the Caribbean Basin

Initiative and being adversely affected by the North American Free Trade Agreement (NAFTA) recently concluded between the United States, Canada and Mexico.

However, I would like to point out two areas that could complement a package consisting of economic development with democratic participation, which has been suggested in some recent interdisciplinary and multilateral studies:[5]

1   The economic development of the *biological diversity* of the Central American ecological zone, which has great potential despite the ecological destruction of the last decades. But biodiversity is threatened by poverty. The ecological subjects which have preserved Central America's environmental riches throughout history – the indigenous and peasant culture – are today in a tragic process of disintegration caused by structural adjustment and the poverty, unemployment and migration that result from it. Unemployed people, uprooted from their communities, are forced to 'eat their future', in an indiscriminate struggle for survival which is damaging the region's natural resources.

   The blind dynamic of the market is affecting the area that could be the very leading edge of Central America's modern accumulation, its biodiversity. The same social subjects that once preserved the region's environment have become its principal enemy. The democratisation of our relationship with nature requires a sustainable economic project with a vision of the future.

2   Because Central America forms a natural bridge between the northern and southern parts of the continent, its *regional geo-economic potential* makes it the geographic link for any hemispheric integration project, particularly with the Group of Three – Mexico, Colombia and Venezuela. The infrastructure of roads, railways, energy and port facilities depends a great deal upon regional stability.

   Central America also forms a natural bridge between the Pacific and the Atlantic. The idea of a new canal or a trans-isthmus land bridge (railways, motorways, oil pipelines, conveyor belts for the transport of solid commodities) opens up prospects for Central America to transform itself into a twenty-first-century Transnational Services Platform, thus complementing its traditional model of accumulation based on natural resources.

   Realisation of this economic potential depends upon the region's stability and governability, which in turn require an economically equitable and participatory democracy. And in the

present phase, the achievement of democracy calls for the integration of economic and political democracy.

Democracy and Regional Integration

Individual solutions, either economic or democratic, for each Central American nation do not exist. Esquipulas incorporated two aspects, economic revival and democratisation, as a framework for the consolidation of peace. Unfortunately, however, the integration process that has occurred since Esquipulas involves only the integration of transnationalised minority elites with few links to civil society in their respective countries. It is also an integration which is more outward-looking than inward-looking. While the European Union maintains nearly two-thirds of its economic links within the European market, more than 80 per cent of Central America's economic links are outside the region and approximately 15 per cent are within it. Integration in its present form is a 'disintegrating integration' as far as the greatest part of Central American civil society is concerned. It does not include the peasant and indigenous masses; it discriminates against women and the overwhelmingly unemployed youth; it puts its main emphasis on the development of the region's Pacific side and has no special project for the Atlantic Coast.

We are enduring an ecologically destructive, disintegrating integration. The incorporation of indigenous people, peasants and, in particular, women is vital if we are to halt ecological destruction. Having survived the tremendous ecological destruction caused by the wars, we now face neoliberalism and poverty as the new great enemies of nature and the environment.

Therefore, democracy in Central America must be integrated into a regional project which can overcome the region's economic problems and can take account of social, cultural and environmental aspects. It is important to recall the recommendations of the Sanford Commission on Central American Recovery and Development (1989). Their basic proposal was a post-war regional project which would enable a *period of exceptionality* in the region, as the Marshall Plan did for Europe in the aftermath of the World War II. Instead, however, the region was forced to deal with a structural adjustment programme without having managed to overcome the crisis – the equivalent of undergoing surgery without anaesthesia. The indiscriminate and asymmetrical opening up of the region to the conditions of international market competition, for which no country in the region – not even Costa Rica – was prepared, has caused serious internal social and economic tensions. Despite the political will for peace-building and the consolidation of democracy, the new economic polarisation and climate of social tension are putting integration and democracy themselves at risk.

After nearly five years, during which its recommendations have been ignored, the realistic, multilateral and far-reaching vision of the Sanford Commission should be reconsidered today. Evaluating current experience, the Commission's recommendations should be taken up again and examined to see whether they might not be even more valid now than they were in 1989.

The Difficult Democracy

In 1992, we in Latin America asked ourselves whether we should not be celebrating the 'Year of the Uncovering of Latin America'. In this context it is important to 'uncover' many false meanings and realities that go by the name of democracies.

Unmasking Democracy

After thirty years of failed development theories and practices, it should not be surprising that there is criticism of a model of development that has so often been false and damaging. As democracy is being initiated in several Latin American countries, it is appropriate to wonder about the *masks of democracy* that have falsified its content, so that they may be removed by the growing demand for participation and genuine democracy. These include the notion of 'restricted democracy', which requires limits to be set not only on economic demands but on demands for participation, for fear of falling into anarchy; 'democracy of the facade', which offers the legal form of democratic rights without having the capacity to implement them; 'democracy under guardianship', which requires a foreign power to protect and guide its construction; and even 'low intensity democracy', which uses democracy as an instrument of domestic interference, under the assumption that the transition to democracy requires a firm hand.

But perhaps the broadest mask of democracy is 'neoliberal democracy'. As Norberto Leichner comments:

> the neoliberal project is anti-democratic. The neoliberal dictator-ship limits public action to the market and terms of trade. The public space is a *common space of reciprocity*. It implies community and requires a citizenship that respects individual differentiation and

guarantees community integration ... citizenship is therefore the practical exercise of democracy.[6]

In the neoliberal project, there is no space for citizenship: the space is the market and its terms of trade, which create competition, but not community.

This is one of the first tasks of the difficult democracy: to be able to unmask limited or false democracies so as to deepen and build a democracy for the end of the twentieth century while learning from the errors and weaknesses of the past. With the phase of political and military dictatorships in Latin America left behind, it is now necessary to overthrow the economic dictatorship over marginalised or excluded majorities which constrains and corrupts the nature of democracy.

The market is a means and democracy is an end and a method for achieving it. The challenge for the end of this century is to *democratise the market* by correcting the asymmetries and enabling community and to restore its value to democracy, deepening its character and its social content.

Democratising Power

On the basis of the Central American experience, democracy is seen as a phenomenon of power and a method of *reconstituting the fragmented community*, particularly from the perspective of a democratisation process taking place in the midst of a deep economic crisis. The *democratisation of power* means overcoming 300 years of colonisation and 200 years of excluding power and embarking on the exercise of participatory power based on concertation. In Central America, we are passing beyond the period of the oligarchic power elite and are experiencing the stage of 'double power' and the distribution, decentralisation and alliances that enable the sharing of power.

Although these issues are crucial in Central America today, they are not yet on the United States' agenda of democratisation, which ends with the end of war, militarism and dictatorships. Changing the conception of power and who participates in it is, however, the main topic on the Central American democratic agenda. Here there is also the problem of insufficient international support for this third phase of democracy in the region.

The 1990s are a period of transition from the old oligarchic power to the new social power and from power strategically linked with Washington to a kind of power that is more autonomous and more Central American in character. If it is to be democratic and peaceful, this transition requires negotiation and alliance-building. The new subjects of democratic power, subjects emerging from Central

American civil society in the last two decades, do not have the capacity to impose a project of power, but they do have the capacity – to varying degrees in different countries – to veto an excluding and impoverishing neoliberal project. And herein lies the essence of the crisis of governability which has become extremely acute in Nicaragua and is not yet resolved in El Salvador, despite the ending of the war and the general elections of 1994.

In Guatemala, the oligarchic power continues, although it is increasingly being weakened by the pressure of the new democratic subjects, especially the indigenous 60 per cent of the population, who are demanding citizenship rights. In Honduras, too, the old oligarchic power remains in place, buttressed by the military and by strong US support and military presence. In Costa Rica, the power transition has been carried out more harmoniously since the restructuring of power in 1948; but neoliberal adjustment policies threaten to shatter the social pact typical of Costa Rican democracy.

In Panama, the US invasion of 1989 reconstituted the oligarchic power seriously weakened during the presidency of General Torrijos (1968–78), who, with the support of the defence forces, tried to carry out a more participatory power transition. However, the corruption, authoritarianism and drug-trafficking of General Noriega, followed by the US invasion, has led to grave national collapse and trauma.

(The situation of Belize is closer to the Caribbean pattern and reflects the legacy of British colonialism and thus does not really fit into the Central American democratic experience.)

Inflecting these national processes as well as the regional picture, the imposition of the neoliberal project, coinciding with the inception of peace and democratisation processes, has created serious difficulties for social cohesion and the formation of community. The market has fragmented civil society even further, provoking competitiveness in societies already drastically asymmetrical. The current dilemma is that there cannot be a democratic reform implying citizenship for all without an economic project which will help the incorporation of the citizenry into the democratic project. On the other hand, orthodox adjustment-oriented economic reform is coming up against the veto power of broad sectors of the community who see themselves excluded from the economic project, not integrated into it.

Neoliberal policy, the conditions imposed by international financial institutions, heavy political pressure being put on Central America by the United States and potential foreign investors are creating the conditions for the recomposition and return of family networks within the dominant bloc: that is, of oligarchic power. These family networks or constellations, built on the basis of successful marriage ties, have begun to reconstitute themselves since the mid-1980s in Honduras, El Salvador and Guatemala and since 1990 in Nicaragua and are becoming the modernised Central American power elites. They are the 'new right': they have supported civilian governments displacing their former military allies; they support political openness and social reform that displaces recalcitrant sectors of the old traditional oligarchy – even including members of their own clan. Moreover, they have a regional vision and look for political solutions to conflicts, favouring dialogue over military action.

Even before the end of the war, these family networks were able to begin a process of economic accumulation based on modernisation, technification and training of the young generation in the best universities of North America and Europe. Some of these 'modernising businessmen' defend a model of democratic transition through concerted agreement even with the revolutionary forces. The neoliberal discourse, the defence of structural adjustment and the political integration of Central America around these elite groups is paving the way for what Marta Elena Casaus Arzú has called 'the *metamorphosis of the oligarchies*, in that the image is changed, but not the domination ... certain class fractions are renewed, but without the traditional sectors losing any of their power'.[7]

At present, most citizens of Central America prefer democracy to any other political system, particularly in the wake of the collapse of state socialism in Eastern Europe. The Central American Left – even its revolutionary sections – has reaffirmed democracy as the framework for political life as we approach the end of the century. If democracy fails or becomes inoperative, the threat of fundamentalism, whether nationalist or *caudillista*, right-wing or left-wing – an extreme example is Sendero Luminoso in Peru – could be the desperate, defensive reaction against exclusion.

The Democratisation of Global Power

The internationalisation of the economy demands the internationalisation of democracy. Today, the demand and the search for community and citizenship cannot be carried out in a single nation, just as the economic project cannot be based on total self-sufficiency. The democratic project of the search for community and citizenship has a global content and scope. This search at the global level will have important implications for the search for true democracy in Central America.

The alliance among social subjects within countries also calls for international alliances and the convergence of democratic projects. In this context, external cooperation should have as a basic element the facilitation of this functional integration of different democratic communities and the collective defence of democracy.

Asymmetrical international economic and political relations have positioned the small group of Northern countries as one of the principal obstacles to democracy in the South. This lack of a sense of the global public, that is, of the common space that is the 'global village' at the end of our century, impedes the creation of a planetary citizenry (and of a world civil society) in a world which is, for the first time, one, yet – owing to asymmetries in wealth, technology and power – is more sharply polarised than ever. Can domestic, national democracy be possible within today's internationalised, globalised context without genuine democracy and citizenship also existing on an international level?

The international crisis of democracy also encompasses the United Nations, the World Bank and the International Monetary Fund. Just as internal democracy within nations has demanded the democratisation of national power, achieving democracy on an international scale requires the democratisation of these institutions.

The 'champagne glass' image of international wealth distribution, to which I referred above, can also be used to illustrate the increasing centralisation of power in all possible forms.

> The restructuring of the capitalist system tends to reinforce this polarisation and asymmetry given that there is no longer a countervailing weight to the West. The increasing division of the world, between a North of few peoples and many resources and a South with many peoples and few resources, is the axis of the current crisis ... Under these conditions, the current model of society in the North – in its style of development and lifestyle – cannot be reproduced throughout the world because it has definite ecological and population limits ... The crisis is not only one of distribution and equity, it is a crisis of values and the direction humanity is taking. For this reason we can call it a *crisis of civilisation*. Society worldwide is neither sustainable nor stable under these conditions ... This model of society is not possible for the majority of the world's population and this fact is leading to increasing ungovernability in many nations of the world.[8]

The way the North relates to the South is one of the more serious problems blocking worldwide democracy and peace.

Some Suggestions for International Cooperation

Central America is a region of small nations with a potential for growth that is strategically located as a continental bridge between the North and the South as well as between the Pacific and the Atlantic. The consolidation of democracy and stability in the Central American nations could have a *multiplier effect* as well as a *demonstration effect* for the rest of Latin America.

The consolidation and deepening of democracy should be included as a basic component of all foreign cooperation, for democracy is the most authentic foundation for the 'DDP' triangle – Democracy, Development and Peace.

From a Central American and, I would dare say, Latin American and Third World perspective, the following would be some priority areas, compiled from countless meetings during recent years, in which foreign cooperation could significantly contribute to DDP:

1   Concentrate on developing the productive capacity of small and medium-scale producers through projects that lead to self-sufficiency in food production and to health and primary education. Contribute to the building of regional and international trade channels for farmers' and artisans' products, which these producers are unable to trade on the international market without support from trade networks, which are currently monopolised by transnational interests.

2   Channel a substantial part of cooperation via non-governmental organisations (NGOs), in order to: promote democratic NGOs – those that are created in support of and in response to the particular needs of the organisations of civil society.

    Encourage horizontal links between these NGOs and people's organisations (indigenous communities, peasants and farmers, women, organisations of the informal sector) on a national, regional and international level, creating networks that will consolidate citizenship, with their own economic base.

    Finance popular credit institutions that will help overcome financial discrimination against small producers, in collaboration with the new rural financing agencies which are emerging in Central America.

    Support third-generation human rights, that is, through the consolidation of civil rights, the development of social and economic rights and the strengthening of the people's right to participate democratically in this planetary city at the century's close. Human rights should include the rights of citizenship and democratic community.

Link Northern and Central American grassroots organisations with like-minded groups in civil society, to create a People-to-People relationship, democratising the exclusivist relationships that operate in transnational companies and economic elites.

3   Include indigenous peoples, women and children in the process of development. The cultural recovery of the historical roots and identity of indigenous peoples is personified in the Guatemalan indigenous peasant leader Rigoberta Menchú. The incorporation of some 60 million indigenous Latin Americans who are socially and economically marginalised is particularly essential for Guatemala, the Andean countries and Paraguay, where they form population majorities, as well as for indigenous minorities throughout the hemisphere.

Investment in women is perhaps the most efficient form of investment and has a greater multiplier effect due principally to women's impact upon children, young people and the environment. Women, indigenous people and peasants are the three social subjects most vital for the hemisphere's ecological recovery.

4   Cooperate in initiatives promoting regional integration, including financing regional institutions which encompass accountability and democratic participation, in order to improve on the current bureaucracy and enabling the creation of regional think-tanks which could transcend the existing 'parallel state' institutions which serve the regional economic elite. Also, support for training and research groups run by national NGOs and organisations of peasants, women and indigenous peoples, contributing to their regional linking via Concertación, a regional network of Central American NGOs.

5   Regional infrastructure. Historically, the Isthmus of Darien has served as a bridge between North and South, Pacific and Atlantic. Today it has a geoeconomic role to play as the link between Mexico and South America, creating a Latin American counterweight to NAFTA. International cooperation could help unite the hemisphere for the first time via railways, roads and ports.

At the same time, it could collaborate in the construction of a trans-isthmus infrastructure, which would enable Central America also to function as the most efficient bridge between the Pacific and the Atlantic in trade, services and even intermediate production.

These suggestions may appear utopian, even romantic. I believe, however, that now that the Cold War is over, the world offers possibilities of thinking seriously, differently, of looking towards the long term, of avoiding collective suicide. US Vice President Al Gore wrote recently, 'An equitable distribution of political power and wealth are prerequisites for any successful attempt to save the environment and society'. The fact that a US vice president can now make such a statement offers hope that things can change in the world.

I close with a sentence from the *Popol Vuh*, the sacred book of the Maya which has given strength and inspiration to Rigoberta Menchú and to the indigenous peoples and which may also inspire in us the political will demanded of us by the common destiny of humanity, as we look towards the twenty-first century:

They began to fulfil the destiny they carried deep in the marrow of their bones.

Notes

1   The Group consists of the FSLN, the UNO Centre Group, the Christian Democratic Union and the United Reconciliation Group, which is composed of members of the Social Democratic parties.

2   *Quinientos años sembrando el Evangelio*, Pastoral Letter of the Bishops of Guatemala, Guatemala, 15 August 1992.

3   CEPAL/UNESCO, *Educación y conocimiento: eje de la transformación productiva con equidad*, November 1991, p. 1. Or: CEPAL, *Bases para la transformación productiva y generación de ingresos de la población pobre de los países del Istmo Centroamericano*, 1991, p. 1.

4   See also George Irwin and Xabier Gorostiaga, *Central America: The Future of Economic Integration* (Boulder: Westview Press, 1989); Victor Bulmer-Thomas, *The Political Economy of Central America since 1920* (Cambridge: Cambridge University Press, 1987).

5   See for instance Eduardo Stein and Salvador Arias Peñate (ed), *Democracia sin Pobreza: Alternativa de Desarrollo para el Istmo Centroamericano* (San José: DEI, 1992); Raúl Ruben and Govert van Oord (ed), *Beyond Adjustment* (The Hague: MAK, 1991); published in Spanish as: *Más Allá del Ajuste: La Contribución Europea al Desarrollo Democrático y Duradero de las Economías Centroamericanas* (San José: DEI, 1991).

6   N. Leichner in *Sociológica* vol. 19 (May–August 1992) (volume title: 'Democracia y Neoliberalismo: Perspectivas desde América Latina', UNAM, Mexico).

7   Marta Elena Casaus Arzú, 'El Retorno al Poder de las Elites Familiares Centroamericanas 1979–1990', *Polémica* (Costa Rica: FLACSO, 1992) p 157.

8   Xabier Gorostiaga, 'Latin America in the "New World Order"', *Iberoamericana* vol. 14, no. 1 (Tokyo: Sofia University, 1992).

6

Pathology and Power: The Failure of Democracy in the Caribbean

Niala Maharaj

For three decades, parliamentary democracy has been like oxygen in the English-speaking Caribbean – a basic ingredient of life that everyone took for granted. 'West Indians have always assumed that things like *coup d'état*, *golpe de estado*, individual dictatorships, are only things that happened in Haiti or Cuba or Santo Domingo', observed the British historian Gordon Lewis in 1991.[1] This has recently become a subject of wonder among intellectuals reviewing the general record of postcolonial nations. Carlene J. Edie, for example, begins her recently published book, *Democracy in the Caribbean*, with the words:

> Among developing nations, the Caribbean has the largest number of liberal democracies. The Commonwealth Caribbean states, with a few exceptions, have maintained competitive parliamentary democracies for over three decades and have largely escaped the kinds of social and political upheaval apparent in many parts of the Third World ...[2]

If one takes democracy as an inherent good in itself, as Jorge I. Dominguez seems to do, one would agree with him that, 'the Caribbean's capacity to sustain liberal democratic polities is impressive. Since independence (beginning with Jamaica and Trinidad and Tobago in 1962) ten of the twelve (Guyana and Grenada excepted) Anglophone Caribbean countries have consistently held fair elections and have been free from unconstitutional transfers of power'.[3] However, it would be a mistake to conclude that the inhabitants of these former English colonies are equally impressed. For, inside the region there is a strong feeling that the Caribbean is an illustration not of the success, but of the failure of democracy: that is, the failure of this political system to guarantee social, political and economic development.

On my 1994 visit to the richest island of the region, Trinidad and Tobago, I found a bitter cynicism towards democratic institutions. Parliamentary politics were regarded as a farce. The Prime Minister is a geologist, people said, that's why he has rocks in his head; the leader of the opposition is no better. A by-election recently threw up such candidates as: the leader of a recent coup attempt who campaigns on the fact that his would-be constituents got household appliances in the looting which accompanied his bid for power; a former journalist in whose speeches the nouns and verbs fail to match; and a man who informed the public that the world would come to an end on May 25.

The media grieved over the corruption of the judiciary; the lawyers were lamenting the tawdriness of the media. On 14 May 1994, the leader of Trinidad's opposition accused the oldest daily newspaper in the country of protecting the drug dealers in the country. 'Refer to your bosses', he said, turning to the press table in Parliament. It was a reference to a widely-held belief that the new owners of that newspaper, the self-proclaimed 'Guardian of Democracy', have bought it with the proceeds of the illegal cocaine trade.

And the fact that the former British colonies have been spared the *kind* of social and political traumas that have overtaken many parts of the Third World does not necessarily imply any unusual commitment to democracy.

'It is now a gun culture', observed Selwyn Ryan, Director of the Institute of Social and Economic Research at the University of the West Indies. 'The judicial system is threatened in a fundamental way, the police system is compromised, the school system is a mess. All the pillars of the society have been corroded in a fundamental way and I don't see anything down the road that will enable us to recover the ground we have lost. The prognosis for democracy is rapidly growing worse.'[4]

Even the US embassy does not bring up the subject of democracy here. For it is clear that the islands' societies have been rapidly going backwards in the last decade, backwards towards the same violence, destitution and colonialism of their beginnings. Instead, the embassy has to rely on intellectual mercenaries such as visiting scholar Dr Juan Del Aguila, Associate Professor of Political Science at Emory University to parrot its current cliches.

'With the end of the Cold War', lectured the Professor in Trinidad in June 1994, 'there is now a tremendous opportunity for the US and its allies to fashion a world in which values of democracy and social justice play a part. Free and open democratic politics have proved the best means by which people can govern themselves'.[5] The man sitting next to me snorted. He turned out to be the representative of the United Nations Development Programme in this region, a Belgian with long experience of the Caribbean islands. 'They might be able to say that elsewhere', he muttered. 'Here, people are too sophisticated to swallow that.'

In fact, Dr Aguila had just come from mainland Latin America, where he could easily peddle his facile truths in the twilight of dictatorship and civil war. He had not troubled himself to examine the history of the English-speaking Caribbean.

The Genesis of this Democratic Mess

'Despite the longevity of democratic institutions there', Carlene Edie remarked, 'Caribbean states have not been frequently analysed as have other regional clusters.'[6] One might argue that it was not despite, but because of, this region's apparent commitment to democracy that few have bothered to examine its internal developments. For those of us who lived through the first three decades of independent nationhood in the region and who are not social scientists, there is no mystery to democracy's tenacity. It does not need to be explained through detailed analyses of constitutional systems, such as the essays in Edie's book conduct, but by reference to history, geography, language and culture. Democracy was, from the first, all these former British colonies knew of politics, something which came with the package called Independence, and was given the same value as the rest of the package. This is a vital connection to recognise if one is seriously interested in understanding democracy in the Caribbean. Having had none of the revolutionary turmoil that other 'developing countries' experienced in order to achieve statehood, the islanders simply poured new wine into the old bottles of the colonial political system, putting local leaders in place of the foreign ones. Their parliamentary institutions were just models of those of the former coloniser. This involved a certain element of play-acting. 'Despite the formal resemblance to Westminster or Schumpetarian canons of democracy', Ryan admitted in 1993, 'the political systems of the Anglophone Caribbean leave a great deal to be desired in terms of how they operated in the post-independence period, although they were considered exemplary models of democratic propriety ... Adherence to these institutional and procedural forms, has, however, been ritualistic and concealed a reality that was masked by artificial prosperity'.[7]

V.S. Naipaul, the region's premier novelist, dubbed the early political leaders 'Mimic Men', who assumed the roles of English parliamentarians, without the conviction that comes from immersion in the historical traditions of that system. Derek Walcott, the region's premier poet and playwright, depicted independent politics as a 'Dream on Monkey Mountain' in a play by that title, in which the new leaders just followed, monkey-style, the rituals of their former masters. Meanwhile, the electorate, who had not read the books their leaders had or observed the English system in action, had to discover what democracy meant.

'Everybody just washing their foot and jumping in this democracy business', a character warned in *The Suffrage of Elvira*, Naipaul's fictional account of the first elections held in Trinidad. 'But I promising you, for all the sweet it begin sweet, it going to end damn sour.'[8]

By the end of the book ordinary villagers had discovered a way to accommodate this new entity among the other known forces in their world – race, religion, black magic, local social status and power-broking. It was a source of easy money. Votes could be bought and sold, patronage dispensed.

They talked of the degeneracy of the modern age; they agreed that democracy was a stupid thing; then they came to the elections and to Baksh. Chittaranjan said:

> This democracy just make for people like Baksh. Fact, I say it just make for Negro and Muslim. They is two people who never like to make anything for theyself, and the moment you make something, they start begging.

So democracy just reinforced the ethnic stereotyping that previously existed. It did not break down the old loyalties of race and religion.

Despite these tawdry beginnings, the region's intelligentsia hoped that Caribbean democracy would eventually evolve into something less farcical. The system was the best possible in an imperfect world, they believed. The smallness of communities and economic resources did not allow for the extravagant levels of corruption that were turning up in other postcolonial societies. Everybody knew everybody and that created a kind of social control. Given a chance, the intellectual elite hoped, communities would become used to the responsibilities of national management and eventually learn how to govern themselves effectively. No one else now wanted to – not the former colonial power nor the giant superpower to the North. So peace was the norm, not war, civil war, uprisings and putsches. To change the norm required effort, risk. Living in one of the most beautiful and bountiful parts of the world was discouraging to risk-taking.

In this attitude, they were encouraged by the nearby champion of democracy. Television followed hard on the heels of Independence and the US horror of any other form of political organisation permeated down into the consciousness of the islanders. Dictatorship, military rule, communism soon became creatures of another Third World, one that spoke Spanish and Arabic and Chinese, translated to the islanders' ears via the media's prejudices. Only Guyana had any direct experience of an alternative political system, but it was part of the Latin American continent and its poverty-ridden state was an object lesson. From Cuba, these islands were shielded by an unstated diplomatic cordon and the aggressive propagandising of the rich, English-speaking US, whose television programmes showed happy, secure families with big cars and numerous household appliances. Many useful scholarships in technical fields which Cuba offered were unadvertised by neighbouring governments; airlines discreetly ignored the geography of the region. So there was no way of investigating whether things were really worse in a communist state or better. Fidel Castro's description in every respectable newspaper was 'dictator'. The islanders were equally insulated from their Spanish-speaking neighbours and Haiti by the poor language-instruction methods they had inherited with their British-oriented educational systems. It is no accident that Castro prepared his guerrilla struggle in Mexico. Grenada was a brief aberration.

The Economic Contradiction

But despite this eschewing of alternatives to the democratic model, independent politics in the Caribbean did not lead to contentment. 'Slaves, the children of slaves, then pathetic, unpunctual nationals, what have we to celebrate?' asked poet Derek Walcott in a literary essay in 1970.[9]

For within less than a decade, it had become clear that the islands were steadily going nowhere – at least nowhere towards the material and social development that was expected to result from self-government. For political independence had not been accompanied by any effective effort at economic independence. Gordon Lewis, among others, pointed out that all of the West Indian states, whatever the variations of their political rhetoric, were following the economic model of Puerto Rico, which did not have political independence and depended on foreign investment for economic growth.

'An intensified industrial programme along those lines', Lewis warned, in the insightful essay that concluded his 500 pages on *The Growth of the Modern West Indies*, 'has still left the island economy a system characterised by heavy external ownership of productive facilities, large-scale mass unemployment, a high-cost import structure, a low percentage of trade unionisation in the new factories, the sacrifice (characteristic of capitalist enterprise everywhere) of agriculture to industry, and much else ...'.[10]

Many regional economists, such as Edwin Carrington, challenged the wisdom of this policy. It was leading, Lewis warned, to 'a dangerous compartmentalisation in the underdeveloped economy between the economic and political spheres of sovereignty'. But weightier voices, such as St Lucia's Nobel-prize-winning economist, Arthur Lewis, favoured this compartmentalisation. So very open economies became the norm. The resources of the state were largely directed, many analysts now argue with hindsight, at the kind of patronage Naipaul described, rather than at establishing a base for long-term economic development. A kinder view is possible: many Caribbean leaders, educated in post-war Britain, adopted the kind of welfare economic model then in vogue in the mother country, investing in education, national health systems and infrastructure. But while these led to a high standard of living compared to many other parts of the Third World, the fundamental economic arrangements of the region suggested a continuation of colonialism. Thus, from very early on, Caribbean people were confronted with a very contradictory notion of democracy, one which included a lack of control over the material resources of their societies.

The result turned out to be an extension of the poverty of the colonial era and educated electorates who felt they deserved better than they were getting. 'This ultimately breeds a double standard of reference', Lewis observed, 'poisoning the moral climate of national life'.

Some ordinary people – my father for instance – soon began to conclude that the region had been better off 'under the white man'. For, in the colonial era, the corruptibility of the democratic system had been too far away for them to see. Now, with or without ballot papers, with or without a free press, constitutional safeguards or legal systems, the children of former slaves still felt trapped in a poverty-ridden fate they could not control.

We climbed (Walcott wrote in verse)
where the inheritors of the middle passage stewed
five to a room, still clamped below their hatch,
breeding like felonies.[11]

To understand the Caribbean, its perversions of the present and probably greater ones of the future, it is absolutely necessary to take account of this profound feeling of entrapment in the psyche of ordinary people, and in particular, among its intellectual elite. Gordon Lewis put his finger very precisely on an important consequence of this policy of divorcing economics from politics: 'What this suggests, disturbingly enough, is that the possession of political sovereignty (which Jamaica has, while Puerto Rico does not) is, in fact, of negligible value, since it is rendered largely nugatory by the surrender of large slices of economic sovereignty to outside forces, both financial and political.'[12]

Independence soon began to seem meaningless to many in the Caribbean. For some people, this also tarnished the attendant concept, democracy, which, in its practical applications, was already beginning to erode. The mass political parties, Gordon Lewis noted, developed more and more an antidemocratic spirit, with leadership transformed into political cults.

Thus, despite having little history of armed struggle, despite the fact that the majority of people display little taste for radical political solutions, there have been numerous sparks of insurrection over the last 30 years. For the most part, mild forms of internal coercion were able to keep elected governments in place: repressive labour laws, a readiness to resort to states of emergency, murders by the police under the guise of crime prevention, political thuggery a la the Grenadian Mongoose Gang. But these did not encourage confidence in democratic institutions as the guardian of citizens' rights. 'Radical critics', noted Ryan, 'in fact point to several incidents or system features which give an entirely different picture of Caribbean democracy. There have been numerous examples of the ruling elites using vigorous repression when serious challenges were made to dislodge them from power in the interest of the broad masses ...'.[13] As Derek Walcott wrote:

All those who promise free and just debate
Then blow up radicals to save the state,
Who allow, in democracy's defense,
A parliament of spiked heads on a fence,
All you go bawl out, 'Spoils, things ain't so bad'.
This ain't the Dark Age, is just Trinidad.[14]

The Regional Contradiction – Hemispheric Politics

And, if internal measures to protect democracy failed, the political elites could always 'call in the marines'. For, added to all the problems that these former colonies share with other 'developing' societies, the islands have a particular one which is articulated regularly. Smallness. Even when the recognition dawned that 'black still poor, though black is beautiful', as Walcott put it, there was nothing that could be done about it if that meant bucking the international system. The islands were, as a Mexican once put it, 'so near to the US, so far from God'.

According to Dominguez, 'the Caribbean has been the one area in the Americas most marked by frequent international, conventional military confrontations since the Second World War'.[15] Thus, those who ruled these islands always had to act as though they had power while knowing that, in fact, their power was only tolerated by their giant neighbour if they kept within certain policy boundaries. One cornerstone of these policies was the adherence to the 'forms of democracy': the parliamentary system, no matter if these impeded efforts towards social and economic development. This was not negotiable.

Jamaica's flirtation with Cuba and socialism, and the resulting destruction of her economy by international institutions, underlined the boundaries. Nicaragua, Honduras, El Salvador lurked like ghosts in the minds of the educated. The invasion of Grenada sealed the matter and the gleefully televised Desert Storm later added insult to injury. Politicians in the region grew used to knowing that they had to fit into the straightjacket of the 'free world'. And so did those who challenged them. 'One reason why the many violent and unconstitutional attempts to overthrow various governments failed', Dominguez noted,

is that at key moments international actors intervened in time on democracy's side. This has happened so often that it can no longer be described just as good luck; it is a pattern of international behaviour in this subsystem.

Prime Minister Charles's government in Dominica owes its survival more than once to timely arrests or weapons seizures by the US Federal Bureau of Investigation (FBI) ... In this context, the most controversial international intervention – the 1983 invasion of Grenada – is consistent with the norms that had evolved in the Caribbean international subsystem to privilege democracy over non-intervention (the opposite of the more common norm in Latin America).

Powerlessness corrupts. The best minds of the region gradually turned away from direct politics, from the constant willingness to compromise it required. So Parliament became the arena for the mediocre, the greedy, the small-minded, those who could live comfortably with the silly excuses for failure to take decisions that would use resources for community development. Those with talent drifted into perpetual opposition, via the trade unions and the university, or to a more indirect form of public involvement, sitting on boards of national organisations, acting as advisers or consultants, nudging the government of the day or castigating it.

Over a period of 30 years this role is debilitating. Those with the power to act do not always take your advice, or take it incompletely, or muck it up when they do. Your proposals get muddied with pragmatic considerations, are spurned for corrupt reasons, or for no reason at all, that is stupidity. The result is bitterness, a growing cynicism and a further retreat from public life, leaving spaces to be filled by the ever more incompetent and corrupt. Arrogance follows, and the inability to grow.

'Few heroes allowed in this vapid crowd', a verse of doggerel published in the *Trinidad Guardian* commented in 1994. So most are forced to flee.

The rest look on with sorrowful eyes,
And cry for their small country.
A place so blessed, a land so rich,
It's a tragic tale to state
That among all these natural gifts
There's a gradual loss of faith.
But who can struggle and who can fight,
If friend is also foe
And of those on top, they try their best
To keep the rest below.

Hence, by the end of the 1980s, the Caribbean had developed one more element in its phalanx of hindrances to effective democracy: a crisis of leadership. 'Grand causes no longer have legitimacy', as Ryan summed up the situation in 1994. 'We don't have leaders like Nehru, Nkrumah, C.L.R. James any more in the Third World.'[16]

Instead, in the southernmost island, Trinidad, the 1990s have thrown up Patrick Manning, a bright, middle-management type, capable only of handling a minor branch office of a large multinational enterprise. He is not an intellectual, a visionary, a social thinker and leader, as was expected from the early leadership in the region, but a technician who gets his confidence from the approval of the increasingly vocal US embassy.

For, by the 1990s, too, the US's profile in the Caribbean had altered. Having agonised over its own economic mistakes and hatched the NAFTA solution, it now needed markets for its goods. Petty considerations concerning sovereignty had to be swept unceremoniously aside.

'Sally Cowell, the US Ambassador, is saying that, in the real world, the sovereignty thing is gone', Ryan noted in discussion. 'We live in a borderless world.' This hemispheric pressure to create an economic bloc to rival Europe's and Japan's has put additional pressure on Caribbean democracies. Nationalism has suddenly become an outmoded concept and all the efforts to create democratic societies have to be violently revised, as the islands become reinvented as outposts of the US market.

'The system here depended on a group of brown Englishmen', claimed Charles Shapiro, chargés d'affairs of the US embassy in Trinidad when I interviewed him in June 1994. 'Those people are dying.'[17] This is something of an overstatement, perhaps based on wish-fulfilment. For these are the very people who question the simplistic definitions of democracy bandied about by the North Americans. Some of them may be stuffy or 'inflexible', as Shapiro calls the retiring Head of the Trinidad's Armed Forces, Brigadier Ralph Brown, who insists that the defence of this region includes the defence of the right to 'social justice and economic development'. Members of this group may still carry about them the flavour of outmoded English public-service traditions. But they are not all dying. What they are doing is retiring from the public arena, recognising that their world has ended. 'Society', as a concept, has been wished away by those with the real muscle in the region.

Thus, in 1994, when I visited Trinidad, the newspapers were full of items about how the country was going to 'fulfil the requirements to join NAFTA' by opening up its markets to US goods. 'There is no such thing as independent development', the Prime Minister stated in my interview with him. 'Our markets are too small to guarantee the viability of industries.'[18]

What industries? I wondered. The country had produced nothing for export except oil. But its leadership did not seem to have any answers to this, just ideology. Competition will force Trinidadians, it seems, to create industries so they can sell something to the US. And, in order to prepare for the miraculous emergence of a productive sector where there was none before, the entire economy of this island was being dismantled. Factories which produced goods for the local market were being closed down *en masse*, the companies which possessed them turning to the import business. Jobs were disappearing by the thousands.

'The best role for the state is to be a facilitator and attract investment', the Prime Minister said. It had been doing this all its life, but these investments (in sectors such as tourism) did not leave enough foreign exchange in the local economy to pay IMF debts. So he was now selling off every state industry, every public utility he could lay his hands on, in order to fulfil the requirements of the current orthodoxy. Longstanding laws – that inhibited foreign ownership of land, regulated the movement of money, controlled the currency, regulated the media – were being swiftly reversed. This was absolute economic revolution.

Revolution always depends on some fantasy about its gains. This island now appeared one bewildering mass of fantasy about export promotion, when nobody had a clue what to export. 'Foreign experts' were there to tell them how they could market products, but no one would answer the fundamental question of what these products would be. Consultants of the shoddiest kind were thick on the ground, informing Trinidadians about the joys of the global marketplace, but middle-management staff had confused looks on their faces as they emerged from seminars. Once, these people – largely women – had a bright, confident look. But in the early 1990s, subjected to innumerable senseless lectures on the flimsiest aspects of international commerce by all kinds of fly-by-night experts, the light had gone out of their eyes. For it was apparent that the last vestiges of independence were being given up.

This requires a restructuring, not just of the economy, but of the mind. This is why the crisis in the Caribbean expresses itself in psychological terms. People are too sophisticated to believe the propaganda that is being put out by the government on behalf of global economic powers, but some have to act as though they do. Thus, in the 1990s, there is as much violence, suicide and chemical addiction in the upper classes as there is in the ghettos of a country like Trinidad. For this choice of a return to colonialism does not have the support of anyone in the country, not even large sections of the capitalist and managerial classes. It is too obvious that it does not make sense. Senior bankers, managers, entrepreneurs, even those running local branches of multinational enterprises, expressed private bitterness when we talked of the changes. They saw their home – Trinidad and Tobago – being destroyed, even if their companies made increased profits and they themselves got giant remunerations.

'You cannot pauperise a country like this', one Citibank executive said to me. These people are aware that what they gain in increased personal benefits they will lose to the destruction of the social climate. But, despite the existence of democratic norms, they felt powerless to prevent themselves become chattels of (primarily) the United States. 'I can see that free trade doesn't benefit a country like this', complained the Chairman of the Caribbean branch of a large multinational in discussion in 1994. 'They talk of open markets but keep up protectionism in their own countries.'[19] He, ironically enough, has been one of the public leaders of the struggle against 'liberalisation' of the economy, on the side of the same trade unionists with whom he has often had bitter negotiations in the past. He knows that the interests of his company may be served by liberalisation, but the local community, of which he is a part, will be adversely affected. When I spoke to him, he vowed to continue his public campaign against the new orthodoxy in the region, despite knowing that he was fighting a losing battle.

Thus the feeling of entrapment in the Caribbean psyche has been given a further twist in the new economic climate of the 1990s. It makes Caribbean democracy seem all the more hollow. Ryan sees this as a potential death blow. As he wrote in 1993:

> The key question of the 1990s, therefore, is whether Caribbean states, faced with the enormous weight of these burdens, will survive in any way which resembles what they looked like in the past three decades. Will liberal democracy survive the onslaught of these new horsemen of the apocalypse? Many Caribbean political elites have expressed pessimism. Jamaican Prime Minister, Michael Manley ... indicated that he had now come to believe that social ethics had little to do with international economic relations and that survival was the principal concern of actors in the international political arena. He had come to believe that it was virtually pointless to appeal to the conscience of man. That was the environment of reality within which Caribbean decision makers must now function. Not to appreciate that was to live in a dream world.[20]

Psycho-social Factors

Dominguez' assertion – that the Caribbean's capacity to sustain liberal democratic polities has been impressive – is therefore somewhat euphemistic. If anything, it has been the capacity of their economic masters to maintain acquiescence for a contradictory system combining internal democracy and international anything-but-democracy which must be admired. Hence my own insistence that, in analysing issues relating to democracy in this region, sufficient weight must be given to psychological, cultural and social factors.

Gordon Lewis has very properly identified the role of the press in keeping up a climate of fear about the possible consequences of any straying from the economic and social paths sanctioned by the US. But beyond that, one of the most useful contributions the Caribbean can make to an understanding of our modern world is in the use of television to manufacture consent in the victims of international politics. After the Gulf War in 1991, there ensued a spate of discussion about CNN's power and potential as a disseminator of 'acceptable' interpretations of events. But for a decade before, CNN had already been demonstrating its ability to mould Caribbean public opinion to its world view, and to generate the pervasive notion that there was only one way of life in the modern world – the American one. The result, of course, was mass confusion, for the realities of the viewers in the islands were somewhat different from the fantasy America on the screen. Loaded on a regional psyche still reeling from the perverted self-image of centuries of slavery and colonialism, this has created a level of psychological and social dislocation that saps the will of any possibility towards sustained political activity.

Studies carried out by Rogler, Hollingshead, Seda, Oscar Lewis and others showed, according to Gordon Lewis, that, in the 1960s, large sections of Puerto Rico's population were 'at once psychologically depressed and socially disorganised, with alarmingly high percentages of mental retardation, psychosis, incest, prostitution and drug addiction; not to mention a collective inferiority complex that comes from the habit, reinforced by the externally-controlled industrialisation programme, of always looking to the norteamericanos to do things, to make decisions as the controlling group in the relationship'.[21]

Lewis predicted that this pattern of social pathology would spread all over the Caribbean, as the Puerto Rican economic model was adopted elsewhere. Most descriptions of Jamaica in the past 20 years, of Barbados in the last ten, and my own observations of Trinidad over recent decades, certainly confirm this.

'Officer', began 17-year-old Denzil Gittens, admitting to the apparently motiveless murder of a neighbour three years ago, 'this thing was more than me'.[22] He was right. In this region, thousands of children are now pathologically violent, involved in shooting, rape and torture, often for no gain, either economic or political. In

Trinidad, with a population of one million, each morning's headlines feature two or three violent deaths. According to a foreign criminologist, Professor Maureen Cain, 14 crimes per 1,000 people were reported in 1993. And this would only have been a fraction of those committed, since most crime is not reported. Ten years ago, Cain noted, there were 1,700 people in custody. In 1993, the number was 33,000. 'Yet', she concluded, 'violent crimes were on the rise and imprisonment appeared not to deter criminals'.[23]

'Violent crime is for young men', stated lawyer Robin Montano in the local press. 'A trip to the Magistrates Court on any morning will show that about 95% of the persons up on charges for violent crimes are young.'[24] These youths, says Camini Marajh, a former crime reporter of the *Trinidad Express* who interviewed them in prison, talk about killing for the sake of 'rank'.[25] To move up in status in their underworld, one has to prove that one is more callous than anyone else. It is the only avenue to self-esteem open to them. Denzil's account of his own act was chillingly casual, vacant in its brutality. Many people in the society have despaired of the youth.

But Marajh has examined the workings of the Youth Training Centre, a prison for young offenders. According to her report, the provision of educational opportunities, literacy training, communication and care seems to be successful in rehabilitating hardened young criminals.[26] But as a result of the economic changes, educational opportunities are dwindling, literacy is falling, communication is eroding and care is a thing of the past. So the violence has been rapidly growing worse. And it expresses itself in many other demoralising ways: increased domestic violence, a spiralling of ethnic tension, abandonment of children, even the daily publication of photographs of grossly brutalised dead bodies on the front pages of newspapers. There is a war taking place here, people believe, but it is not a war between the haves and the have nots. Denzil Gittens did not murder his neighbour because she had any material possession he desired. She was just a poor woman. But she did possess something – a concept of morality. She had referred to him as a thief. What was impressive about his explanation of his crime, however, is that he expressed very little anger over this. He didn't kill her in the middle of an argument, or while in the grip of passion. He did it just to prove he could do so to a friend who had said he couldn't.

In any practical discussion of democracy, one must ask whether a collection of people in such a psychological state are really capable of exercising democratic rights and responsibilities. This is the question which the intellectual elite in the region are now forced to confront. An effective democracy is one in which systems and institutions reflect the will of the majority of the people. But in the Caribbean, that will has been on the receiving end of a number of powerful attacks. Democracy has survived here for so long, I contend, not just because of the checks and balances that are supposed to be part of that system, but because of the smallness of the societies. Traditional values in the village ethos made for some measure of social stability. People lived close to each other both literally and figuratively. They did not look to rules and regulations to protect them as much as to the humanity of other people who had to confront vulnerable groups and individuals in an everyday setting.

'The democratic system in this region has survived for this length of time because of that brown middle class we once derided as Afro-Saxon', political scientist Selwyn Ryan stated in our 1994 discussion. 'There were family values involved in the way they administered things. There was a certain ethic of responsibility. But today, there's no notion of something that you can build and expect to be around down the road. Everything is a hustle. Many people are not volunteering for public causes any more.' The very identity of many members of this class has been bound up with the ethical codes of democratic social management. Lawyers, senior civil servants, journalists, depended on democratic institutions for their livelihoods. Materially secure by virtue of their high professional skills, they could have left this backwater. But they chose to remain – for the weather, the comfortable life, the exuberant culture. So, for a long time, they kept up some defence of the institutions which were supposed to guarantee democratic codes of conduct: the Parliament, the free press and the independent judiciary.

In the last decade, however, this group has been forced to change its perspective radically. In 1993, for instance, Desmond Allum, a member of Trinidad's Parliament, called for the imposition of a state of emergency and the suspension of civil liberties.[27] There were no threats to the state when he made this call, no major civil unrest. He himself is no fascist, but rather a liberal, humane and responsible man, a lawyer who, in earlier times, led the resistance to any attack on the political rights of citizens. Why did he make this call? To fight crime. Did the Bar Association object, denounce him, summon up the constitutional jargon they had used to ward off such calls in the past? No. Did the trade unions? No. Allum wanted the state of emergency to apply to 'certain parts' of the country – that is the ghettos, where the unemployed are concentrated. In other words, a form of social apartheid in a country where South African apartheid has always been the most popular international issue. And the only reason why the appeal was not successful was that it was regarded as impractical. And during the week that this essay is being written, this call has been made again, twice. The first was by a member of the Upper House in Parliament and the second time by a left-wing intellectual.[28]

Thus we now have a situation in which the very people who once defended democratic rights and freedoms are prepared to renounce them voluntarily. The reason – a perception that crime has gone totally out of control. How can you continue to uphold the rights of citizens – or would-be citizens – who do not respect any law, even the law of the jungle? Among wild beasts, the weak are killed for food. Here, human beings are killed for the act of killing. Freedoms are believed to have already been lost – to the criminals.

Crime, Cocaine and Culture

'The criminals in this country seem to be in charge', lamented a letter to the *Trinidad Express* on 26 October 1993. 'They are the government. They run everything.' For several years now, Trinidadians have been talking about 'living in a state of seige', for the crime has resulted in an unofficial curfew. Most people do not venture out after dark. Even in broad daylight, people remain imprisoned in their iron-barred homes. In the house where I write this, one must switch off an electronic alarm system before venturing upstairs to get a drink from the kitchen as though one is in a high-security prison. Social and cultural life has become truncated. A quiet beach is a danger zone. Large social functions such as weddings are held up and everybody robbed. In a country where conversation was the primary cultural activity, radio talk shows are now a major means of exchanging ideas, for, instead of circulating freely, people prefer to remain at home. Children are guarded closely, escorted everywhere, for in today's Trinidad, a bully carries a gun, or at least a knife. A child might be stabbed just to be made to hand over his sneakers. Women have to give up on freedom of movement for the sake of safety. This has led to numerous attacks on the constitution, and a readiness to abandon the checks and balances of the democratic system.

Express editorialists have called for a Gun Court to be established similar to that in Jamaica, where anyone found with even a single bullet in their possession is thrown into a large, high-security prison for life without trial. 'Unfortunately', the *Express* chided the Jamaicans, 'legal challenges to the constitutionality of the Gun Court soon took precedence over the fact that violent crime was on the decrease'.[29] Hence the law, the constitution, is now regarded, not as a means of handling crime, but as an obstacle to fighting it. All the proposals for change now being put forward involve restrictions on the rights and freedoms of all citizens, since, in the public mind, there is no way of distinguishing who is a criminal and who is not. According to numerous investigations, including one carried out by Britain's Scotland Yard, the police service is riddled with corruption. So is the judiciary, according to legal experts. But, instead of dealing with these matters the government wants to change the constitution. This seems to be in accordance with the views of the US embassy. 'The institutions that were set up in 1962 (the year of Independence) were based on assumptions that just don't work', its chargé d'affaires, Charles Shapiro, stated in an interview.[30]

Those assumptions involved the separation of the judiciary from the executive, and a police commission which was independent of government control.

'The systems for ensuring that people get justice and for investigating crime are corrupt. Instead of addressing this problem, they want to change the law, and this will lead to a totalitarian system', argued Harold Chang, former President of the Medical Board. But because crime now appears to be endemic in large parts of this hemisphere, Caribbean governments are being encouraged to see it as normative. 'Trinidad's crime problem is a generation behind that of the United States', stated US embassy official Shapiro. 'It is part of a worldwide phenomenon', echoed the local Prime Minister. Historian Kusha Haraksingh pointed out, however, that while it is true that the situation in Trinidad now resembles that of many American inner cities, in the US there is relative safety in the suburbs. In this small country, there is no cordon of police protection between the ghettos and the residential areas occupied by the more well-off.

'What is happening is that Trinidad is being turned into one large American inner-city', Haraksingh says.[31] This remark explains much of the cultural change that is taking place. The centre of focus is rapidly shifting for the middle and upper classes. Those who are not planning to leave the region for the safer suburbs of North America are preparing their children for life abroad. The future leadership is being exported *en masse*, denuding these islands of the human potential to keep democracy going in the future. The cultural landscape has radically changed in the past five years. Fundamentalist religion of every variety – Christian, Muslim, Hindu – is growing like weeds in the rainy season, eroding the liberal culture that began to develop in the first two decades of independence. This is connected with a retreat into ethnic identification, as the economic stresses increase competition for resources and tempers fray under social strain.

'Many school teachers are now Christian fundamentalist', reported Janice Philip, a veteran educator. 'Children in prestige schools now reach the age of seventeen without knowing about Darwin's theory of evolution, at the same time that they are pushed to use the latest computer programmes.' 'It is a descent into the middle ages', mourned Public Health specialist, Camini Naraynsingh. Principals are bringing in exorcists to chase out demons in top schools of the country. The newspapers feature long articles attributed to Satya Sai Baba, a self-proclaimed incarnation of God who lives in South India. Meanwhile, Catholics sight the Virgin Mary regularly when she touches down on a spot to the west of the country's capital. For many analysts, all the features of the current changes are a result of the rapid incorporation into the current hemispheric economy.

'There are no jobs and the black underclass is growing', Ryan stated in discussion. 'There's no ground for optimism. It's a crisis of expectations. The confidence with which we faced the future – our children can't have it. There is an inexorable process at work internationally. That's the only game in town, and you have to wait until that cycle exhausts itself. The new orthodoxy requires x-y-z. The most you can do as a small state is to find the cracks and exploit them.'

For a small Caribbean country, however, the legal cracks are unavailable. The international system revolves around big bucks. And the biggest bucks that are being offered are by the drug-cartels in Latin America. So that is the crack the Caribbean is finding.

> Oh Trinidad is a pleasant place,
> For them that's always high,
> But Trinidad is a better place
> For them that's crooked and sly ...

goes a verse of doggerel poetry written by the local weatherman, Robin Maharaj, and published by the *Trinidad Guardian* on 18 June 1994. 'The world trade in illicit narcotics is said to be in the vicinity of $500 billion per annum', Ron Sanders has pointed out.[32] The scale of these funds, linked to illegal business, is deeply subversive to any system of values connected with upholding law and order. At the same time that incomes are dropping through the floor in the Caribbean, there is increasing money to be made by getting involved in drug-trafficking. So many Caribbean economies are now based, to a greater or lesser degree, on cocaine trading. This requires corruption. According to numerous commissions of enquiry in the region, many public officials, including prime ministers and senior cabinet members, have succumbed in the past decade. As Sanders noted:

> The Commissioner of Police in Antigua and Barbuda – one of the better-off small island states – earns no more than $2,000 per month, and a senior customs official makes $483 per month. By comparison, pilots flying light aircraft on behalf of the Columbian drug barons are reported to earn $5,000 per kilogram, and their planes carry an average of 300 kilograms; this translates to $1.5 million per shipment. If we take the pilots on the one hand and the police and customs officials on the other as the representatives of the front line in the battle of drug trafficking, it becomes clear that small countries cannot win. Police and customs officials are simply not compensated sufficiently to resist bribes.

The entire system of criminal justice has been put under additional strain to cope with all the criminality that has blossomed as a result of the illegal economy. The more spectacular crimes, which have encouraged many people to abandon their defense of democratic rights, are the results of turf-wars by rival drug-trafficking gangs. The governments' willingness to enact legislation which will reduce the privacy of all citizens is an effort to satisfy the US obsession with money-laundering. Since many of the smaller islands have been turned into offshore banking centres over the past two decades, the region as a whole is now regarded as a centre of dubious financial dealings.

The cocaine trade has also brought with it arms. Both small and large conflicts are now often settled in a deadly manner. This has increased the sense of social chaos and unbearable tension. No one knows what to expect in the future; community structures have been broken down, and no authority is to be trusted. Violence has rapidly become a way of life. Civilization in this region seems to be dying.

Conclusion

'I have left death, failure, disappointment, despair in the wake of my dreams', stated the Caribbean leader at the end of Derek Walcott's 1968 play, *Dream on Monkey Mountain*. Today, it seems foolish to talk about structures of democracy in Trinidad. The population wants relief from the seemingly unbearable social stress at any price. For most people, the world that they inhabited has vanished almost entirely. The dream of a dignified democratic future now seems to have been an illusory one.

'I think that the future will be worse because a lot of people are being killed!' wrote nine-year-old Christopher Chang, when asked to describe his country:

> There are some nice people but there are more bad than good! The future might also be worse for me because I might be killed. When I grow up I will probably live away, where there is not so much violence. Sometimes it is scary to know you will die, so that is why I might go.

When people cannot depend on the state for basic protection – including protection from the rapacity of global commercial forces and the provision of services, what role is left for it? Only control. You cannot even talk of a police state at the moment, since the police service does not function. You have a choice between the anarchy of the present and the development of a totalitarian, colonial state that can suppress criminality through rigid brutality. This is one option that people in Trinidad are bracing themselves for.

For the crisis has forced people to look at the fantasies they have lived with in the past. It has caused them to examine the reality underlying the democratic ritualism in which they have indulged for 30 years. The destruction of civilisation here has also destroyed ideology and, from left and right, you hear the same explanation of the crisis: global imperialism. The forms of democracy were not enough to defend Trinidad against this. Even as the island gets scooped up into the US market, its inhabitants are discovering that they are not part of that society.

'Between me and thee, America, is a great gulf fixed! Truly I am from "the other side"', lamented the liberal poet, Wayne Brown, after a stay in the US in 1994.[33] Formerly Head of Information at the US embassy in Trinidad, Brown was shocked to discover how far apart the realities of liberal artists of the two places now are. He tries to talk to old friends there: '… but then something happens', he writes, 'and I wonder if even he is capable of sharing my incomprehension … Well, there were always two worlds, I guess. And they were never geographically discrete either. But until a couple of years ago, it was possible to see Trinidad as belonging, predominantly, to one, and not to the other.'

Other poets and novelists of the region had always said that there were two worlds below the structures of democracy here. They had said that, in this postcolonial society, a system had to be fashioned which would suit the needs of the entire population. It had to be a real democracy, not a figment of the colonial imagination. They had hammered on about the importance of economic democracy, about opportunity for all. But the political pundits, who had more weight in the sphere of action, had never listened.

But today, in the midst of the violence, there is a certain gentleness in middle-class Trinidad, a certain humility, as people prepare for the end of their world. 'That's the contradictory thing', political scientist Ryan observed in discussion, 'In spite of everything, there's still a sense of community here.'

On this, real democracy can perhaps be built at some time in the future. For democracy starts with a notion of community. And, as Walcott put it in *Dream on Monkey Mountain*, 'your dream touch everyone, sir. Even in those burnt-out coals of your eyes, there's still some fire. Dying, but fire. If a wind could catch them again, if some wind, some breath ...'.[34]

Notes

1   Essay published in the *Trinidad Express*, 18 August 1991, soon after an attempted coup in Trinidad and Tobago.

2   Carlene J. Edie (ed), *Democracy in the Caribbean* (New York: Praeger, 1993).

3   Jorge I. Dominguez, Robert A. Pastor and R. Delisle Worrel (ed), *Democracy in the Caribbean. Political Economic and Social Perspectives* (Baltimore: Johns Hopkins Press, 1993).

4   In discussion, June 1994.

5   Public lecture given at the residence of the US Ambassador, June 1994.

6   C.J. Edie (ed), *Democracy in the Caribbean* (1993).

7   Selwyn Ryan, 'Problems and Prospects for the Survival of Liberal Democracy in the Anglophone Caribbean', published in Edie, *Democracy in the Caribbean* (1993).

8   V.S. Naipaul, *The Suffrage of Elvira* (London: Andre Deutsch, 1958).

9   Derek Walcott, 'What the Twilight said', published in *Dream on Monkey Mountain and other plays* (New York: Farrar, Straus and Giroux, 1970).

10 Gordon K. Lewis, *The Growth of the Modern West Indies* (New York: Monthly Review Press, 1968).

11. Derek Walcott, *The Castaway and Other Poems* (London: Jonathan Cape, 1965).

12 Gordon K. Lewis, 'The Challenge of Independence' in *The Growth of the Modern West Indies*.

13 Ryan, 'Problems and Prospects'.

14   Derek Walcott, 'The Spoiler's Return', in *The Fortunate Traveller* (London: Faber and Faber, 1982).

15   Dominguez, *Democracy in the Caribbean*.

16   Discussion with the author, June 1994.

17   Discussion with the author, June 1994.

18   Discussion with the author, June 1994.

19   Discussions with Gary Voss, Chairman of the Caribbean branch of Unilever and former Chairman of the Trinidad and Tobago Manufacturers' Association.

20   Ryan, *'Problems and Prospects'*.

21   Lewis, *Growth of the Modern West Indies*.

22   From an article in the *Trinidad Express*, 10 January 1994.

23   From an article in the *Trinidad Express*, 10 January 1994.

24   *Trinidad Guardian*, 15 June 1994.

25   Reported in the local press. The response to this call was also reported in press clippings from 1993.

26   Press reports, June 1994.

27   Reported in the local press. The response to this call was also reported in press clippings from 1993.

28   Press reports, June 1994.

29   Editorial, *Trinidad Express*, 16 October 1993.

30   Discussions with the author, June 1994.

31   The statements on this page were made in a series of discussions held with the author in June 1994.

32   Ron Sanders, 'The Drug Problem. Policy Options for Caribbean Countries', in Dominguez, *Democracy in the Caribbean*.

33   From his column 'In Our Time', published in the *Trinidad Guardian*, 18 June 1994.

34   Acknowledgements
      This essay was based on discussions with the following people in Trinidad:
      Gaurie Mohabir – Centre for Free Thought and Meals
      Kim Johnson – Specialist Writer on Legal Affairs, Trinidad Express Newspapers
      Dr Harold Chang – Former President, Medical Board of Trinidad and Tobago
      Patrick Manning – Prime Minister of Trinidad and Tobago
      Dr Camini Narayansingh – Mother and Public Health Specialist
      Camini Marajh – Former Crime Reporter, *Trinidad Express*
      Alva Viarrel – Crime Reporter, *Trinidad Express*
      Dr Selwyn Ryan – Director, Institute for Social and Economic Research, University of the West Indies (UWI)
      Dr Kusha Haraksingh – Department of History, UWI

Jones P. Madeira – Editor-in-Chief, *Trinidad Guardian*
Charles Shapiro – Chargé d'Affaires, United States embassy
Janice Philip – Teacher
Bruce Paddington – Director, Educational Television Unit, Ministry of Education
Sunity Maharaj – Investigative Reporter, *Trinidad Express*
Suzanne Lopez – Features Editor, *Trinidad Express*
Keith Smith – Editor-in-Chief, *Trinidad Express*
and others whom I may not name.

In addition, I wish to express my gratitude to the following:
For help in research: The staff of the *Trinidad Express* library, Camanie Naraynsingh, Bruce Paddington, Selwyn Ryan, Suzanne Lopez. For coffee, forebearance and incredible hospitality: Tamira Chang and family.

7

Communalism and the Democratic Process in India

Achin Vanaik and Praful Bidwai

Communalism is a combined process of: competitive desecularisation in a religiously plural society – a competitive striving to extend the reach, power and importance of religious institutions, religious ideologies and religious identities – which along with non-religious factors helps to harden divisions and create or deepen tensions between religious communities.[1] Communal politics is the mass politics of religious identity. While all communalisms feed upon each other and therefore require to be fought against simultaneously, majority communalism, that is Hindu communalism, is the most dangerous in India. It is on this that this article will focus. The ultimate logic of minority Sikh or Muslim communalism is separation – the creation of Khalistan or another Pakistan. But it is only Hindu communalism that can transform altogether the character of the Indian state and society pushing it towards viciously authoritarian forms.

The most important form of Hindu communalism is Hindu Nationalism. Hindu Nationalism is a politico-religious movement and ideology which, like others of the same ilk, seeks to transform the state and civil society of a Third World country. But is it a kind of fundamentalism? That depends of course on how one defines fundamentalism. Certainly it is possible to give a broad, generic definition which would encompass not only such politico-religious movements but also non-religious 'fundamentalist' movements. The definition of fundamentalism is thus somewhat heuristic. For our purposes it would seem more appropriate to restrict the label of religious fundamentalism to those movements which stress either a return or a reinterpretation of foundational or fundamental holy texts in order to resolve contemporary political and social problems. In such a reckoning, Hindu and Buddhist nationalisms are not fundamentalisms and cannot be, given the non-scriptural character of the two religions.

But otherwise Hindu Nationalism, as a form of cultural exclusivism, shares many similarities with fundamentalisms. All these movements fight on the terrain of modernity itself. They do not exist on some ground between tradition and modernity. Communal politics is a modern form of the politics of religious appeal. Nationalism, and therefore Hindu Nationalism, is by its very nature a modern phenomenon. Religious symbols and themes (many of which are traditional) are used to pursue ends which are modernist and anti-modernist but never non-modernist or pre-modernist. Meanwhile, the means of mobilisation used by such movements or forces are invariably modern.

Politico-religious movements in the Third World are not atavisms. They are contemporary reactions to the failed promise of modernisation, to ideological confusion and to incoherent and often authoritarian governance. They are also anti-modernist in seeking to undo and reverse the powerful thrusts in modernity towards minimal secularisation (the basic separation of religion and state) and towards democratisation based on a principle of institutionalised individual rights. Certainly this is so of Hindu Nationalism, the right-wing and reactionary (but not conservative) form of Hindu communalism.

Hindu Nationalism seeks to construct a pan-Indian, monolithic 'Hindu community'. But if it does not have roots in 'traditional India', neither does secularism, its ideological counterpoint. Both emerged in the colonial period and have been contesting each other since. But it is really in the postcolonial period, primarily in the last 15 to 20 years, that this form of communalism has risen to such dangerous proportions. It is at this time that the failure of the postcolonial project – the failed promise of developmentalism – has become evident. In India the name given to this postcolonial project was the 'Nehruvian Consensus'.

The underlying principles of this project were socialism, democracy, secularism.[2] By socialism was meant nothing more than a welfarist capitalism with some genuine commitment to striving for social justice, but at least that. By secularism was meant at least the safeguarding of a non-denominationalist and non-religiously affiliated state even if the state's actual practice of religious impartiality left a great deal to be desired. It was the Congress both as movement and party that most strongly embodied this Nehruvian Consensus and developmentalist project. The failed promise of that project is also the failed promise of the Congress. More than anything else it has been the decline of the Congress (itself rooted in basic socioeconomic transformations since independence) that has created the vacuum in which Hindu Nationalism as a politico-religious movement and ideology has flourished.

Today, it is not just the Nehruvian Consensus as a way of fulfilling the postcolonial project that is being rejected but the foundational principles of social justice, democracy and secularism of which it was a flawed embodiment. The neoliberal economic turn is a repudiation of the first. The forces of Hindu Nationalism – constituted above all by the Rashtriya Swayamsevak Sangh (National Volunteer Corps) or RSS (the semi-militarist, cadre-based hub of the whole Combine, set up in 1925) and its various front organisations, most notably its political wing, the Bharatiya Janata Party (BJP) – are redefining democracy to mean majoritarianism or promoting 'Hindu interests'. And they are redefining secularism as Westernised pseudo-secularism which needs to be replaced by a Hindu Rashtra or Hindu Nation with a Hindu State, which by virtue of being Hindu will be naturally and genuinely tolerant and therefore genuinely secular. The story of Hindu Nationalism's emergence can now be briefly traced.

From the National Movement Era to the Late 1960s

An element of Hindu Nationalism was never absent from the consciousness of the National Movement. It was sometimes embodied in the language of appeal by Mahatma Gandhi, that is the equation of independence with Ram Rajya or the benign kingdom of King-God Rama. This was because of the nature of mobilisation carried out by the Congress. The latter was an umbrella organisation which sought the widest possible base by appealing to a variety of groups largely on the basis of their pre-existing identities yet which aimed to link these communities' interests to the achievement of independence from British rule. Thus Muslims, Sikhs and Hindus were often appealed to as Muslims, Sikhs and Hindus so that a nationalist identity was seen as resting upon a religious identity rather than as transcending it.

For the first two decades after independence the considerable success of India in institutionalising democratic rule and in carrying out a degree of welfarist industrialisation enabled the Congress to survive as the dominant political institution in the country. Indeed, the Congress and its leadership largely oversaw this period of successful transition to a relatively stable democracy. A variety of factors were responsible for the subsequent emergence of the peculiar paradox of India's polity – endemic political instability encased within a framework of remarkable democratic durability. On the one hand a democratic political system had been institutionalised with strong mass commitment to its preservation. On the other hand there was the partial decay and mutation of a variety of democratic institutions such as the legislature, civilian bureaucracy, judiciary and press.

Above all, the principal overseer of political stability, the Congress, had entered a period of slow but historic decline. For decades a Congress alliance with rural landed elites had assured it decisive control over the countryside while it also carried a populist appeal among the poorest sections of Indian society. Given the enormously segmented character of Indian society – no other country in the world is criss-crossed by such a range of community affiliations and identities – the Congress was the centrist formation par excellence. It was the one party that could appeal to the widest cross-section of the Indian population, thus confirming the view that Indian political democracy to be stable could not rest on some unachievable two-party competitive system, but required the constant popularity of a dominant centrist formation.[3]

Challenges from above and below undermined Congress dominance. Historically, the electoral base of the Congress were the Brahmins and forward castes, along with the 'core minorities', that is Muslims, Dalits (Untouchables) and tribals. The very successes of Indian development in the first two decades transformed the situation. New rural elites from the middle or backward castes emerged and pressed for their aims both within and outside the Congress Party. At the same time growing dissatisfactions in relation to growing expectations made the support of large sections of the core minorities for the Congress increasingly volatile. The Congress itself had also transmogrified. In the first two decades after 1947 the Congress had moved from being a mass movement and organisation to being an increasingly corrupted party of governance and patronage. Organisationally, it had become an electoral machine to be cranked up only around the time of various local, regional and national elections.

The Reign of Mrs Gandhi and the Emergency Interregnum

The crisis of Congress hegemony became obvious and therefore the inauguration of the era of 'endemic political instability' took place in the late 1960s when for the first time in its post-independence history the Congress Party split under Mrs Gandhi, with her wing proving triumphant eventually. Ever since, the basic dilemma has remained the same. On the one hand there is the historic decline of the Congress in the sense that its consistent dominance as the centrist focal point of Indian politics cannot be taken as assured. On the other hand there has been the consistent inability of any other political formation to replace it as a dominant and stable point of reference.

In retrospect the Emergency is best understood as Mrs. Gandhi's failed attempt to resolve the endemic crisis of political instability through an authoritarian transformation of the polity. But that has only meant that one is clearer on what should not be done to address the problem of instability, not about what should be done. There have been six general elections since 1971. All of them have been referendum-like in character. In the absence of any clear and convincing ideological perspective from any side the electorate has been presented with issue-based differentiation between the main claimants to power. This has only now begun to change with the rise of the strongly ideological BJP, with the RSS behind it.

In those six elections either the Congress or a centrist alternative – usually a patchwork formation united by anti-Congressism rather than any positive principle of unity – has come to power. The Congress has lost twice but the alternative to it has not lasted a full term. Congress victories by massive seat majorities in the first-past-the-post system in 1971 and 1984 (when Mrs Gandhi was assassinated) were themselves, ironically enough, indicative of the growing volatility of voter support which could swing this way or that from one referendum-like election to the other. In 1990 the Congress for the first time in its history came to power as a minority government. For the first time the dimension of a specifically parliamentary instability had been added to the general problem of endemic political instability, until the Rao government engineered the necessary defections.

By the late 1970s and early 1980s the Nehruvian Consensus itself had come to be seriously questioned and increasingly regarded as a failed project. But its basic principles were not as yet questioned. That would come only with the rise of political Hinduism whose principal components were, firstly, the steady expansion of RSS influence in civil society through the extension of networks of *shaka* (neighbourhood chapters where cadres are recruited and given physical training and a Hindu Nationalist politico-religious catechism) and, secondly, the political rise of the BJP and its forerunner, the Jan Sangh.

It was the Emergency and the mass-scale anti-corruption movement that preceded it and partly provoked the declaration of Emergency that gave the forces of Hindu Nationalism an unexpected lease of life. The cadres of the RSS found a cause – opposing corruption and then the Emergency – that gave it energy, mobilisational experience, and public legitimacy on a much greater scale. The Jan Sangh, hitherto a fringe right-wing party, by becoming a part of the political coalition called the Janata Party which overthrew Mrs Gandhi and the Emergency regime in the 1977 elections, secured more seats for its chosen candidates standing under the common Janata banner (over 90 in a Lower House of around 540) than it had achieved in all previous elections put together. It also secured legitimacy as a 'responsible' party as well as practical political power for a time during which it could misuse this to place adherents and sympathisers of Hindu Nationalism in various positions in the bureaucracy.

The Janata party was to break up over the unwillingness of the Jan Sangh, as one of its original components, to sever its links with the RSS, an extra-parliamentary organisation with no commitment to the Janata Party as such. In the 1980 elections, won by Mrs Gandhi's Congress, the Jan Sangh's seat tally fell to 16. It was still a part then of the renamed Janata (S) which got 60-odd seats and was routed by the Congress.

Between 1980 and the next general elections in 1984 the dilemma facing the Jan Sangh (which had reconstituted itself as an independent party) was the classic one confronting any party seeking to come to power in New Delhi through the electoral route. Given the segmented and sectional character of Indian society how could any non-Centrist party hope to do so, or even to fare well? Should the BJP weaken or strengthen its links with the RSS whose agenda could not be the same as that of a political party, even one with a commitment to Hindu Nationalism? The RSS would support even the Congress (as it has done on occasions) if it felt that this would promote the advancement of Hindu cultural nationalism in civil society. Should the Jan Sangh try to be the party of the Great Hindu Rally/Rassemblement, or should it try to be the Hindu equivalent of a right-wing Christian Democratic party of Western Europe? Only more Hindu than Christian Democracy is Christian, and less democratic? Should the Jan Sangh, as the political representative of Hindu Nationalism, move towards the centre of the Indian political spectrum thereby diluting its Hindu Nationalist message? Or should it swing towards a much more aggressive and communalist posture where it would tie itself much more strongly to the parent cadre organisation, the RSS, and accept in the final count the latter's authority?

Between 1980 and 1984 the Jan Sangh sought to weaken its links with the RSS, to move to the centre and to dilute its ideological message through advocacy of a largely incomprehensible 'Gandhian Socialism'. This was eventually to give way to 'Integral Humanism', a covering label coined by Deen Dayal Upadhyaya, a Hindu Nationalist leader of less self-confident times, and then to an aggressive and open

Hindu Nationalism. The 1984 elections were the turning point. The Jan Sangh fared dismally. It got only two seats. There was a change of leadership with the current leader L.K. Advani replacing the 'moderate' A.B. Vajpayee; a change of orientation; and eventually a change of name to the Bharatiya Janata Party (BJP).

The Rise of Hindu Nationalism: 1984 Onwards

The Jan Sangh/BJP had now settled on the message it would push. From 1984 onwards its growth in power and influence would surprise itself. It was not the case that its message was new. It was the fact that the *receptivity* to its message was new. It was not the rise of the BJP that explained the decline of the Congress but vice versa. In the ideological vacuum created by the decline of Congress hegemony and the absence of a replacement for it, the BJP was the one party which along with the other forces of Hindu Nationalism was promising an altogether new project for the resurrection of 'Indian-Hindu greatness'. This was a project attacking the very foundations not only of the Nehruvian Consensus but for the construction of any decent and humane vision of Indian society. But the *fact* that it was a new project is what aroused and continues to arouse such passion both amongst its supporters and amongst its opponents.

Establishing 'Hindu unity' was to be the key to the construction of a strong India. But there are only two ways to go about constructing such 'unity'. Either there is some principle of coherence internal to Hinduism, which given its diffuse and agglomerative doctrinal and ritual character, could only be a loose and accommodating Brahminism. The trouble with this is that it can only take Hindu communalism so far. The divisions within 'Hindu society' are too many and too strong, particularly the all-important hostility of lower castes to upper-caste and Brahmanical domination. Far more important has been the other principle of coherence – the construction of an 'enemy' outside the fold of Hinduism and Hindus which can serve as a unifying rallying point. The only serious candidate for this in the Indian context is Islam.

Between 1984 and 1989 the BJP was to achieve remarkable success in spreading this pernicious message. Since Muslims are only 12 per cent of the population and are disproportionately represented amongst the poorest and most illiterate sections of Indian society, there is no way that a message of direct domination by Muslims over Hindus can be sold. Instead the focal point of attack has been different. The (weakly) secular Indian state has been attacked for 'appeasing' Muslims, and thus treating Hindus 'unfairly'. In selling this message the forces of Hindu Nationalism have been greatly abetted by the fact that the Indian state, especially under the Congress, has not so much appeased Muslims but appeased *all* communalisms. Indian secularism has been an admixture of Western notions of separation of religion from state institutions, and a peculiarly Indian notion of the state treating all religious groupings equally through active intervention and support. In practice this has meant that successive governments have played a game of 'balancing' communal favours to the leaderships of the different religious communities.

Thus the absence of a uniform civil code of even an optional nature has been a concession to Muslim fundamentalist leadership adamant about the sanctity of a very conservatively interpreted Sharia. While the refusal of governments to carry out a purge of pre-dominantly Hindu paramilitary forces which have themselves attacked predominantly Muslim communities, has been the other side of the picture. In 1986 the issue of a uniform civil code came up when the Supreme Court insisted that the provisions of the Indian penal code on maintenance take priority over the Sharia for an elderly Muslim divorcee, Shah Bano, who had petitioned it. The Congress government's decision to overturn the ruling in favour of preserva-tion of Muslim personal law sparked mobilisation and counter-mobilisation by fundamentalist Muslim leaders and by the forces of Hindu Nationalism. This transformed what was essentially an issue of women's oppression by personal laws of all kinds into a battleground of identity politics between 'appeased Muslims' and 'aggrieved Hindus' although Hindus themselves could not suffer from such a government decision – the victims were Muslim women and children.

To counterbalance this concession to Muslim communalism, the government sought to appease Hindu communalists by lifting the locks of a disputed shrine in Ayodhya where Hindu devotees were given full access to worship while Muslims, rightly regarding the shrine as a mosque which had long been desecrated by the surreptitious placement of Hindu idols, were denied such access. In the early 1980s religious front organisations of the RSS, most notably the Vishva Hindu Parishad (VHP) had carried out a series of mass mobilising pilgrimages of a semi-religious/semi-cultural nature aimed at consolidating a common Hindu identity. The forces of Hindu Nationalism were in effect the only formations confident of carrying out mass mobilisations of a kind that had an implicit or explicit anti-Muslim thrust. But what was missing was an issue that could not only focus with some degree of plausibility on the state's 'appeasement'

of Muslims but simultaneously also arouse a strong sense of Hindu
deprivation and grievance.

The government provided it with just such an issue with its action
in Ayodhya, the mythical site of the birthplace of the Hindu God-
king Rama. For decades there had been a localised belief,
unsubstantiated by any serious empirical evidence, that a temple
dedicated to Lord Rama had been destroyed by the first Mughal
Emperor, Babar, in the sixteenth century and a mosque built in its
place. Local disputes after 1947 had led successive governments to
restrict entry to the disputed shrine in the 'interests of law and
order', though elementary justice demanded full restoration of its status
as a mosque which had been defiled by nocturnal introduction of
idols in December 1949.[4]

In the wake of the government decision, the RSS, BJP and VHP spear-
headed a remarkable campaign for the destruction of the mosque and
its replacement by a new temple dedicated to Lord Rama as a symbol
of respect for 'Hindu wishes' desecrated by past 'Muslim perfidy' and
sustained by a state bent upon 'appeasing' Muslims, who by their
opposition to such a 'restoration' showed themselves to be 'con-
temptuous and hostile' to 'Hindu sentiment'. Carried out in a variety
of forms, this campaign was among the most significant campaigns
in India's post-independence history. More than anything else it
polluted the political and democratic atmosphere of Indian society.
It was to deliver huge political and social dividends to the forces of
Hindu Nationalism though in time it was to offer diminishing and
even negative returns.

By the time of the 1989 elections, which were won by the new
centrist alternative to the Congress, the Janata Dal (headed by V.P.
Singh on an anti-corruption platform – Rajiv Gandhi's implication
in the Bofors arms sale scandal), the BJP had clearly become a
powerful new actor on the political stage. The peak of its Ayodhya
campaign and the unmasking of Hindu Nationalism's ruthlessly
authoritarian, communal and anti-secular face was yet to come.
Nonetheless, by 1989 the BJP *going it alone* in the elections won 88
seats, propping up a minority Janata Dal government that it would
soon enough bring down.

From the 1989 Elections to the Destruction
of Babri Masjid

1989 saw the installation of the minority V.P. Singh government which
was dependent on both the Left (consisting primarily of the

Communist parties) and the BJP, for its survival. The BJP had by then identified the mosque/temple issue as a high priority on its agenda, indeed it had decided to concentrate on it. The centrality of the mosque/temple issue to the BJP's agenda was premised upon a qualitative change in the relationship between the party and its 'sister' organisations – the Vishwa Hindu Parishad, the Bajrang Dal and the Rashtriya Swayamsevak Sangh, especially the VHP. The VHP is the broad religious-cultural 'front' organisation set up in 1964, and the Bajrang Dal is a recent addition to the 'family'.

It is the VHP which originally launched the Ayodhya campaign in the early 1980s and controlled it until 1988. The campaign's adoption by the BJP meant that the VHP, a rag-tag coalition of assorted sadhus, leaders of obscure Hindu sects and plain fanatics, had become much more important within the 'Sangh Parivar' – the RSS-led 'family'. In some ways, this obscurantist non-parliamentary grouping was able to dictate its own agenda to the BJP. The RSS, meanwhile, consolidated a particularly close relationship with the BJP from the mid-1980s onwards.

At the RSS's goading, the BJP astutely exploited the potential the mosque/temple issue offered, first to mobilise people politically on a mass scale, and secondly, to combine non-parliamentary activism with its parliamentary work, thus bringing the pressure of its mass campaign to bear upon the weak V.P. Singh government. By mid-1990, numerous forms of mobilisation by the BJP-VHP-Bajrang Dal-RSS combine could be identified: collection of 'consecrated' bricks from villages and towns in a symbolic gesture of support to the planned construction of a Rama temple at Ayodhya; public meetings where fiery anti-Muslim rhetoric would flow freely, and which would be used to recruit cadres and activists; processions of *Ram jyotis*, literally, oil lamps dedicated to Rama, which would be organised late at night in and across neighbourhoods to focus sharply on the temple, often in a provocative fashion to hold out the threat of violence and aggression to Muslims.

In parts of north India, an overtly militant and particularly menacing form of mobilisation was organised: the wielding and brandishing of the *trishul*, or the trident, Lord Shiva's weapon, and its use as a symbol of a new militant Hindu consciousness. A whole industry manufacturing propaganda material – posters, stickers, mini-trishuls as well as colourful and fanciful accounts of ancient and medieval Indian history mushroomed, which sustained this mobilisation.

In the autumn of 1990, the BJP succeeded in multiplying the scale of mobilisation many times and imparting to it a particularly aggressive edge. This happened with L.K. Advani's *rath yatra* – literally a chariot tour which covered more than half of the country. The chariot – an imitation of ancient horse drawn carts from the *Mahabharata*, in reality a decked-up Toyota van – took Advani to more than 20 communally sensitive cities as well as to hundreds of small towns and villages, where volunteers could drum up support, and organise rallies and public meetings on an overtly anti-Muslim platform of hatred and vituperation. Advani boldly displayed the election symbol of the BJP – the lotus flower – on the *rath* and made no effort to hide the link between the *yatra*, religion and politics.

The *rath yatra* left a trail of violence and devastation in its wake. Right from Somnath in Gujarat in the west, where it started, it was plain that the *yatra* was calculated to provoke: there were accompanying rituals using human blood; the most horrifying and belligerent chants and slogans were raised; and Muslim-owned shops and names were openly targeted. V.P. Singh came under pressure from the Left and the secular media to ban the *yatra* on the ground that it was calculated to provoke violence, and was indeed doing just that.

Singh dithered. He would vacillate between tough action to affirm the law of the land and trying to placate the BJP leadership. Ultimately, and belatedly, Advani was arrested and his march halted – not by the central government of Singh, but by the government of Bihar, then also under Janata Dal rule. The manner in which the episode was handled strengthened the BJP immensely. Singh's hesitation and indecision in taking on Advani, and preventing wholly preventable violence, lent credibility to the party's boastful assertion that it was the unstoppable, invincible force.

In his own way, and thanks to his political weakness, Singh perpetuated the central government's policy of appeasement of the BJP. This was to further boost confidence in the Hindu communal camp. As soon as Advani was arrested, the BJP announced it was withdrawing support to Singh in Parliament. By September, the government was tottering and counting its last days. Then, in October the VHP launched another offensive, this time in Ayodhya itself. It organised a *karseva*, or voluntary service, to make a symbolic beginning to build the temple. Unwilling to prevent it, although it was in blatant violation of court injunctions against a change in the Ayodhya status quo, the government allowed *karsevaks* to gather in large numbers right next to the Babri mosque. On October 30, a frenzied mob climbed over the compound wall of the mosque, and some volunteers climbed on top of one of the shrine's domes to plant saffron flags. Once again, a weak and vacillating state had allowed the forces of extreme right-wing communalism to score a victory. No one was prosecuted for this criminal act.

The V.P. Singh government was followed by an unstable coalition, which soon made way for elections in May 1991. The Congress Party returned to power at the Centre, in a minority government, this time without Rajiv Gandhi, who was assassinated during the election campaign. The new prime minister, Narasimha Rao, was a weak compromise candidate, never known for convictions or firmness, and in favour of a 'soft Hindu' rather than a principled secular approach.

The preceding months of mobilisation had brought the BJP handsome electoral gains: the party won 119 seats against the 88 it had bagged in 1989. Its share of the national vote rose to over 20 per cent, way beyond its own expectations, and breaking all previous patterns of sudden spurts in electoral support. Thanks to the fragmentation of the rest of the non-Congress vote between factions of a splintered Janata Dal, the BJP emerged as the single largest party in the lower house of Parliament. It also took power in the state of Uttar Pradesh where Ayodhya is located.

Rao's greater proclivity towards appeasement, his dependence on non-Congress MPs in crucial parliamentary votes, and his weakness within the ruling party, were cynically exploited by the BJP's leaders who played their cards skilfully, extracting concession after concession, occupying more and more political ground. A situation of collaboration or informal alliance/understanding between the BJP and the Rao faction of the Congress soon emerged, which permitted the BJP to tilt the scales in its favour time and time again.

An important factor sustained this informal alliance. In mid-1991, the government embarked on a new right-wing oriented economic policy, which was largely unpopular and strongly opposed by the Left. The BJP by and large endorsed the policy, which meshed well with its own orientation, although some if its hardcore RSS leaders had reservations about its emphasis on liberalisation of foreign investment and trade. Rao came to depend more and more on the BJP for support for his policy in and out of Parliament.

By 1992, a larger-than-life BJP commanded a degree of political influence far in excess of its actual weight in Parliament, politics and society. It used this influence deftly, through the media and the bureaucracy, to advance its Ramjanamabhoomi campaign. It calculated that the effete, vacillating and compromised Rao government would not be willing or able to stand its ground and resist the BJP-VHP-RSS-Bajrang Dal's encroachments into Ayodhya.

It planned a strategy of making such physical encroachments and in July 1992, undertook a *karseva* to construct a platform on a plot of land within the mosque complex, as part of its temple construction campaign. The government's response to this patently illegal and provocative move was supine. It allowed the platform to be built, thus sanctioning and legitimising the encroachment. And it pleaded with obscure religious leaders and assorted sadhus that they should counsel reason and tolerance upon the leaders of the temple agitation.

The post-July run-up to the demolition of the Babri mosque on 6 December 1992 is a story of retreat after ignominious retreat by the government, and of further intrusion on the BJP's part; of negotiations, special pleading and entreaties directed at an unrelenting Hindu communal leadership, of disinformation and dissimulation and plain lying on the government's part; and deception, devious manipulation and rogue tactics on the part of the BJP and its allies. Subsequent disclosures make it plain that the government had adequate warning from its own intelligence agencies as well as from the Hindu communal leaders with whom it was negotiating, of the likelihood of a planned assault on the Babri mosque on 6 December.

However, it failed to take precautionary measures, to get the state government of Uttar Pradesh – then under the BJP's control – to deploy adequate central paramilitary troops, secure injunctions from the law courts, or to arrest BJP-VHP leaders who, it well knew, were engaged in a conspiracy to destroy the mosque. The carnage of December 6 sent shock waves through all of South Asia. The BJP parliamentary leadership's first response to the events was apologetic: Advani resigned as Leader of the Opposition in the Lok Sabha and the chief minister of Uttar Pradesh also quit. However, the party soon moved to a more defiant, militant posture justifying what had happened, and blaming the lethargic legal system for its inability to resolve the Ayodhya dispute. Rao dismissed three other state governments where the party ruled – Madhya Pradesh, Rajasthan and Himachal Pradesh – for their involvement in the razing of the mosque and support to *karsevaks* – an action the BJP claimed was undemocratic.

After the Demolition: The Current Conjuncture of Uncertainty

December 1992 marked the peak of the BJP's militant activism. Since then the party has been in a state of uncertainty, although by no means so demoralised or weak as not to benefit occasionally from the Congress Party's prolonged crisis and the government's difficulties. A major test for the BJP came in November 1993 when elections were held to the legislatures of the four states where the party ruled until December 1992. In many ways, the party failed the test. The election results signified the BJP's decline and the emergence of a new trend in Indian politics, based on an alliance between plebeian, oppressed layers of the population which have a stake in secularism and pluralist democracy.

The BJP did not fight the November elections just to return to power in the four states. It contested them as a referendum on the legitimacy of the movement to build a temple to Lord Rama at Ayodhya, on the demolition of the mosque, on its claim to be the 'natural' representative of the Hindus, indeed on its 'Hindu Rashtra' platform of a Hindu nation/state.

It clearly lost the referendum on all these issues. According to its own leaders, the BJP may have been set back by a decade. It can no longer claim that it sets the north Indian, or national political agenda. Or that it enjoys a unique status in India by virtue of its claim to represent the 'soul of Indian nationhood'.

Constituency-wide results from the four northern states suggest that the BJP's base among the lower castes has significantly eroded; its vote has become geographically more skewed; and its support has proved unstable and volatile. None of this is compensated by its gains in the centrally administered Delhi capital region, where the new assembly does not even enjoy full municipal powers.

Not only did the BJP lose both in terms of seats and votes in Madhya Pradesh, Rajasthan and Himachal Pradesh – in the last case, a whopping 82 per cent of the seats it held. It performed poorly in India's biggest (and the world's fifth most populous) state, Uttar Pradesh, too, with the exception of its western region.

The party's support base proved essentially unstable, lacking in durability and loyalty. A 'wave' – or sudden burst of popular support based on a changing electoral mood – can earn the BJP votes from the unlikeliest of social strata. India has had many such waves in the past two decades, and the nature of the vote has tended to be plebiscitary on many occasions. But as soon as the wave recedes, the BJP is back to low scores. This is the past experience with other right-wing parties in the country, too.

After the November elections the BJP has once again become a party that is much more urban than rural, and upper caste in its orientation, as it was in the pre-1985 period. This also places a limitation on its ability – in the absence of a wave – to generate rural support which alone can help it garner the votes needed, to set the agenda regionally or nationally.

It seems highly unlikely that there will be another wave on the mosque/temple issue. Today, a flimsy structure, with a canvas canopy and tin-sheet walls, exists where the Babri mosque once stood. The BJP and VHP demand that a permanent Rama temple must be built on that very spot. Narasimha Rao has prevaricated on the issue. On 7 December 1992 he declared that the mosque would be rebuilt at the site and also that a Rama temple would be built close by. He later announced that two separate trusts would be set up to undertake the construction of the two shrines. Rao's latest move is to deny that he had made a solemn public commitment to rebuild the mosque at the same site.

The BJP-VHP has once again threatened to agitate the issue by mobilising fanatical Hindus and by beginning the construction of a full-scale temple soon. It has drawn up grand architectural plans for such a temple. However, the *construction* of a temple – a slow, boring, undramatic process where not much mob activity is possible – lacks the appeal of *demolition* – of an enemy symbol, a clearly identifiable object of hate.

Why did the BJP lose the 1993 assembly elections? BJP leaders have wholly incompatible analyses of the party's defeat. Some believe the party lost because it concentrated excessively on the temple issue. Some believe just the opposite. The tension between the two views, and the differences between the RSS and the BJP, are likely to sharpen in the future.

Already the RSS is distrustful of the BJP leadership's 'soft' pro-liberalisation position on India's new economic policies recommended by the IMF and the World Bank. The RSS favours indigenous industry and opposes foreign capital. It follows a xenophobic, autarkic model of growth. The RSS refrained from openly criticising the BJP leaders because of the elections. But since then, the dispute has tended to come into the open, further weakening the BJP's and the 'family's' claim to being a united, disciplined, coherent force.

There are three principal reasons for the BJP's defeat. First, there was an *effective* challenge to it in Uttar Pradesh, Madhya Pradesh, and to some extent in Himachal Pradesh – in contrast to 1990–91 when the Congress adopted a 'soft communal' line. In Madhya Pradesh, the Congress, under leaders not belonging to the Narasimha Rao faction, itself confronted the BJP head on. And in Uttar Pradesh, the party was strongly opposed by strongly secular non-Congress rivals.

Secondly, the winning combination typically involved an alliance between significant sections of the Dalits, low-caste Hindus ('backward' or 'Other Backward Classes' (OBCs) in constitutionalese), and Muslims, who feel particularly threatened by the BJP's communal politics. The three groups represent roughly 15, 45 and 12 per cent of the Indian population. If even half of them back a party – and that is saying a great deal, because in India voting is rarely *en bloc* – that party can reasonably expect to win.

The third factor was the BJP's poor record of governance in all the four states. It ran regimes that were bankrupt in social policy, ineffective in promoting development, and as corrupt and venal as Congress governments. They antagonised poor people, and in some cases, even sections of the elite. The voter judged the BJP's record of governance and found it wanting.

Of these three factors, the emergence of the multi-caste alliance is the most significant. At its root is self-assertion by the lower orders of the Hindu hierarchy and their struggle for equality and freedom from exploitation. This is a historic trend that started in the south of India in the 1930s and has now reached the north. It has been an integral part of the social reform movement in the country. It is in part a consequence of the continuing rigidity and persistence of the caste system. Given the growing awareness of their rights among Dalits and OBCs and the emergence of a new radical leadership, this trend seems irrepressible.

It got a big boost in 1990 when the New Delhi government under V.P. Singh announced the acceptance of a 1978 report of the Mandal Commission on OBCs, which recommended that 27 per cent of all government jobs be reserved for them in addition to the 15 and seven per cent respectively provided for the Dalits and tribals by the Indian Constitution. Singh's announcement of the implementation of the Mandal Report touched off a furore in the North, with upper-caste Hindus taking to the streets.

The agitation not only challenged the 27 per cent quota for the OBCs, but the very principle of reservation and affirmative action for the Dalits and tribals (on which a consensus had existed until then). This helped bring the Dalits and tribals, on the one hand, close to the OBCs on the other, and to an extent overcome their mutual suspicions. The development gave a big fillip to parties and groupings that base themselves exclusively or mainly on Dalit or OBC support. The most noted among these is the Bahujan Samaj party (BSP – or the party of the non-upper castes) led by Kanshi Ram. The BSP has made inroads into every northern state. In some, such as Uttar Pradesh and Punjab, it commands ten per cent of the vote.

How is the BJP to adjust to the new realities? It is the classic dilemma again. It can either evolve into a hardline Hindu communal party which essentially exploits the revanchist sentiments of a narrow stratum of upper-caste Hindus. Or it can fashion itself into a more broad-based party of the Right, defined mainly by a non-religious agenda. The first choice is favoured by many RSS leaders. The second seems to be the preferred option of the so-called moderates. It, too, is fraught with problems. There is a space for a right-wing party in today's India: the property-owning elite and sections of the middle class that have benefited from Structural Adjustment policies are looking for a pro-Western, pro-globalisation political articulation of their views and interests.

But in a society of want, mass deprivation and rising political awareness among plebeian layers, such a party is unlikely to gather the popular support needed to contend for power. The BJP will opportunistically try, especially in the second scenario, to appropriate the Dalit-OBC platform and project itself as the representative of the 'backwards'. However, its ideology, leadership and organisational hierarchy are heavily upper-caste and anti-Dalit-OBC. It is unlikely to succeed beyond recruiting a few token OBCs. The Dalits largely remain hostile to the party. Unless the present mobilisation of these forces collapses altogether, the BJP is unlikely to be able to counter or co-opt the trend.

Whatever it does the BJP is unlikely to get any closer to fulfilling its dream of moving to the centre of power by mixing religion with politics. It will have to depend more on its opponents' faults than its own virtues for any potential major successes. It has reason to feel happy at the further disintegration in the northern states of the Janata Dal which in 1990–91 had already split into factions. Also significant is the growing tension between components of the ruling coalition in Uttar Pradesh. But the OBC-Dalit alliance has held so far and the political space for the Janata Dal or for formations of its type continues to exist.

The Congress has been the principal short-term beneficiary of the BJP's losses. In that party, the Narasimha Rao group has been strengthened. But the Congress's gains are likely to be transient. The party has no coherent policies that address the root cause of the Hindu-communal-sectarian upsurge. Its organisation is in poor shape, its old electoral base in tatters, especially in the north, and its leadership crisis is pervasive. If it returns to appeasing the BJP, gets involved in financial scandals, or allows a major crisis to develop in Kashmir, the BJP stands to benefit and will once again go on the upswing.

In brief, the BJP's future does not lie in its own hands. It has ceased calling the shots. A new secular window of opportunity has opened up in India, along with new possibilities of realignment of social and political forces, which leads us logically enough to making a concluding overall assessment of the future prospects for Indian democracy.

Prospects For Indian Democracy

In the former colonial world, India's experiment has been unique. No other country has had such an enduring democracy, albeit a violent one and a weak one relative to those of the advanced democracies. In assessing the continued durability of Indian democracy, especially in the light of the communal challenge, the sources of this uniqueness must be understood. There are both historical and structural reasons for this.

The main historical features belong to both the colonial and post-independence period. There was the distinctive character of British rule with a mere 100,000 troops controlling the fortunes of a sub-continent for over a century. Such rule was simply not possible without the encouragement of an administrative infrastructure manned largely by Indians themselves to help govern the country in the name of the crown and its proclaimed ideals. This also affected the character of the National Movement for independence. Only the Chinese and Vietnamese national liberation struggles bear any comparison with the National Movement of India in longevity and in the scale of mass support and mobilisation.

However, in the Indian case the struggle was essentially non-violent and dedicated to the transfer of power from the structures of colonial administration rather than to the overthrow of the institutions of colonial rule. Through a prolonged process of demanding greater rights for Indians within colonial rule which gradually moved up to the demand for independence, the instruments of self-governing and democratic rule were built up – the rule of law and an independent judiciary; a 'depoliticised' steel frame of an administrating bureaucracy; a military apparatus kept separate from the liberation struggle and subservient to political command and authority; the elements of a Westminster-style legislative system. Of course, the role of the Congress itself was paramount. The importance of this pre-1947 legacy to the preservation of Indian democracy has now systematically declined to the point where its impact can no longer be deemed significant. It is the post-independence historical factors that must henceforth be given decisive weight.

Since independence there has been a combined and complex process of both further institutionalisation and de-institutionalisation of Indian democracy which has given it a distinctive character. Hence the unique paradox of endemic political instability encased within a quite remarkable democratic systemic durability. Some important aspects of this de-institutionalisation process have been remarked upon earlier, above all the decline of the Congress itself. But quite the most important institutionalised force behind the sustenance of Indian democracy must also not be forgotten – the absorption of a democratic ethos and commitment to the preservation of its basic institutions on the part of the Indian people. It is the expression of the real awakening of the lowest classes and castes of Indian society.

It would be romanticism, of course, to believe that this alone could ensure the preservation of the democratic system. But when this is allied (among other things) to the most important structural feature of Indian society then we do arrive at a more important basis for democratic durability. This latter feature is the single most powerful 'negative' obstacle to the establishment of a centralised and national authoritarian structure. It is the uniquely segmented and sectionalised character of Indian society, a segmentation that makes extremely difficult both 'unity from above' (amongst the various dominant classes, castes and parties) and 'unity from below' (of a kind that can promise revolutionary social change). Indian society is both strongly resistant to centralised macro-authoritarianism and very open indeed to the institutionalisation and spread of micro-level authoritarianism.

This segmentation of Indian society is a 'permissive' and not an 'efficient' cause of its democracy. It is not sufficient to guarantee its durability. Indeed, the overall trend line of Indian political life has been opposite to the general trajectory of Third World politics. This general trajectory has, no doubt, been subjected to very considerable variation, country-wise and even region-wise, but the overall direction has been towards greater democratisation of Third World societies.[5]

This is a controversial thesis in that the greater economic marginalisation of a large part of the Third World both counteracts and diminishes the political consequences of the drift towards quasi-democracy and near-democracy. This is a valid enough point but it does not alter the fact of such a political drift overall; nor of the specific benefits of greater political rights and freedoms of various kinds, even if rights understood above all as civic and political rights remains an unsatisfactory and far too narrow conception.

In India, compared to the past, the centre of gravity has shifted to the right, and for the worse, in three crucial spheres: the economy, secularism and democracy. Regarding the economy, the New Economic Policy inaugurated in 1991 is a virtual guarantee of the institutionalisation of a deeply iniquitous dualist economy which marks a qualitative leap backward even from the earlier dualism of the Indian economy. Such a right-wing economic shift greatly increases the need for a corresponding right-wing political representation for ruling elites that breaks from the traditional populism of Indian politics. This growing space (within limits) for right-wing political formations does not mean a space for the equivalent of conservative-liberal parties of the West European and OECD type, but of more anti-democratic, reactionary right-wing formations.

Regarding secularism, enough has already been said about the nature of the communal challenge to Indian democracy. From the late 1960s/early 1970s onwards perhaps the most accurate characterisation of Indian politics was that there was a clear drift towards a more 'authoritarian democracy'. But given the paradox of the polity, it was necessary to equally emphasise both the authoritarianism and the democracy. One could still feel secure that although the brush fires of authoritarian practices and developments were increasing in size, frequency and intensity, they were still brush fires unable to come together on a really system-threatening scale. The social and political preconditions for such conscious organisation of national-level and centralised authoritarianism was still absent.

The general argument of this article has been that this can no longer be so easily or confidently assumed, that such preconditions have been in the making. At the same time the emergence of countervailing forces and the strength of the existing structures opposing a generalised authoritarian involution of the Indian polity must not be underestimated. The situation may be summed up by saying that where once in characterising the overall drift towards an 'authoritarian democracy' it was necessary to maintain a parity of emphasis on both terms in this apparent oxymoron, now it might be more accurate to suggest that the first term be more emphasised. On the continuum between strong democracy and strong authoritarianism/fascism India continues to lie on this side of the critical point marking varieties of democracy from varieties of authoritarianism. But it is a little closer to the critical point that it once was.

The basic democratic mould of Indian politics established since 1947 has not been broken. But it has been shaken, cracked in many parts and also patched up in many ways with glues of unclear strength. In Kashmir, India faces the strongest secessionist movement in its history as an independent Union. But so many are the variables in operation, national and international, that it would be foolhardy to make confident predictions that this will lead either to a break-up of the Union or to generalised repression to prevent growing centrifugal pressures from getting out of hand. Secessionist pressures remain confined to the geographical periphery of India. A more serious problem is the possibility of an anti-secular reaction in other parts of India to growing Islamic militancy in Kashmir and the more general antidemocratic and brutalising effects of a state repression which is legitimised in the name of preserving 'national unity'.

Perhaps the safest claim to make, the best vantage point to take in judging the future prospects of Indian democracy, is to remember that within the catch-all term of 'The Third World' meant to signify a collective unit sharing some common characteristics, India is both the most Third World and the least Third World of all 'Third World' countries. It is among the most Third World in the character of its mass poverty and in various forms of extreme social backwardness. But this must never be allowed to hide the fact that in the general sophistication of its economic and political structures it is in so many ways much closer to the advanced industrialised democracies than it is to developing Third World countries.

Is that reason then to be more than a little optimistic about the future of Indian political democracy? One might tentatively suggest that it is.

Notes

1   The original theoretical debate on the definition of communalism was really sparked off by B. Chandra, *Communalism in Modern India* (New Delhi: Vikas, 1984). Chandra sees communalism as 'above all an ideology'. For critiques of this, see R. Singh, 'Theorising Communalism', *Economic and Political Weekly*, 23 July 1988; and A. Vanaik, *The Painful Transition* (London: Verso, 1990) Chapter 4. The above is a minor modification of the definition first presented here.

2   The fourth principle of the Nehruvian Consensus was non-alignment as applied to India's foreign policy.

3   For the original and classic formulation of the thesis of the centrality of Congress 'On Party Dominance' to the Indian political democratic system, see: R. Kothari, 'The Congress System in India', *Asian Survey* (1964).

4   A detailed presentation of the historical background to the dispute is provided in: S. Gopal (ed), *Anatomy of a Confrontation* (New Delhi: Penguin India, 1991).

5   P. Anderson, *A Zone of Engagement* (London: Verso, 1992) p. 350.

8

Oil, Islam and Israel: US Policy and Democratic Change in the Middle East

Joe Stork[1]

Customary formulations of United States policy towards the Middle East by White House or State Department officials foreground two concerns: access to the region's oil resources at 'reasonable' prices and the security of Israel. Concern for democracy, even the pro forma obeisance that usually accompanies policy articulations for other regions of the globe, have been noticeably absent – so much so as to become rather conspicuous in the present post-Cold War era of 'democratic expansion'. Recent utterances have dutifully added democracy to the official litany of goals, but in a manner that compels a question: to what extent has US policy in fact contributed to or hindered democratic change in the region?

There is, perhaps, a presumption here that the Middle East has seen and does contain liberalising tendencies and democratic possibilities. This, I would argue, is certainly the case. But I also want to avoid any suggestion of a simple and uncomplicated instrumentality with regard to US policy. The question is not whether US policy is primarily responsible for the absence – or the presence – of democratic systems or trends in the region, or in any particular country. It emphatically is not. The political character of a particular state or society is the product of a complex mix of factors and forces – economic, social or cultural; indigenous and external. The question, rather, is this: as we look at the history of the Middle East in the second half of the twentieth century, has US policy shown a concern to inflect the unfolding political sequences in the direction of democratic accountability? Or has the pattern of policy behaviour been in the direction of authoritarian scenarios?

This is an appropriate moment for such an inquiry. The collapse of the Soviet Union has left a triumphalist aftertaste to the prevailing political discourse in this country, a discourse that, until very recently at least, bespoke visions of a political reordering which would feature liberal democracies and market economies across the globe. The US military victory against Iraq, and subsequent reluctant military humanitarianism in Iraqi Kurdistan and Somalia, was tinged with presumptions of a rekindled American commitment to 'good government', with its overtones of democratic accountability. The US foreign aid establishment has adopted 'Democratic Initiatives' as its rubric for the 1990s. 'Our goal in this era', says Anthony Lake, the Clinton administration's national security adviser, 'is to expand democracy and take advantage of the democratic tide running in the world'.[2]

When applied to the Middle East, though, this vision runs up against a commonplace notion among political, policy and media elites that the Muslim character of the region represents a unique and serious impediment to the development of a democratic political culture. Democratic procedures in Israel only accentuate, by contrast, the prevailing image. Turkey's intermittent parliamentary experience could be accommodated provisionally by defining Turkey – a NATO ally, after all – as Western, and by not paying too much attention to the martial law regime that has ruled Turkey's eleven mainly Kurdish provinces since 1980. Iran since the revolution of 1979 only reinforced the broader stereotype, despite the fact that the revolution overthrew a monarchy and proclaimed a republic: the Islamic qualifier was decisive in this regard.

For many Americans, anyway, 'Middle East' is practically coterminous with 'Arab' or 'Arab-Israeli'. And for politically attentive liberal Americans, readers of *The New Republic*, *The Atlantic* and *The New York Times*, the notion of 'Arab democracy' has been, in Michael Hudson's phrase, 'virtually an oxymoron'.[3] Against this stereotype, sympathetic analysts such as Hudson cite the fact that over the last several years, six major Arab countries – Algeria, Egypt, Jordan, Morocco, Tunisia and Yemen – have experienced contested national parliamentary elections. These countries have a combined population of approximately 130 million, amounting to some 65 per cent of the total Arab population. The Palestinians of the Israeli-occupied West Bank and Gaza, the Arabs with the highest political profile in the West, are committed to national elections in 1994 as part of the accord negotiated in Oslo between the Palestine Liberation Organisation and Israel. In Egypt, a high-level civilian court recently threw out charges against Islamist militants accused of terrorism on the grounds that the government's case had been compromised by its resort to torture and forced confessions.

For those who see pressures for liberalisation in the Middle East as coming from the 'triumph' of Western capitalism over Soviet socialism, and from the US military victory against Iraq, this paradox of democratic practice operating in Muslim and Arab societies is easily explained, as was 'Arab socialism' in the 1950s and 1960s, as an essentially imported political fashion. This perspective meshes well with the Islam/democracy incompatibility thesis: it denies any significant agency to indigenous social forces and dynamics; contemporary manifestations of liberalisation are thus feeble, necessarily superficial grafts. For a significant segment of the American political class, American encouragement of such tendencies are dangerous and delusionary, for they risk bringing to power Islamist currents which are inherently fanatic and intolerantly anti-Western.

Those of us who contest the incompatibility thesis would do well to avoid assuming too much. For one thing, elections are not equivalent to democracy.[4] Many such developments should be more properly considered as phenomena of liberalisation. Democratisation and liberalisation are two distinct, though often overlapping and sometimes contradictory, processes. It will be helpful to make the distinction explicit.

Democracy denotes a mode of governance in which decision-making power is shared by 'the people' or citizenry rather than concentrated in the hands of a single ruler or a clique. Today the term refers almost exclusively to representative democracy, in which 'the people' yield power to a political elite checked by periodic elections. (Interestingly, one of the few modern instances of attempting 'direct democracy' on a large scale occurred in Libya in the mid-1970s, but this *jamhariyya* experiment soon became subordinate to the 'Revolutionary Committees' set up by the Gadhafi regime to restore direction and control.) In any case, the issue of who comprises 'the people' – women as well as men, poor as well as propertied – has been the occasion of recurring struggles in those societies that have appropriated the adjective 'democratic'.

'Liberal' in the classical sense refers to limitations on the power of a ruler or state to intervene in the individual and collective lives of people. Historically identified with individual rights of property, liberalism also underlies modern doctrines of political and human rights, as expressed in the amendments to the US Constitution, the French Revolution's Declaration of the Rights of Man and more recently the UN Declaration of Human Rights. A democratic state is not necessarily liberal and vice versa.[5] It is worth recalling that until the twentieth century, democracy had a distinctly pejorative connotation among political elites in the West, with its sense of a popular majority 'oppressing' a privileged minority.[6]

We are witnessing in the Middle East what Michael Hudson calls a process 'through which the exercise of political power by regime and state becomes less arbitrary, exclusive and authoritarian',[7] but this is at least two parts liberalisation to one part democratisation. Most of the electoral openings we have witnessed have been controlled, if not calibrated, by the respective regimes. In Algeria, where the elections actually threatened to change the regime, the army took over and a bloody, protracted civil war has ensued. Yemen's remarkable experiment suffered a grievous setback with the inability of the regime to accede to constitutional checks, plunging that country into its civil war. Everywhere in the region the 'shepherds of democracy' are monarchs or military men. Even where elections have encompassed wide sectors of the population and included opposition forces, they have been for parliaments with little power vis-à-vis the president or king. The Mubarak regime in Egypt has sidestepped the meddlesome independence of the civilian high court by assigning virtually all cases of 'Islamic terrorism' to military tribunals.

But the presumed incompatibility of Muslim culture with democracy extends, in most versions, to liberalism as well. I will summarise my critique of the Islam/democracy incompatibility thesis in the following propositions:

1   No religion is democratic; no political culture is solely determined by the religion of its majority; and no set of social and political practices survives unchallenged and unchanged from one era to the next. I subscribe to the succinct formulation of Francois Burgat, a French scholar deeply familiar with Islamist political currents in Egypt and North Africa: 'Was Muslim civilization democratic? No more, one is tempted to respond, than Christian civilization was, before it became so'.[8]

2   Islam is politically, culturally and theologically diverse. There is no 'position of Islam' on governance, notwithstanding the (competing) claims of many Islamist writers and spokesmen to the contrary. The language of religion can be used and is used, in Muslim countries as elsewhere, both to support and to oppose the prevailing order. A classic instance occurred last year in Saudi Arabia, when King Fahd banned a new organisation calling for greater regime accountability: the king was not fooled for a minute by the name of the group, the Organisation for the Defense of Islamic Rights.

3   Neither is Islamism a unitary or monolithic phenomenon. To cite Burgat again: 'Islamism manifests the displacing of the entire range of political ideologies towards the religious terrain more than it

does the simple emergence of a political current'.[9] One can find articulate rejections of pluralism in the writings of leading Islamist leaders and theorists, but these theses cannot be fairly imputed to all who might fall under the broad category 'Islamist'.

4   Islamism is an expressly modern political phenomenon, notwith-standing a tendency towards social conservatism and a penchant for seeking sanction for political positions in scripture and/or in 'tradition'.[10] There is the not particularly Islamic notion of 'republic' as the substantive noun in revolutionary Iran's proper name.[11] Islamism's modernist character is also apparent in its modes of organisation and mobilisation. The institutional site of Islamist mobilising has been the university. In the words of Tunisian Islamist leader Ahmida Enneifer, 'competition with the ideology of the university left was decisive in the ideologi-cal and political structuring of the [Islamist] current'.[12] The social profile of Islamist cadre, moreover, bears an uncanny resem-blance to that of radical nationalists and communists in earlier eras.

5   A strong egalitarian current has contributed to the vitality of Islamist politics from Iran to Algeria. These groupings are tied to programs, not to charismatic leaders. It is significant, moreover, that a wide range of Islamist activists feel the need to declare their attachment to democracy and to argue that there is an Islamic path to a democratic and pluralist society.[13] The modernist features within Islamism can be discerned in, for instance, the effort to equate *shura*, or consultation, as a mode of democratic practice.

My argument is not that Islamism is a culturally specific expression of liberal democracy or liberation theology. I am speaking only to the thesis that democracy and pluralism are not compatible with Muslim political culture. The fact that prominent Islamists propound the same ahistorical arguments as do Western Orientalists about an unchanging essence of Islam does not make those arguments any more valid.

My point is simply to stress the dynamic character of Middle Eastern politics. Authoritarianism is also compatible with Muslim political culture. Some Muslims see certain prevalent Islamist currents – Sudan's ruling National Islamic Front, for instance – as fascistic in character, resembling the fusion of religion and politics that produced the Francoist dictatorship in Spain. The point is not to see Islamism as politically virtuous, but rather to see it as a complex response within

Muslim societies, one whose varied manifestations are responses to the manifold pressures and stresses of the modern era, including pressures of Western intervention.

Within Arab and Middle Eastern societies, and even within currents broadly characterised as Islamist, there is a widespread and growing concern with issues of governance, accountability and democracy. Opposition to corruption and authoritarianism are key strands running through Islamist as well as secularist political groups. In this regard, we should note the complicity of Middle Eastern regimes and political elites in constructing an image of Islamism as an essentially violent and intolerant force. We should beware of the claims of Mubarak in Egypt, King Hussein in Jordan, the Algerian junta and the Saudi regime, that they are the last defence of civilisation against a totalitarian Islamist wave. These claims conveniently obscure and justify the violence, repression, and intolerance over which the regimes themselves preside, for the most part with the material and political support of the United States.

I would like to insert, provocatively perhaps, an alternative working hypothesis: the key question should not be whether democracy is compatible with Islam, but whether democracy is compatible with oil.

The compatibility of democracy, or political liberalisation, with oil can be posed on two levels. The first has to do with the ways in which the bases of political authoritarianism in the Middle East lie embedded in political and social structures associated with the 'monocrop' economies and rentier states. While such an inquiry would focus first on the oil-exporting states and statelets themselves, after the early 1970s it can be applied to the region generally.[14]

The thesis is basically this. The infusion of money wealth, in the form of oil-generated rents, helped the exporting regimes, and subsequently in the 1970s and early 1980s the region as a whole, to defer the consequences of socioeconomic crisis that provoked earlier political reform movements, such as those in much of Latin America, for instance. Legitimacy through much of this period was sustained by access to oil monies, either directly in the case of the oil-exporting states or indirectly via state-to-state aid and worker remittances.

By the mid-1980s, with the sharp downturn in oil prices and revenues, individual regimes and the Arab region had entered a severe crisis of economic viability and thus of political legitimation. This is the essential background to the liberalisation that has occurred. Political reform is on the agenda now because important sectors of the population have forcefully put them there. The states which we noted earlier had conducted contested national elections were compelled to do so by, among other things, dramatic popular mobilisations and mass insurrections (Egypt in 1977 and 1986; Tunisia and Morocco in 1984; Algeria in 1988; Jordan in 1989; Yemen in 1991). In Saudi Arabia, the defection of key merchant, professional and political families has prompted King Fahd finally to appoint a 60-member consultative council – a mere 30 years after his predecessor, King Faisal, promised such a step. The underlying issue, in all cases, has been falling living standards, growing inequities of wealth and opportunity, and absences of regime accountability.

What postponed the crisis of accountability in the Middle East was not Islam but socioeconomic structures and a political order fed by oil revenues, and by military and financial support from outside powers largely motivated by the oil factor. The states that have experienced the crisis most acutely and have responded with liberalising reforms, are those where the wash of oil monies has most quickly and most completely receded, well before the impoverishing consequences of the Gulf War exacerbated these conditions regionally. Today even Saudi Arabia confronts the need to modify its absolutism as it cuts back services and subsidies and contemplates levying taxes.[15] This all suggests the obverse of the American revolutionary war slogan: No representation without taxation (or entitlements at risk).

The second level at which we question the compatibility of oil and democracy goes to the heart of our topic – the US policy record. Another way of posing the question is this: Is democracy in the Middle East compatible with American determination to maintain a hegemonic position in the region generally and in the Persian Gulf in particular? Former US Secretary of Defense and CIA chief James Schlesinger spoke for more than himself in a recent issue of *Foreign Affairs* when he asked:

> Whether we seriously desire to prescribe democracy as the proper form of government for other societies. Perhaps the issue is most clearly posed in the Islamic world. Do we seriously want to change the institutions in Saudi Arabia? The brief answer is no: over the years we have sought to preserve those institutions, sometimes in preference to more democratic forces coursing throughout the region.[16]

Schlesinger goes on to cite, as justification and endorsement of this view, King Fahd's assertion in the wake of the Gulf War that, 'The prevailing democratic system in the world is not suitable for us in this region, for our people's composition and traits are different from the traits of that world'. Noblesse oblige.

At the beginning of 'the American century', as indigenous challenges arose to the colonially imposed order in the Middle East, Washington sometimes manoeuvred for advantage on behalf of US companies vis-à-vis their European counterparts, and generally endeavoured to supplant European commercial power with its own. Arab (as well as Kurdish and Armenian) self-determination had figured among Woodrow Wilson's famous Fourteen Points, but in the end the US accepted the British and French political map of the region. Towards the end of World War II, the US supported Lebanese and Syrian independence vis-à-vis Vichy France. Washington made tactical efforts to distinguish itself from both Britain and the Soviet Union during the Allied wartime occupation of Iran and immediately afterwards, in the name of promoting democracy and self-determination. Washington also attempted to align itself to some degree with Egypt's Free Officers against the British-supported monarchy, and later opposed the British-French-Israeli aggression against Egypt in October 1956.

Sometimes the issue was self-determination and the right of a regime to choose an American over a European firm, but at no point was the issue democracy. The question of democracy has been basically irrelevant in determining the specifics of US foreign policy, not only in the Middle East but throughout the so-called Third World. The thrust of US policy has historically been one of extending American commercial, political and military presence in a region whose oil reserves had long been recognised as a strategic prize. After World War II, the discourse of American foreign policy was framed almost entirely in Cold War terms, which were expandable enough to encompass virtually any local or indigenous threat to the status quo.

Washington's reasons for supporting one government or movement and destabilising another have to do with issues of access and control, of markets and resources and in the Cold War context with political alignment and military availability. The rhetoric of democracy and democratisation may affect, at the edges, what Washington feels it can or cannot do in a given situation. The American intervention to restore the Sabah family to power in Kuwait, for instance, has brought with it, unintentionally, considerable pressure to liberalise despite the opposition of Saudi Arabia. David Mack, chair of the national security policy department at the National Defense University, recently commented that 'for domestic political reasons' Washington must 'promote reforms that widen political participation and social justice in the [Gulf] region'.[17] As for the current emphasis on democracy as part of the conditionality for foreign aid, this is at least in part a device for rationalising disbursements in an era of shrinking aid budgets. Current revelations of corruption and human rights abuses among US client regimes in the Third World reminds one of the scene in *Casablanca* when Claude Rains strides into Rick's club and declares he is 'shocked, shocked, to find gambling going on here'.

The distance between rhetoric and practice, when it comes to US support for democracy, stems from the fact that democracy involves a measure of mass politics. Liberalisation is frequently something else: a recalibration of regime hegemony with the aim of managing and containing mass politics. Issues such as control of resources have historically been at the forefront of mass politics in poorer countries. The reason John Foster Dulles and other denizens of post-war American foreign policy were so quick to conflate nationalist, populist and neutralist movements and regimes with Communism is that, for them, the results were equivalent: they all reduced in some measure the availability of a given territory for US corporate acquisition of resources and markets. William Elliot, one of Henry Kissinger's Harvard professors, stated the core dispute with admirable succinctness: Soviet success, he wrote, represents 'a serious reduction of the potential resource base and market opportunities of the West owing to the subtraction of the communist areas from the international economy and their economic transformation in ways which reduce their willingness to complement the industrial economies of the West'.[18] It does not require an enormous leap of political logic to appreciate why nationalist leaders like Arbenz in Guatemala or Mosaddeq in Iran or Nasser in Egypt could be seen as equivalent dangers. The fact that such movements or regimes tended to ally themselves defensively with the Soviet Union only seemed to confirm the correctness of this analysis.

Within this framework, the US approach in the Middle East is pretty much indistinguishable from policy in Central America or South East Asia. What we can say about the Middle East is 'the same, only more so'. The stakes in the Middle East have historically been seen from the administrative corridors in Washington and the corporate boardrooms in New York as much greater, owing to the vast inexpensive oil reserves of the Persian Gulf and to the region's proximity to the Soviet Union. It is no mere coincidence that virtually all of the post-World War II doctrines of intervention bearing presidential names, from the Truman Doctrine to the Carter Doctrine, were articulated in relation to questions of access to and control over the Middle East. (The one exception, the Nixon Doctrine, was formulated to rationalise US military power in Indochina, but the Nixon Doctrine's 'gendarme' approach to imperial maintenance was most successfully applied in the Middle East, in relation to Iran and Israel.)

August 1993 marked the fortieth anniversary of what could be called 'the mother of all interventions' in the region, the US-sponsored coup against Iran's last secular parliamentary regime, the National Front government headed by Prime Minister Mohamed Mosaddeq. It was the first successful US covert effort to destabilise and overthrow a legitimate popular government in the post-World War II period, and no less an authority than former CIA director Richard Helms has cited Operation Ajax as a model for covert operations that followed.

The particulars are worth recounting briefly, for they embody the major components of our overview – oil, Islam and US subversion of democratic change. On the morning of 19 August 1953, two CIA officers passed US$10,000 to Ayatollah Abul Qassem Kashani, who then arranged to have an anti-Mosaddeq crowd march from the bazaar into central Teheran. There they were joined by crowds organised by two Iranian agents who had been running a US$1 million per year propaganda and 'political action' operation for the CIA since 1948. The demonstrators and pro-Shah military columns marched on Mosaddeq's home. A nine-hour battle ensued, in which some 300 Iranians were killed and the walls around the prime minister's house were levelled by tank and artillery shells. Mosaddeq escaped over the roof but surrendered the next day to Zahedi, who had emerged from the CIA safe house where he had been hiding.[19]

Was the Eisenhower administration's prime motivation to open up Iran's oil industry to American firms, or was it to foreclose a popular liberal political experiment in which the pro-Soviet Tudeh Party might have come to power? The question may bear on a distinction without a difference. Mosaddeq's successful campaign to nationalise the Anglo-Iranian Oil Company represented the cutting edge of Third World economic nationalism – already equivalent, in the eyes of servants of the Seven Sisters like Foster and Allen Dulles, to 'International Communism'. The demonstrated power of multinational firms to neutralise and accommodate economic nationalism makes such fears appear quaint today, but at the time the American companies, like their British counterparts, feared the 'demonstration effect' in the region and beyond if the Iranian takeover were allowed to stand.

The 1953 coup holds a central place in the unfolding dynamics of revolution and counterrevolution, war and intervention, that have characterised US relations with the region over the past four decades. The British and American embargo of Iranian oil sales under Mosaddeq had 'softened up' – that is brought close to ruination –

Iran's economy. The companies could easily do without Iran's production; they simply turned up the taps across the Gulf, in Iraq and Kuwait. Following Iraq's revolution in July 1958, the game was reversed: the companies held Iraqi production down and increased their take from Iran. In the late 1960s and 1970s, the Shah collaborated with US (and Israeli) efforts to destabilise the Ba'th regime in Baghdad by arming and financing a Kurdish rebellion. After 1979, Iran's Islamic revolution appeared to be the greater threat to Western interests, and Iraq happily (though ineptly) took up the campaign to contain and overthrow the Islamic Republic.

The book is not yet closed on the consequences of the 1953 coup. The US role in constructing and sustaining the Shah's regime largely accounts for the venomously anti-American character of the revolution of 1978–79. It previewed the policies of deceit and imposition by which the US has attempted to preserve political and economic divisions and hierarchies so convenient to Western interests. It wrecked for at least half a century the chances of Iran's secular left and liberal forces to set the political agenda for that country and perhaps for the region.

The 1953 coup, moreover, was instrumental in engendering the radical Islamist political currents that currently serve to justify US support for the petty monarchs and dictators who rule the region. Mandarins like Samuel Huntington are busy today, well endowed by conservative corporate foundations, constructing serviceable doctrines of intervention based on the notion of irreconcilable hostilities between 'Western' and 'Islamic' civilisations.[20] It was events like the August 1953 coup that Palestinian political philosopher Azmy Bishara had in mind in discussing the appeal of radical Islamism in Middle Eastern societies today. 'They accepted modernity', he observed. 'Modernity did not accept them'.[21] The political fault lines of today are not the result of some generic Muslim hostility to democratic rule, but at least in part a consequence of Western refusal to allow a country like Iran the democratic option.

If Iran is the emblematic register of the perverse priority the US gave democracy in its early superpower period, it is certainly not the only case in point. Douglas Little has documented over a decade of US covert activity in Syria designed to produce a regime there that would support US oil interests (at issue was Syrian right-of-way for ARAMCO's Trans-Arabia Pipeline), negotiate peace with Israel and align with Washington against Moscow.[22] Syria's decade of revolving-door regimes commenced with a US-backed military coup in March 1949. Little's account offers no evidence of US concern for democratic niceties, but rather a distinct preference for the military quick-fix.

This is understandable, since popular opinion in Syria (as measured, for instance, by parliamentary elections in September 1954) ran contrary to US wishes regarding ARAMCO and Israel.

The early interventions in Iran and Syria set the pattern for US behaviour in the decades to come. US policy was geared to supporting friendly regimes and quietly destabilising hostile ones. Democracy and modes of governance were not explicit issues. Evidence of the slightest concern for democracy would be hard to discern in US policies – overt and covert support for King Hussein's regime in Jordan despite a three-decade-plus ban on political parties; endorsement of Turkey's junta when the generals there overthrew elected governments in 1970 and again in 1980; arranging Iranian and Israeli support for a Kurdish insurgency against Iraq in 1972 and then leaving the Kurds to the tender mercies of Saddam Hussein's regime three years later, are just a few examples.

Some of these interventions clearly derived from US concern to maintain or improve its political and military standing in the Persian Gulf region. In the mid-1960s, for instance, the US worked behind the scenes in Saudi Arabia to help ensure the ascendance of Crown Prince (later King) Faisal as against his dissolute older brother, Saud, following an abortive 1962 effort by a group of so-called 'Free Princes' to establish a constitutional monarchy. Washington had also stepped up its military aid to the Saudis following the September 1962 republican revolution in Yemen, which attracted the support of Nasser's Egypt.

More broadly, US concern was to preserve a favourable balance of power in the region, in the sense of preventing the development of a leftist or nationalist consensus or dominant coalition that could force the regimes of the oil-exporting states, for instance, to pursue more independent pricing policies. It was not a good time for democratic forces in the region. For this the US cannot be held responsible, but there is every reason to think Washington preferred things this way. Liberals and democratic leftists languished in prisons of regimes allied to Washington (Iran, Saudi Arabia, Jordan) as well as of those opposed to the US (Syria, Iraq, Egypt). It is safe to say that democratic openings would have raised some unwelcome issues with regard to basic issues of resource control, economic development, and Western support for Israel.

The essence of how Israel enters this analysis can be briefly put: as the coincidence of US and Israeli interests developed after 1948, US support for Israel increasingly became a theme wherever mass politics surfaced in the Arab world, and particularly in the 'frontline' states of Egypt, Syria, Jordan and Lebanon. An issue as potent as this

– indeed, as potent as the issue of control of oil resources – was one to keep out of the street as much as possible, notwithstanding the persistent and indulgent demagoguery on the question by most of the regimes. One cannot say that, had Israel not been a factor, the Middle East would be a garden of democracy, but surely the presence of Israel, the manner of its establishment and the increasing alignment of US and Israeli interests all helped to undermine Arab popular support for the pro-Western parliamentary regimes in many countries in the early 1950s. Hostility to Israel has been a feature of mass politics. A small sign of this is that in Egypt, following Camp David, it was illegal for a political party to advocate opposition to Egypt's treaty with Israel (until an Egyptian court ruled this restriction unconstitutional in May 1988).

Israel becomes a prominent feature of US policy in the region after the June 1967 war, in the context of the continuing rivalry between the US and the USSR. The decisive Israeli victory over Egypt, Syria and Jordan had five clusters of consequences that bear on our analysis.

1   The 1967 war led directly to a reconfiguration of the balance of power in the Arab world, strengthening the conservative oil-exporting Gulf regimes allied with the United States and weakening the radical nationalist bloc allied with the Soviet Union. Among other things, this coincided with Saudi-led efforts to replace pan-Arab nationalism with Islamic state solidarities. Significant Saudi funding of Islamist groupings dates from this period. The June war set the stage for Egypt's dramatic realignment – internationally, regionally and domestically – under Anwar Sadat beginning in the early 1970s.

2   The war contributed to the radicalisation of Arab nationalist forces and helped precipitate the emergence of an 'Arab new left' within the liberation movements of Palestinians, Yemenis and Gulf Arabs. In their critiques of the liberatory potential of Nasser's nationalism and Soviet socialism, they evaded the question of democracy in program and practice. The radicals criticised the regime's failure to implement programmes of strong and militarily proficient states, rather than the content of those programs.[23]

3   It prefigured the Nixon Doctrine by presenting Israeli military prowess as a 'strategic asset' in support of US objectives in the region. This directly contributed to Israel's refusal to entertain political settlements with Arab adversaries on terms other than complete surrender, on terms, in other words, that might have

lent some legitimacy to 'moderate' and liberal elements on the Arab side.

4   The June 1967 war contributed heavily to a dynamic of rapid militarisation of the region, with consequent effects on the equilibrium of state and civil society in the region as a whole. Closer US-Israeli military-strategic relations also came to have corrosive effects on the democratic practice of Israeli Jewish society. Militarisation of the region involved more than the Israeli-Arab dimension, of course. It also relates to US policy regards the recycling of oil revenues, for instance, and the broad issue of arms sales to enhance US influence in key states.

5   It dramatically reconfigured the Israeli-Palestinian dynamic by unleashing new political formations and social forces in the occupied territories and in the Palestinian diaspora. It is out of the dialectic of occupation and resistance that fields of democratic practice have developed among Palestinian activists and intelligentsia, in some of the main constituent organisations of the PLO but especially in the occupied West Bank and Gaza. Democratic politics in Israel, particularly the emergence of anti-occupation and anti-militarist popular forces there, has been an important ingredient in this process. But it is not the intentional result of the policies of the state of Israel or its chief patron. On the contrary, successive Israeli governments have, with US indulgence, consistently tried to undermine and destroy Palestinian efforts to build democratic political institutions.

Of these factors, Egypt's realignment deserves further discussion, for it allows us to consider the impact of the very large American presence as a factor in the country's limited moves towards liberalisation. Significant US economic and military aid to Egypt dates back to the late 1970s and the conclusion of the Camp David accords. US government officials and mainstream media generally present Egypt as a country with a government doing its best in the face of opposition from increasingly popular Islamist forces to 'democratise'. The reality is not quite so benign. Anwar Sadat, as part of his 'open door' initiatives on the economic front, took some half-hearted steps towards modifying Egypt's one-party political system, but made sure that the effective monopoly of the state party machine was never impaired. The formation of new parties was heavily controlled, and opposition access to mass media restricted. Sadat, moreover, lent support to Islamist elements to offset opponents on the Left. The government quickly cracked down with mass arrests and martial law whenever its political control was challenged.

Husni Mubarak, after succeeding Sadat in October 1981, moved to buttress his regime's legitimacy and credibility by distancing himself from Sadat's autocratic behaviour. Mubarak's first term was characterised by a refreshing emphasis on constitutional process, freedom of the press, and multi-party procedures. Under pressure from creditor countries and multilateral institutions, Egypt has been compelled to liberalise its economic institutions. Official American concern in all this seems to be that the Mubarak government should maintain a 'democratic cover' for the main goal of economic restructuring. There is no recorded American dissent to the new tone Mubarak brought to his second term: the extension of emergency laws decreed after Sadat's assassination; the law on political parties which has precluded the formation of a single new party; the electoral laws introduced in 1988 to reinforce the ruling National Democratic Party's monopoly nationally and locally; the ban on public meetings and rallies by opposition parties even during supposed campaigns. 'I am in charge', Mubarak said bluntly in his May Day speech of 1988, 'and I have the authority to adopt measures so long as the majority approves'. As for majority approval, he went on, 'I have all the pieces of the puzzle, while you do not'.[24] In October 1994, Mubarak began his third term, following his 'victory' in a referendum in which he ran unopposed. To listen to his latest inauguration speech would be to think that the only serious problem facing Egyptian society is 'terrorism', an affliction totally attributed to Iran and Sudan.

There is one more thing to say about nearly two decades of US political sponsorship for the Sadat-Mubarak regime. Egypt has been the main Middle Eastern laboratory for applying American neoliberalism as a strategy and ideology for the 'structural adjustment' of nationalised, parastatal economies to complement the increasingly transnational and multinational character of global capitalism. As an alternative to a repressive Pinochet-style autocracy, which probably would not work, USAID has come up with something it calls the Democratic Institutions Support Project which will enable important sectors of the population to 'participate in the design of their own pain' (in the words of an AID-commissioned 'political economy review' of Egypt). The dilemma for the AID democrats is that, as one Near East Bureau document acknowledges:

> only a limited segment of these [Middle East] populations would be constituencies for critical economic reform ... The [AID] project therefore limits provision of resources under the public accountability objective to activities that will enhance rather than undermine short term reform priorities.[25]

Perhaps we should be grateful for any combination of circumstances that has compelled the US government to endorse the concept of democratic accountability, but let us recognise that this is an entirely instrumentalist view of democracy, one that brings us back to our earlier distinction between democracy and liberalism. Egyptian political scientist Mustafa Kamel al-Sayyid has written that the bene-factors of the small-scale privatisation programmes the government has already initiated are the provincial elites who form the backbone for the ruling National Democratic Party.[26] There seem to be few policy makers and analysts arguing that trade union democracy and the right to strike should be part of these reforms.

Underlying the reform rhetoric of AID is the proposition that structural adjustment and privatisation can provide the economic growth that will generate employment and rising incomes and that this private sector expansion can only materialise in a climate relatively free of political repression. Alan Richards, a co-author of the AID 'political economy review' of Egypt cited earlier, has argued eloquently elsewhere that a participatory political system that relies on contract and rule of law is 'a necessary condition for a function-ing market economy'.[27] The need for structural reform seems undeniable, but what needs consideration is the assumption that poor and working people must pay the greatest share of the cost. This, as Argentinian social scientist Carlos Vilas points out, 'is not due to any technical requirement but to their political weakness ... who suffers the consequences [of structural adjustment] is a matter of the class nature of policy decisions'.[28] The implications of this sort of critique require another sort of enquiry than this, but we could do worse than recall the circumstances that led to the defeat of the Arab parliamentary liberalism of an earlier era. 'What is democracy?' Nasser asked an Indian reporter rhetorically in 1957:

We were supposed to have a democratic system during the period 1923 to 1953. But what good was this democracy to our people? ... Landowners and pashas ruled our people. They used this kind of democracy as an easy tool for the benefits of the feudal system. You have seen the feudalists gathering the peasants together and driving them to the polling booths ... I want to liberate the peasants and the workers, both socially and economically, so that they can say 'yes'. I want the peasants and the workers to be able to say 'yes' and 'no' without this in any way affecting their livelihood and their daily bread. This in my view is the basis of freedom and democracy.[29]

Concluding Remarks

How should we understand the interface of oil, Islam, Israel and US policy today? Is there any reason to expect that one of us, addressing this topic in 1999 or 2004, will declare the end of the Cold War a watershed that produced a markedly different, 'pro-democracy' American policy in the Middle East? Let me conclude with several propositions.

1   The dynamics of political change in a region such as the Middle East can be inflected by American power, but not determined by it. The people of north and south Yemen did not check with James Schlesinger before unifying their two states and introducing multi-party elections and unfettered political debate to the Arabian Peninsula. And neither was US policy, as far as one can tell, in any way responsible for the collapse of the Yemeni experiment in May 1994.

2   The question of US support for democracy in the Middle East cannot be abstracted from US policy elsewhere. Can one discern, for instance, US support for democracy in El Salvador, or in Russia? When I visited the Middle East in October 1993, I found Egyptians and Palestinians impressed with the full and unconditional endorsement of the US government and major media for Boris Yeltsin's assault on the Russian parliamentary opposition. You can imagine how confident they feel of Washington's support for their own efforts for democratic change in the face of regime resistance.

3   The region faces double crises of weak regimes and weak democratic opposition. One of the most significant developments, as a result, has been the emergence of indigenous human rights organisations and agendas, a phenomenon which has created such space as exists for liberal and democratic politics in a number of countries. In this regard, the selective and indulgent attitude of the Clinton administration to human rights abuses by friendly regimes – Turkey, Egypt and Israel, for instance – shows more continuity with than change from the past. One can also observe what happened in Iraq, in the spring of 1991, when the US stepped aside to allow Baghdad to suppress the rebellions in the north and south of the country. It is worth noting that at no point in the US campaign against Baghdad has free and democratic

elections been among the demands put to Saddam Hussein's regime as a condition for ending international sanctions.

4   The subcontracting of US Middle East policy to declared partisans of Israel – in the Clinton administration, notably the appointment of Martin Indyk to the Middle East desk at the National Security Council – virtually guarantees a fundamentally hostile American attitude towards democratic change and political liberalisation in the region. Indyk is on record as advocating an 'agnostic' response: 'Neither encourage nor discourage democracy but rather leave the choice to the regimes and their subjects'.[30]

5   Finally, we could devote another entire chapter to how oil, Islam, Israel and US policy in the Middle East have subverted democratic change not in the Middle East but in the United States.[31] For years Washington blocked a policy of mutual recognition between Israel and the PLO, all the while financing the mutual recognition of Saudi and Israeli arms dealers and gun runners. US laws against providing military or economic aid to regimes, like Turkey, practising and condoning torture are observed mainly in the breach, not to mention laws against the use of US weapons for aggression, such as in Israel's repeated invasions of Lebanon – most recently in July 1993. How well can the US Constitution withstand a few more experiences like the Iran-Contra affair or Iraqgate, not to mention the much-maligned 'October surprise', the covert interventions supporting the Shah or the interventions restoring the Kuwaiti royal family?

Notes

1   This paper was adapted from remarks prepared for the Delaware Valley Peace Council's First Homer Jack Memorial Lecture, Swarthmore College, 29 January 1994.

2   *New York Times*, 31 October 1993.

3   Michael Hudson, 'After the Gulf War. Prospects for Democratisation in the Arab World', *Middle East Journal*, vol. 45, no. 3 (Summer 1991).

4   Guy Hermet (ed), *Elections Without Choices* (New York: Macmillan, 1978). Such elections can tell us a great deal about the specific political dynamics of an authoritarian system. See, for instance, Volker Perthes, 'Syria's Parliamentary Elections. Remodeling Asad's Political Base', *Middle East Report* (January–February 1992).

5   Norberto Bobbio, *Liberalism and Democracy* (London: Verso, 1990).

6 David Held, 'Democracy' in Joel Krieger (ed), *The Oxford Companion to Politics of the World* (New York: Oxford University Press, 1993); Raymond Williams, *Keywords: A Vocabulary of Culture and Society* (London: Fontana, 1976) pp. 93–98.

7 Michael Hudson, 'Democratisation and the Problem of Legitimacy in Middle East Politics', *MESA Bulletin*, no. 22 (1988).

8 Francois Burgat and William Dowell, *The Islamic Movement in North Africa* (Austin: University of Texas Press, 1993) p. 124.

9 Burgat and Dowell, *Islamic Movement*, p. 100.

10 On the political functions of 'tradition', see Eric Hobsbawm and Terence Ranger (ed), *The Invention of Tradition* (Cambridge: Cambridge University Press, 1984).

11 Sami Zubaida, 'An Islamic State? The Case of Iran', *Middle East Report*, no. 153 (July–August 1988).

12 Burgat and Dowell, *Islamic Movement*, p. 92.

13 Gudrun Kramer, 'Islamist Notions of Democracy', *Middle East Report*, no. 183, (July–August 1993).

14 Giacomo Luciani has developed this thesis in some detail. See, for example, 'Economic Foundations of Democracy and Authoritarianism. The Arab World in Comparative Perspective', *Arab Studies Quarterly*, vol. 10, no. 4 (Fall 1988).

15 F. Gregory Gause, *Oil Monarchies. Domestic and Security Challenges in the Arab Gulf States* (New York: Council on Foreign Relations, 1994); Fareed Mohamedi, 'The Saudi Economy. A Few Years Yet Till Doomsday', *Middle East Report*, no. 185 (November–December 1993).

16 James Schlesinger, 'The Quest for a Post-Cold War Foreign Policy', *Foreign Affairs*, vol. 72, no. 1, p. 20.

17 In a 18 November 1993 lecture at the Middle East Institute, as summarised in the Institute's January 1994 newsletter.

18 William Y. Elliott, *The Political Economy of American Foreign Policy* (New York, 1955), p. 42.

19 This account draws on Mark Gasiorowski, 'The 1953 Coup d'Etat in Iran', *International Journal of Middle East Studies*, no. 19 (1987).

20 Samuel Huntington, 'The Clash of Civilizations?', *Foreign Affairs*, vol. 72, no. 3 (Summer 1993).

21 Azmy Bishara's remarks at a Transnational Institute conference on democracy and intervention in the Middle East, Amsterdam, May 1993.

22 Douglas Little, 'Cold War and Covert Action. The United States and Syria, 1945–1958', *Middle East Journal*, vol. 44, no. 1 (Winter 1990).

23 On this point, see Isam al-Khafaji, 'Beyond the Ultra-national-ist State', *Middle East Report*, no. 187-188 (March–April–May–June 1994).

24 This account draws mainly on Ann Lesch, 'Democracy in Doses. Mubarak Launches his Second Term', *Arab Studies Quarterly*, vol. 11, no. 4 (Fall 1989).

25 Al Miskin, 'AID's "Free Market" Democracy', *Middle East Report*, no. 179 (November–December 1992).

26 Does democracy in the North require autocracy and oligarchy in the South? Is American democracy compatible with a democratic foreign policy?

27 Alan Richards, 'Economic Imperatives and Political Systems', *Middle East Journal*, vol. 47, no. 2 (Spring 1993) p. 226.

28 In *NACLA's Report on the Americas* (May 1992).

29 Roger Owen, *State, Power and Politics in the Making of the Modern Middle East* (London: Routledge, 1992) p. 230.

30 Indyk's concluding remarks at the 1992 Soref Symposium on *'Islam and the US: Challenges for the '90s'*, (Washington Institute for Near East Policy, 1992) pp. 50–51.

31 See Christopher Hitchens, 'Tilting Democracy', *Middle East Report*, no. 174 (January–February 1992).

9

Democratisation in the Middle Eastern Context

Azmy Bishara

There is no logical possibility of establishing a deductive or any other derivative correlation between any religion and democracy.[1] Both categories belong to different levels of abstraction. Religion can only mean a social organisation of the relationship to the holy. Its relationship to democracy, which refers to a certain organisation of power and government, can only be established through checking certain types of religiosity, that is specific patterns of social practice of religion.

If the researcher insists on establishing an exclusion or inclusion relationship between 'Islam' or 'Christianity' as such on one hand and democracy on the other, then he will find himself reaching an exclusion relationship, which is not substantial nor essential, but rather tautological with no theoretical use, because it only means that where is there no correlation there is no inclusion and 'no inclusion' could mean exclusion. The question of compatibility between 'Islam' and democracy is as meaningless as the question of inclusion. There are two remaining choices which may still provide a solution to the compatibility delusion: first, to assume a trans-historical essence of 'Islam' which is incompatible with democracy, an essentialist approach to which neo-orientalists and neofundamentalists adhere; second, to impose current categories, conceptions and interpretations retroactively on different historical contexts, or to use old categories and conceptions, the way we understand them today to cope with modern realities – an approach usually advocated by reformists, but which is a somewhat moderate variant of the first choice because it too is ahistorical.

In any case we cannot draw a direct line – causal, deterministic, or even modifying – between religion as a category and social phenomenon and democracy. These belong to two very different levels of abstraction. Research should begin with patterns of religiosity, that is with the specific historical forms of practicing religions. This Chapter has chosen three main types or patterns of religiosity to be distinguished and studied in their relationship or potential relationship to democracy:

1   popular religion or folk religion;
2   political religion as one type of 'fundamentalism';
3   theological and religious orthodoxy.

These patterns could also be differentiated and divided into subcategories – but this is the farthest a researcher can go with generalisations – one step more and we will find ourselves making generalisations concerning an essence of a certain religion.

The prevailing opinion often heard in Western journalism and pseudoscientific texts is that 'Islam' and democracy are incompatible. We have already established that religion, any religion, as such is incompatible with democracy. The question is, what type of religiosity can coexist with democracy, or even be supportive for its emergence?

In a much debated article, S. Huntington attributes new functions to the exhausted concept of civilisation as a trans-historical subject, as a primary unit, a building stone and as an analytical category for explaining our world, but the reductionist attitude has no bottom limit; civilisation is actually culture and culture is primarily religion. Civilisation is: 'The highest grouping of people and the broadest level of cultural identity people have short of that which distinguishes human from other species'.[2] But 'civilisations are differentiated from each other by language, culture, tradition and, most important, religion'. Does not culture mean all the mentioned above? If we go back to a previous article by Mr. Huntington,[3] we discover that for him political culture is a determinant of political systems. He quotes S. Verba.[4] Political culture is 'the system of political beliefs, expressive symbols and values which defines the situation in which political action takes place'. Huntington adds that this political culture is rooted in the broader culture of society involving both beliefs and values *often religiously based*, concerning the nature of humanity and society, the relationships among human beings and the relation of individuals to a transcendent being.[5] Culture at large determines political culture and political culture determines political systems. In this form of 'civilised' reductionism, culture remains a trans-historical unit, not unlike race, which was the building unit of the human universe for some in the first half of this century. 'Islam' is for Huntington, needless to say, such a civilisation-culture-religion.

The Hegelian notion of a sequence of civilisations and religions each representing a category, a *Prinzip*, an idea in his philosophy of right or his system of logic still prevails in Eurocentric models of inter-pretation of differences in our world. Ernest Cassirer once wrote that no philosopher had such a deep impact on later politics as Hegel did. Much later, and coincidental with the collapse of the socialist bloc that rested ideologically, in part, on the unity of the logical and historical in the system of the Prussian philosopher, along came Fukuyama; this former official in the US State Department wrote a parody of Hegel describing the march of democracy in history up to its victorious end. 'The end of history', he calls it – which only serves to show that Cassirer's assertion retains its vitality. According to this caricature of Hegel, Islam remains an obstacle to the final triumph of liberal democracy. In an interview with Fukuyama by the Israeli political scientist Shlomo Aineri published in the Israeli newpaper *Davar* (19 October 1991) Fukuyama claims:

> I am pessimist concerning the options that the Arab states ever join the modern world. Athough these societies are economically more progressive than the African ones, they harbour more obstacles on the way to democracy. A main factor for that is Islam ... Moreover, there is incompatibility between Islam and Capitalism in many aspects. That is why I do not expect that the democratic revolution will spread to this part of the world in the near future.

For Huntington too, Islam remains unreceptive to democracy.[6]

An essentialist approach to 'Islam' is presented by M. Yamauchi. 'Islam'[7] is presented as an easily identifiable reality and value system bare of any qualifying quotation marks. It is unique, and due to this 'unique' nature of Islam 'the situation in the Middle East cannot simply be considered analogous to that of Western society at an earlier stage in its history. For one thing, the two guiding principles of the Enlightenment – the belief in social progress and the devotion to secularism – are incompatible with Islam'. As a result of that 'various governments now find themselves in a head-on confrontation with Islam and its relationship to democracy'.[8] As a matter of fact there were and still are differences between 'the situation in the Middle East' and 'Western society at an earlier stage' in more than 'one thing' and liberal democracy owes its birth, genesis and formation in the last 200 years to more than 'one thing'. It is also true that 'various governments' find themselves involved 'in confrontations', but not with 'Islam' nor for 'democracy'. Different Islams were involved and engaged in political and social conflicts in the Middle East, the most antagonistic of which to democracy is the variant, which claims simply to incarnate Islam and to represent its essence and is accepted unquestioned by orientalists, even if they are from Japan.[9] (Orientalism is not a geographic category).

However, the problem of ahistorical thinking, usually performed with trans-historical categories, is more far-reaching than the unavoidable necessity of committing historiographic errors by relying on trans-historical subjects to do the work for the researcher. The real problem lies in the totalitarian approach inherent in any assumption of trans-historical subjects of history. Islam, which encompasses all spheres of life and politics, does not harbour its alternative, which can be imposed only from the outside. The 'West' is identified with democracy, even in the sphere of foreign policy. In Yamauchi's above-mentioned article a total confusion prevails, which is typical of bad Western journalism but not thinkable in disciplinary Orientalistic periodicals. Saddam Hussein and Gadhafi are brought as examples of Islamic extremism[10] and supporting the 'peace process' is synonymous with supporting democracy and its critics are considered antidemocratic.

Another approach seeks compatibility between 'Islam' and democracy. According to this approach, democracy has to be put in quotation marks, as there can be many kinds of democracies, amongst which there should be a place for Islamic democracy. Only one 'Islam' or one true 'Islam' exists and it is democratic. For A.R. Olayiwola, Islam:

> as a religion and a complete way of life ... encourages the practice of 'democracy' in all its ramifications. There is no doubt that there are some apparent similarities between the Islamic and Western conceptualisation of 'democracy', nevertheless there are major differences between the two perspectives and, in particular, the Western approach to 'democracy' contains un-Islamic elements.

It is not 'Islam' that contains undemocratic elements, it is 'Western' democracy that contains un-Islamic elements. 'Islam' remains an essentialist category, but democracy defies definitions. 'As a concept, "democracy" is pervasive in modern value systems but elusive in definition'.[11]

The modern apologetic attitude towards 'Islam's' relationship to modern enlightened values is anxious to prove to the 'West' that 'Islam' is civilised according to Western categories; 'Islam' liberated women, liberated slaves and founded the first socialism or the first democracy (the choice varies with speaker and context) on earth.[12] In this approach meaning and function of early Islam is pulled out of its historical context and democracy and other categories lose their specificity or their concreteness. Their universality of value and application is replaced by a harmless 'universality' of interpretation. In this process both historical 'authenticity' and modernity are lost.

One of the interesting examples of this approach is delivered by Abdel-Rauf in his critical remarks about Novak's *Democratic Capitalism*, for not mentioning 'Islam' alongside 'Judaism' and 'Christianity' as one of the sources for the development of capitalism.[13] Instead of criticising the notion of a Judao-Christian tradition leading to capitalism and the later to democracy, some Moslem intellectuals admonish it on account of the exclusion of their own tradition. Two hundred years after Adam Smith, Abdel-Rauf tries to show that the hidden hand of God is another name for the invisible hand of the market. In the introduction, S. Naser joins him in refuting claims of Moslem writers who insist that 'Islam' is neither capitalist nor socialist. For them 'Islam' has a capitalist value system.

This approach is a reminiscent of the much more serious Islamic reformism of the nineteenth century. Al-Afghani, Abduh, Al-Kawakibi and At-Tunissi were less systematic and more eclectic than today's theoreticians. Nevertheless, their concern was neither apologising to the 'West' for the Islamic history and value systems nor apologetic in relating to Islamic traditions. Their concern was to reform Islamic thought and politics, for which two main strategies were applied: first, a return to the 'fundamentals' of religion as a purifying step against myths and superstitions; second, the domestication of modern categories and concepts including democracy. By trying to find the common values shared by *shura* and democracy (anti-despotism), they did not target a self-satisfied preservation of or perservance in the *shura* as an Islamic sort of democracy, nor did they mean to apologise for the lack of democracy by inventing one and imposing it retrospectively on Islamic history. They looked for a point of contact, a point of acquaintance between democracy and their own history.[14]

Neofundamentalists (political-religious movements) refrain from using concepts from foreign languages for totally different reasons. They emphasise the difference, the incompatibility between the concepts of the Islamic heritage and modern 'imported' ideas. Democracy in this case is incompatible with *shura*, which means nothing more than unbinding consultation with experts.[15] Irrespective of the fact that the notion of consultation with experts is a modern representation of an old, actually pre-Islamic principle of tribal organisation and decision making, which was operative also in early Islamic periods, and apart from the later development of Islamic despotisms that emptied the *shura* of all content, the neofundamentalists are no less modern and no more authentic than representatives of the first approach, for example. In their assault against modernity they impose concepts like *al-islam din wa dawla* (Islam is state and religion) on Islamic history, a statement which presupposes the separation between them. They impute modern meaning to old categories such as *ummah*, which used to mean something close to community of believers but now receives the false but modern attribution of nation. A legitimate translation of the word 'nation' to the word *ummah* without its religious connotations becomes for the neofundamentalists a semantic base for turning the religious community into a political nation. In the late 1980s and at the beginning of the 1990s we witness an interesting attempt to reconstruct the reform movement especially by leaders of Islamic movements who, not unlike the reformists of the nineteenth century, are concerned with practical questions, mainly political ones. In the writings of H. At-Turabi and R. Al-Ganushi we can detect beginnings of a genuine attempt to deal seriously and positively with democracy.[16]

Not only are there differences between different types of religiosity and their relationship to democracy, but differences in the same pattern, so called 'fundamentalism', are also impossible to ignore.

Democracy From Above

The democratic reforms in Jordan and Algeria came after social unrest in April 1989 in Jordan and during October 1988 in Algeria.[17] They are both examples of democratic reforms occurring after a strong legitimacy crisis of the political system, with a background of lasting social crisis and failing modernisation in two very different contexts: the first is a monarchy which suffered from a strong legitimacy crisis as an artefact of colonialism, especially at the tide of Arab anti-imperialist nationalism in the 1950s and 1960s. The second is a republican product of that period with anti-imperialist foreign policies, socialist jargon, secular policies and a centred state economy.[18] These countries are so different that they constitute two extremes, between which the rest of the Arab countries could be scaled. Both had to undertake wide-reaching and supposedly necessary social and economic adjustments demanded by the IMF as conditions for rescheduling debts.[19]

The same process of failing modernisation – huge unproductive state sector, highly centralised state power, corrupted bureaucracy and a state of fear and a paralysed civil society – that led to the crisis of ruling systems, also encouraged the alignment between popular indigenous Islam and elitist political Islam. This alignment is not as natural as it looks. It is an historical result of certain economic, political and social conditions. But the bottom line shows that the process that produced the crisis of the contemporary state – a failing and perverse modernisation process – produced also its undemocratic alternative, the Islamist movements in their present form.

The paradox of Arab democracy lies in the fact that it introduces a choice between two undemocratic options: the ruling regime or political Islam. Moreover, the choice itself is unreal because winning elections does not necessarily mean the capture of power. Elections alone do not establish democracy. It is democracy that establishes elections as the only modern possible way for choosing and over-throwing governments.[20]

Some Arab countries initiated elections from above to solve their own legitimacy crisis and to establish democracy. People and political movements took these reforms seriously through active participation. But the destiny of this kind of 'democracy' could resemble that of its predecessor, Arab 'socialism', if it continues to alienate simple people by being cynical. An example of such a low intensity democracy is Egypt, a country which is witnessing a growing alliance between folk religion and elitist political neofundamentalist religion, with the religious establishment using its indispensability for the political system in its confrontation with the former alliance, in blackmailing the government for more concessions in affairs of religion and state.

Gills and Rocamora[21] believe that the success of the new wave of democratisation which is sweeping the globe 'is built upon the failure of "development" both in the Third World and the former second world'. But we ought to see also that paradoxically the failure of 'development' led to both the crisis of the dictatorships and their undemocratic alternatives. Some of the dictatorships themselves were mostly a reaction supported by the Western superpowers to a different kind of popular dictatorship, that came to power in many Third World countries and at least had at the top of its priorities a national agenda and not Western interests. Examples of this was Nasser of Egypt, who was politically defeated by the direct use of power in 1967 war, as well as Arbenz of Guatemala, Mosaddeq of Iran and Sukarno of Indonesia. Allende of Chile could not escape a similar Western reaction although he was not a dictator but the only really democratically elected president in Latin America in his time.

The move from the national agenda did not always take a bloody form, but it always shifted towards mixed economies, opened markets with reduced state involvement but without reducing the state's or public revenues' share in the GNP. The people got only new exploiters in the form of a capitalism mediating between foreign capital and domestic economies. This kind of capitalism does not introduce a democratic agenda because democracy grows first from national interests – democracy is a form of national politics – it presupposes as its *sine qua non* the nation as the sovereign and the nation. Needless to say, it excluded more or less people (slaves, women, non-proprietors) according to the historical phase, but the democratic criteria of our days can only be the universal citizenship as a formative building block of modern nations.

Who could become the carrier of the democratic idea in the Arab Moslem countries of the Middle East (except of course the historical process as implied by Fukuyama and except American foreign policies like the Gulf War, as implied by many Western commentators)? The bourgeoisie does not seem anxious to play the role of its European vanguard as it did in the eighteenth and nineteenth centuries. Some even claim that it is prevented economically from playing that role,[22] because it did not become an organised and independent business class. What is the degree of independence needed in order to qualify for the role of democratic agent of change? Apart from the need to answer this question, we should not forget that in Eastern Europe the democratic reforms were carried out by the state and party bureaucracy, not by any business class. Also, some reforms were accomplished in some Arab countries, but they did not exceed the state's initiative and the business classes in these countries are not only reliant on the state, but also dependent on foreign capital.

The simplistic answer to the question posed above is: the carrier of democracy is civil society, an answer which has become fashionable lately, again as an echo for heated Western debates on civil society which offer another Eurocentric model of analysis. However, this kind of answer is akin to turning one's back to the question. The alternative it suggests for lack of democracy in the state lies outside the state. Usually in the context of these debates civil society is defined as the institutions and associations and organised forms of social life outside the state. In practice, however, civil society is demoted from occupying all the social space between the individual and the state (that is presupposing both) to the status of NGOs, that are usually sustained by ruling parties or by foreign aid. The civil society concept also plays the notorious ideological role of leading the theoretical and practical disputes on democracy, out of the state; however, democracy has a meaning only in the state as a system of government.

On Civil Society

From Ferguson to Hegel on Kant and Adam Smith, and from Hegel to Gramsci's *salta* over Marx, civil society never meant simply NGOs.[23] It mediates between the individual and the state and separates them at the same time. If civil society means mainly the social organisation outside the state, two variants of 'civil society' could be envisioned: First, the traditional and organic structures, like the tribe, the clan, the extended family, the *waqf*, the confession, the traditional neighbourhood. All these are more independent from the state and from foreign aid, all are more self-reliant than the NGOs. Secondly, we have the modern Islamic movements and their grass roots and community services, which are sometimes financed indirectly by government money, but usually due only to their or their constituency's influence in government ministries.

Intellectuals of Islamic revivalism in the Arab world pay considerable attention to these collective organic structures and consider them to be specifically Islamic. They represent the Islamic way of organising autonomous society:

> The history shows that the Islamic society was crowded with entities and associations that performed this function from *ulama* groups ... to guilds and fraternities ... the mosque was a cultural center, and the *waqf* was a major institution financed by peoples' contributions and played an important role in providing social protection for the nation ... That is how Moslem society ran its own affairs centuries before the idea of civil society emerged, and gained the longings of some people today.[24]

Unlike what some Arab intellectuals think, the European middle ages were not a total chaos. Similar structures may also be detected in pre-modern European history. They are not specifically Islamic but pre-modern. They were not civil society, but they were substituted by civil society. The bourgeois revolution destroyed the old organic structures of personal loyalties and dependencies and replaced them by inorganic legal structures based on the citizen-individual, and not the collective, as a legal subject. This is exactly the point which makes the difference and explains the longing that 'some' Moslem intellectuals have for the original or 'authentic' forms of civil society, and that some even call Islamic forms of democracy.

The attraction of these intimate collectives and the nostalgic feelings they stir up should be related to the specificity of the Arab Islamic present, not to a distinguished unique or peculiar past, which, although it did exist, does not provide a model of explanation. The modernisation in the Arab Islamic world undermined the old recognised legal collective subjects of traditional society and trans-ferred them to the private sphere, without replacing them with the individual-citizen in the private sphere. What actually matters about the idea of civil society is not simply its presence outside the state, albeit in the public sphere. Civil society is outside the state in its narrow meaning but very much inside it in its full extensive meaning. The barriers that stood between the state and the single person, thus signifying and presenting a protected sphere, the only sphere of freedom, were removed by the process of modernisation, leaving the single person alone to face the violence and arbitrariness of the state.

The alienation of the modern Arab individual from his organic belongings was not compensated for by his individuality, privacy and legal personality, but was complemented by the state of fear and arbi-trariness. The sphere of freedom seems not only to lie outside the state, but also in the past or in its simulations. The yearning for freedom, however, becomes a struggle for democracy if it is pursued inside the state. The old traditional structures did provide protection and still provide intimacy, but they did not only prevent an encounter between the state and its single subjects, they also prevented the single person from meeting 'his self' privately, that is turning into an individual.

Many Islamic thinkers and preachers of the present resort to the rhetorical question: what is democracy? in order to justify the pos-sibility of presenting yet another form of democracy, the Islamic one. After all, every totalitarian party used the label of democracy. Needless to say, the word Islam was not misused less than the word democracy. It may be useful to remember that the debate is neither semantic nor philological and that the real problems of the Arab world cannot be avoided by another misuse of the concept of democracy.

It may also be constructive to increase the confusion by pointing out that in spite of the etymological discussions of the word democracy and despite the long historical background and the different forms of democracy in history, we cannot consider the Athenian democracy a democracy in our contemporary sense of the word.[25] In Athens' historical democracy there was no separation between the private and the public sphere, no separation between state and religion and a citizen's rights and obligations were not a consequence of his autonomic personality but of his belonging to the organic collective, the *polis*, which expresses itself in his rights and duties. Moreover, there has never been an historical subject under the name of democracy that marched along an historical route leading from Athens to London and New York, as may appear in the Eurocentric meta-narrative.

The acculturation of the concept of democracy took place under Western dominance and hegemony. But this was not always the case, at least in the awareness of thinkers. The beginnings of acquaintance with the concept took place prior to the colonial period, at a time when Arab intellectuals looked to Europe with hope. The only 'liberal' phase in Arab politics was under the influence of colonialism. In the collective memory it has remained associated with dependent politics and corrupt politicians. A long period of dictatorship had to follow until democracy returned as a political option. In the meantime Arab society became disillusioned by development, secularisation and modernisation that were, alongside Arab unity, the main slogans of undemocratic nationalist regimes.

The middle class that raised the ideas of nationalism and Arab socialism and practiced relatively secular and rational policies in the 1950s and 1960s was confronted with traditional Islamic conservative forces supported by the main Western powers. After the failure of nationalist modernising politics, the whole political discourse was 'Islamised': successive political regimes looked for legitimacy using an Islamic rhetoric and seeking acceptance by folk religion through an alignment with the religious establishment or even directly with political Islam, and these steps contributed even more to the process of Islamisation.

The middle class, which is still the only agent of change, has at least two 'strategies' for change, but both do not deserve the name strategy: "Islam is the solution" is the slogan of Islamic elites, a slogan which can mean a lot of things and nothing, which is why it could be a strategy for mobilisation, not for change. "Democracy is the solution", reckon the secular elites of the opposition, an assertion which has the same deficiencies of the first, generality and emptiness, but which lacks its pathos.

The first 'strategy' suggests the view of civil society as a setback instead of heading towards a democracy in an Arab Islamic context and the second looks for civil society in the NGOs away from real, political struggles for power, a sphere which is occupied more and more by Islamic political movements.

Presenting democracy in the Arab world as the solution without exposing the link to the failure of modernisation and development does not only mean presenting an abstract democracy, one which incorporates ideas about English and American democracies. In the

Arab Islamic case, a democracy without social justice and without the historical context can only mean a democracy for the economic and political elites, from which the poor are excluded, or in other words, one that resembles democracy in India, the only stable democracy in the Third World and yet the most avoided and the most easily skipped example. It is easier to decorate a political agenda with an abstract democracy than with an Indian democracy.

A Refuge

Folk religion never exists as a doctrine, let alone as a state doctrine, even when it was possible to describe it loosely as a 'way of life', because an all-embracing way of life does not leave room for ideology. If 'Islam' could be considered a way of life then it would be a paradox to consider it as ideology. In this case, the world of symbols and meanings, the hierarchical structure of society, and the apotheosis of community are all united under the rubric of religion. This world of symbols and meanings differs from one place to another, it varies according to culture and to the types of material reproduction of society, it changes from nomadic communities to peasant societies and from village life to urban life. Having said change, we have already said differentiation between the world of ideas and that of the production of material life. The first product of this discrepancy is ideology, and thus ideological elements enter the world of religion.

The more religious life differs from 'real' life, the more emphasis it puts on the character of 'tradition' – the first form of popular ideology is tradition. Whereas among elites of society tradition continues to exist, an exclusively elitist religiosity claims another form: that of the retrospective utopia of a lost harmony, a utopia which claims to be a state doctrine and political ideology. Folk religion remains very much alive as a tradition which demonstrates not only tenacity or persistence, but also a considerable capacity for adaptation. It can provide a refuge of intimacy in an alienating fluctuating reality, exactly because of its ability to change its meaning and function. It is stable in an unstable world and defined in a permanently shifting reality due to its ability to change and to redefine itself.

Unless it meets with the elitist, more political and doctrinist religiosity, folk religion can adapt to dictatorship and democracy. In order to be accepted, democracy does not have to become a value system. People do not have to believe in democracy in order to be able to live with it, accept it or even participate actively in the democratic process. Democracy is neither a value system nor an alternative to folk religion. It is the elites that are supposed to carry the democratic change which should pass through a value upheaval. A change in the values of the elites took place before, during and after the democratic changes in Europe in the eighteenth and nineteenth centuries. But we should not forget that economic and cultural rising elites (the bourgeoisie) in Europe usually had a direct interest in democratisation and participation. Religion did not become democratic as a consequence, nor did democracy become a value system. People did not become democratic in the English country-side nor in the slums of London as a precondition for parliamentary democracy; as a matter of fact they were excluded from participation for a long time.

Democracy is primarily a system of government supported by a democratic value system based on power interests and ideologies of elites; it is not *primarily* a value system. It regulates one's relationship to the other and to political power although it does not necessarily control one's relationship to oneself. Democracy includes elements of coercion; it changes the ways of legislating and of electing a government, it changes the modes of legitimacy but exalts the rule of law and imposes a set of obligatory rules on both rulers and ruled.

Moslem believers have participated in the democratic process when they were given a choice: in Syria between national independence and the first military *coup d'état* in 1949 supported by the CIA;[26] in Egypt when the British and the *khidewi* (king of Egypt) cynically manipulated parliamentary democracy for their own interests; in Jordan during the elections of 1956, the results of which were anulled by the king and the American Sixth Fleet; and most recently in Algeria. The threat to democracy never came from the so-called 'masses', but usually from economic and political elites who felt threatened by democracy and were supported and even stimulated to action by Western policies and intervention. The question which should be asked does not relate to the incompatibility of democracy with folk religion but to the incompatibility of Western interests and mediating elites with unpredictable democratic processes when material and strategic interests are at stake.

The sphere in which we can establish with certainty a meaningful modifying, and even conditioning, relationship between folk religiosity and democracy is the sphere of individual liberties, without which democratisation will not reach the private sphere. The space which is controlled by religious tradition is not stable – it also varies in different historical contexts and it also responds to economic and political conditions. Lack of democracy, for example, coupled with an alienating modernity, is a certain prescription for increasing the pressure on the family as the last 'bastion' of the man who is deprived of rights and of dignity (his manhood) outside the nuclear family. His rejection of modernity takes a conservative antidemocratic form especially over issues that have become a component of democracy in a later stage of its development in the West: the right of choice inside the family, women's rights in private affairs, for example. The common reaction of folk religiosity to modern alienation very much resembles that of the religious establishment's response to the democratisation of the private sphere, which is the last bastion of the clergy. The position of contemporary Islamic establishment theologians in questions related to 'personal and family affairs' has become much more rigorous and conservative than the positions of their pre-modern predecessors were.

The tendency to concentrate on the axis of tradition versus democracy leads to another form of depoliticisation of the quest for democracy in Islamic countries, and to a misguided reversal of priorities. Democratisation of the public sphere relieves the pressure of tradition and narrows the scope of influence of religion as tradition. For political regimes, the depoliticisation of the democratic process is a cause for satisfaction for three good reasons: it keeps the struggle out of the sphere of power; some of the burden of combating democracy is carried by the clergy; it gives the political system a golden opportunity to appear as the protector of tradition and religion.

A Bunker

It is a conventional belief of students of Islamic and Middle Eastern studies that in the Islamic middle ages there was no differentiation between religion and politics or that political power was dominated by religion. This article takes an opposite point of view:

1 We assume a unity of Islam and politics in the 'golden age' of the prophet and the first four *caliphs* as a stipulative definition of that period. The prophet and his first four successors did not rule according to religion; their words and deeds are religion itself;

2 After the establishers' age and with the differentiation that took place through turning the *caliphate* into a specific form of monarchy, the religious institutions and the *ulama* became subordinated to political power, but there were always exceptions. Orientalists and 'fundamentalists' usually believe that the opposite is the case, but lately also secular Arab writers agree to use the

paradigm whereby 'Islam' unlike 'Christianity' does not know the difference between 'God and Caesar'.[27]

From the early stages of the secularisation of political power in Islamic history – which means mostly the differentiation between political interests and deeds and religious beliefs and practices, and subjugation of religion to mundane political power – from early stages on, the bulk of the religious establishment withdrew to defensive positions, especially when political power thrived. In crisis situations, the defensive, conservative positions become offensive ones, in which cases the lost harmony of state and religion is not simply reconstituted but the religious establishment gains a bigger share in mundane power.

The religious establishment developed three defence mechanisms that compose its specific conservative mode of coping with the split reality of politics and religion, which it generally coexisted with, in fact it is a creation par excellence of the split reality, without which it ceases to exist. The three mechanisms are:

1   The closure of *bab al-ijtihad*, which means the proclaimed prohibition of creative interpretation of the Qur'an and the *sunna* in a creative way to cope with new realities, a paradigm that does not imply that interpretation stopped since the third Islamic century, but rather the inauguration of a conservative class and institutions of *ulama*. Some Moslem thinkers[28] consider this step, which affected the bulk of religious institutions until the nineteenth century, to be an act of protest against subjugating religion to the changing, arbitrary, momentous caprice of the despot. This interpretation is reasonable but it does not change the fact that the protest's form and content were conservative.

2   The invention of *hadith* (statements and deeds related to the prophet) to cope with new realities. Instead of acknowledging the fact that the words and deeds of the prophet as delivered in the Islamic heritage are not sufficient to face the new world and that creative thinking should find the answers, the religious establishment chooses the most conservative variant: inventing a *hadith* for the insoluble without innovative thought in the framework of the *shari'a*.

3   Consolidation of its position as custodian of the private sphere of the family. The first form of secularisation is not the privatisation of religion, but the privatisation of theology, in which the private sphere of the believers becomes its main affair. In the public domain, it appears in charge of public morals, that is objectified

outside the personal morals. The religious establishment assumes the role of censorship. It remains outside the political domain and enters only as invited by the secular power which needs its *fatwahs* (religious judgments) for justification of unpopular political steps at times of crisis.

This is the general pattern of conservatism of the religious establishment. Islamic history is full of examples of rebellious theologians who refused to accept the split reality or to tolerate the 'un-Islamic' practices of the rulers. In the collective memory of the oppressed they remain as heroes, as exceptional theologians who were ready to suffer and even sacrifice their lives in challenging the arbitrary will of the despot. The heroic and exceptional confirms the rule and the general picture of subordination to the political rule and to the split reality.

Can the religious establishment be subordinate to the democratic government as it is to the despotic one? The answer to this question has to take into consideration that the democratic government seeks different sources of legitimacy, a fact which should, theoretically at least, free the establishment from delivering *fatwah*s to order. The democratic government should not intend to subjugate the religious establishment to itself but to the law. The question that remains to be asked is: what kind of law? Beginning with the private domain would mean a frontal attack on the religious establishment which could also unite it with folk religion against democracy. The democratisation of the private sphere should be gradual and theological pluralism in private affairs should be encouraged. The democratisation from the outside has to be accompanied with religious reform that renders it acceptable.

The religious establishment is not able to become a democratic power but it could be integrated within democratic policies if no room is left for it to build alignments with folk religion and, most importantly, with political religion.

An Offensive

In his book *Islams and Modernity*, A. Al-Azmeh defines the attitude of political Islamist groups towards democracy in the following way:

> Islamic groups menace the fledging of the democratic process by their totalitarian Rousseauian notion of general will ... From this Islamist political parties derive their notion of democracy: democracy

becomes a totalitarian passion whereby the Islamist party substitutes itself for the body politic, conceived as a social protopasm which remains formless until it is endowed with an Islamic order.[29]

The writer, who is under the influence of statements of the leaders of FIS (the Islamic salvation front of Algeria) on the eve of 1991's elections, does not take into account that the FIS did express the 'general will' at least of the majority and that the secular officers imposed themselves as the nation's body politic and as representatives of the *volonte general*. He also does not pay enough attention to the structural and the subsequent theoretical changes that the Islamic movements have to go through by looking for representation of the so-called general will, through elections.

In fact, the willingness of political religious movements to reach political power through elections in a party system indicates a real change, although this does not mean at first a change in the deeply antidemocratic, antiliberal character and political doctrines of these movements. The first modern Islamic movement in the Arab world, the Muslim Brotherhood of Egypt, was generally in favour of parliamentary elections from its emergence in 1928 until the July revolution of 1952.

This movement, like the other political-religious movements and unlike the religious establishment, refuses to succumb to the split reality of religion and politics. It seeks to reunite the mundane with the secular and moves to the offensive, behind the programme of re-establishing the caliphate as the symbol of the lost unity. But its beginning the opposite of the reform ideas of the nineteenth century in which the *shura* principle could be developed or adapted to democracy; the Muslim Brotherhood's concern is to adapt democracy to the *shura* principle. Moreover, there is no Islamic religious commandment that even hints against elections. The sovereign remains God and the elected authority cannot disobey his laws embodied in the *shari'a*. Democracy remains reduced to its electoral aspect, while all other facets are limited to the rules of the *shari'a*.[30] In the best case, democracy is *included* in the *shari'a*. Democratic elections are one way of establishing God's will and it is unimaginable, of course, for God's will to be just another possibility in a multitude of political variants in a democracy.

The 'moderate' beginnings of the political Islamic movements in the Arab liberal age were soon changed beyond recognition in the confrontation with the secular nationalist forces which came to power in the 1950s and 1960s with an agenda of modernisation and rationalisation through the state. The bloody confrontation between the Islamic movement and the nationalist regimes in Egypt and Syria, for example, led to a process of change and a radicalisation. The clash with the highly popular nationalist anti-imperialist politics did not contribute to the popularity of the political religious movements. The fact that the Western policies at that time played the card of Islamic politics against the progressive national regimes and the aspirations that they invoked only added to their image as 'Arab purveyors of the Truman doctrine of the 1950s and 1960s'.[31]

The turning point is usually represented by the rise of the ideas of Sayyed Qutb, who in his person and work symbolises the radical condemnation of contemporary Moslem societies and rulers as un-Islamic, considering the struggle against them as a struggle against heresy. The divergence from Islamic ideal and utopia was never sensed and articulated so deeply. Islamic history became nothing but a constant deviation from the fixed ideal of the past. A total gap between politics and ideals together with total alienation and a strong belief in the possibility of a redemptive meeting of the ideal with the real leads almost necessarily to totalitarian politics.

With the crisis of nationalist modernisation politics two main factors changed the picture for the Islamic movements:

1   New regimes emerged that could not supply what the nationalist regimes through highly inefficient state capitalism could: Arab nationalist ideology of legitimation and the basic needs of the population including free education. Islamisation of political discourse became the gradual solution of legitimacy crisis. Later, liberalisation became a possible tactic of legitimation,[32] albeit under the hegemonal Islamicised discourse.
2   The Islamic movements received a new reinforcement and constituency from the newly educated classes, sons of the peasants and other adherents of folk religion.

Under the new circumstances the Islamic movements themselves developed in two different directions:

1   Splinter groups continue the radicalisation process using Islamicised categories of the national discourse. They adopt an antidemocratic doctrine. Democracy seems in this light only as a heretical system, that can only be used tactically. This position is shared by militants from the main Islamic movements too.[33]
2   The main large Islamic organisations adopt a more pragmatic approach. They use any given opportunity, whether it is elections for a municipal council or for a professional trade union, the

control of the administrative cadre in a ministry or the domination of the smallest *waqf* in the most remote village, in order to consolidate their power.

The debate around the obligation to democracy remains undecided. Some theoreticians of the Islamic movements, who are motivated by the argument that after the Iranian revolution a violent seizure of power has become more difficult than before and also by a genuine change in modes of thinking, are experimenting with democratic ideas. Some of them go so far as to think that their reform is indispensable to any future democratic change. It is commonsensical to assume that a real democratic reform cannot be carried out without reforming the principal attitude of the main political actors towards democracy.

Part of this task has already been done by the reformers of the nineteenth century and some thinkers of the liberal phase in the twentieth century, like Abas M. Al-Aqad. Nevertheless, the reform by and the debates among leading figures and Islamist militants in questions concerning democracy gains a special significance, not only because their reforms can have an immediate influence on political programs, but also because their long practical experience and their relative proximity to wide segments of the population could render a synthetic effort feasible.

Al-Ghanushi from the banned Tunisian An-Nahda movement emphasises the differentiation between the 'form and content' of democracy,[34] a differentiation that has also been made by nearly all variants of totalitarian thinking in this century. And although al-Ghanushi prefers the democratic form to any other un-Islamic form of government, his differentiation opens the option for any government to claim that it represents the content of democracy although it does not respect the form. The obligation to democracy should first of all be to its form.

Reformers from the Islamist movements pay most of their attention in the democracy debate to questions of legitimacy and the election of governments,[35] a concern which is understandable due to their long confrontation with dictatorship, and needless to say, not all draw the same conclusions from the brutal oppression. Questions of citizenship, civil liberties and pluralism outside the *shari'a* limits are left unanswered by the reformers. Crucial questions that could decide the future of democracy in the Third World, such as social justice, national sovereignty and dependency, deserve also a more concrete answer than 'Islam is the solution'.

Notes

1 One is tempted also to delimit democracy by adding 'any' democracy, which presupposes that there are different sorts of democracy, but I want to stay with this category, which nowadays means nothing other than liberal democracy.

2 S. Huntington, 'The Clash of Civilisations', *Foreign Affairs*, vol. 72, no. 3 (Summer 1993) p. 24.

3 S. Huntington, 'Will More Countries Become Democratic?', *Political Science Quarterly*, vol. 99, no. 2 (Summer 1984).

4 S. Verba, 'Comparative Political Culture' in L. Pye and S. Verba (ed), *Political Culture and Political Development* (Princeton, 1965) p. 513.

5 Huntington, 'Will More Countries', p. 207 (my emphasis, A.B.).

6 Huntington, 'The Clash', p. 280.

7 Islam appears as an eminently protean category. It appears among other things to name a history, indicate a religion, ghettoise a community, describe a 'culture', explain a disagreeable exoticism and fully specify a political program. A. Al-Azmeh, *Islams and Modernities* (London and New York: Verso, 1993) p. 24.

8 M. Yamauchi, 'Prospects for a Peaceful and Democratic Middle East in the Post-Gulf War Era', *Japan Review of International Affairs*, vol. 6, no. 1 (Spring 1992) p. 67.

9 For a more balanced, informed and differentiated approach of a Japanese scholar, see Y. Kosugi, 'The Future of Islamic Revivalist Movements and Democracy', *Japan Review of International Affairs*, vol. 7, no. 1 (Spring 1993).

10 Yamauchi, 'Prospects', p. 77.

11 A.R. Olayiwola, 'Democracy and Islam', *Islamic World Quarterly* (Third Quarter 1993) pp. 190–1.

12 H.A. Amin criticises this approach from an interesting Islamic point of view in his book '*dalil al-muslim al-hazin*' (*A Guide of the Sad Moslem*) (Cairo, 1987) p. 37. Amin further claims that the holders of such an approach would be surprised to read the old classical biographies of the prophet, whose writers lived the same historical context and did not need to embellish or beautify the then prevailing value system.

13 M. Abdel-Rauf, *A Moslem's Reflection on Democratic Capitalism* (Washington and London: American Enterprise Institute, 1984) pp. 27, 29, 31.

14 For further discussion of the reform movement, see A. Hourani, *Arab Thought in the Liberal Age* (London, Oxford and New York, 1970); M.A. Al-Jabiri, *wijat nazar* (*A Point of View*) (Casablanca,

1992) pp. 125-6; A. Lurui, *mafhum alhuria* (*The Concept of Freedom*) (Casablanca, 1981) p. 36; At-Tuwni, Al-Azm and Ihmudeh, *ath ath – thawra al-faransiyah fi fikr an-nahda* (*The Impact of the French Revolution on the Reform Thought*) (Tunis, 1991).

15 H. Saleh, *ad-dimuqratyah wa hukm al-islam fiha* (*Democracy and Islamic Judgment on it*) (Beirut, 1988) p. 68.

16 See Al-Ganushi, *mahawer islamiyya* (*Islamic Pillars*), no date; At-Turabi, *tajdid al-fikr al-islami* (*The Renewal of Islamic Thought*) (1993).

17 See M. Hudson, 'After the Gulf War. Prospects for Democracy in the Arab World', *Middle East Journal*, vol. 45, no. 3 (1991).

18 Both processes took place before the Gulf War. After the Gulf War a setback took place in both countries, especially in Algeria. Nonetheless, an immense number of Western writers and commentators insist on considering the Gulf War as a turning point in the direction of democratisation. The declaratively oil war became retroactively a war for democracy.

19 Hudson, 'After the Gulf War', p. 418. Jordan has to pay debts that are per capita higher than Brazil's or Mexico's.

20 The author is aware of the discussions and debates on questions like radical democracy, direct participatory democracy and social democracy, but insisting on the parliamentary democracy, reflects a position that sees all other forms as complementary and not as a substitute for the representative democracy, which is a necessary, though not sufficient, condition for any possible democracy in modernity.

21 The concept of low intensity democracy is borrowed from B. Gills and J. Rocamora, 'Low Intensity Democracy', *Third World Quarterly*, vol. 13, no. 3 (1992).

22 See S. Zubeida, 'Islam, the State and Democracy. Contrasting Concepts of Democracy in Egypt', *Middle East Report* (Merip, November–December 1992), p. 9.

23 See A. Seligman, *The Idea of Civil Society* (New York and Toronto, 1992); J. Cohen and A. Arato, *Civil Society and Political Theory* (Cambridge: Massachusetts, and London, 1992).

24 F. Huweidi, 'al-islam wad-dimuqratiya' ('Islam and Democracy'), *Al-Mustagbal al-Arabi*, no. 166 (December 1992) p. 10.

25 See also D. Held, *Models of Democracy* (Stanford, 1987), pp. 15–16.

26 See G.E. Perry, 'Democracy and Human Rights in the Shadow of the West', *Arab Studies Quarterly*, vol. 14, no. 4 (1992) pp. 6–10.

27 B. Lewis, 'Introduction' in Gilles Kepel, *Muslim Extremism in Egypt: The Prophet and Pharaoh* (Berkeley and Los Angeles, 1985) pp. 10–11. See, for example, H. Khashan, 'The Quagmire of Arab

Democracy', *Arab Studies Quarterly*, vol. 14, no. 1 (1992) p. 21.
For Khashan the *caliph* was only an executive power, 'therefore
there is very little left for humans to improvise, since almighty
god has taken care of every thing'. It would be hard to find a
more simplistic delineation of the so-called unity between state
and religion.

28   See, for example, T. al-Bishri, 'al-masaala al-qaniniyya bain ash-
shari'a al-islamiyya wa al-qanun al-wadi'i' ('The Legal Question
between the Islamic and Positivist Law') in *at-turath wa tahadiyyat
al-asr fi al-mujtama' al-arabi* (Beirut, 1987) p. 642.

29   Al-Azmeh, *Islams and Modernities*, p. 29.

30   As representatives of this classical position of 'moderate' political
Islamism, see: J. Iqbal, 'Democracy and the Modern Democratic
State' in J. Esposito (ed), *Voices of Resurgent Islam* (New York, 1983),
pp. 257–58; and Y. Al-Qirdawi, *al-hlul al-mustawrada wa keif
qadat ala ummatina* (*The Imported Solutions and how they subverted
our Nation*) (Cairo, 1985), pp. 68–9.

31   Al-Azmeh, *Islams and Modernities*, p. 32.

32   The process which begins, according to the model of Schmitter
and O'Donnell, with the readiness of the moderate wing of the
authoritarian rule for compromise usually ends with unpredictable results or, to be more accurate, with the worst imaginable
results usually predicted by the hard-liners of authoritarian rule.
G. O'Donnell and P. Schmitter, *Transitions from Authoritarian Rule*
(Baltimore and London, 1991). The process which began from
above in the Arab world is, by comparison, still under control.

33   See the examples introduced by J. Esposito and J. Piscatori in their
article 'Democratisation and Islam', *Middle East Journal*, (Summer
1991), pp. 435–6. Hafazallah Nuri, for example, supposes that
democracy has equality as its primary condition, but 'Islam' does
not accept equality between man and woman, healthy and ill,
knowledgeable and ignorant. See also the position of Ali Ben-
Haj, one of the most prominent leaders of the FIS in H. Ayyashi,
al-ilamiyyun al-jazairiyyun (*The Algerian Islamists*) (Dar al-Hikmah,
1992), pp. 58–9.

34   Al-Ganushi, *mahawer islamiyya*, p. 50.

35   See for example the democratic positions of one ex-leader of the
Syrian Islamic Brotherhood, Adnan Sa'ad ad-Din, 'min usul al-
a'mal as-siyasi lil-haraka al-islamiyya al-mu'asira' ('Of the
Fundamentals of Political Praxis in the Contemporary Islamic
Movement'), in A. an-Nafisi (ed), *al-haraka al-islamiya ruia mus-
taqbaliyyah* (*The Islamic Movement. A View of the Future*) (Cairo,
1989) p. 79.

10

Democracy and Development in the 1990s

Basker Vashee

To Western decision making officials in governments and international agencies, the post-Cold War era should usher in a spread of democracy in the Third World. In many ways the insistence on multi-party democracy and human rights standards may well have been tied to the attempt at the New World Order, as proclaimed by President Bush. Or it may have been an attempt at the search for a new ideology to guide the foreign policy of the Western powers.

Democracy in its Western form began to be seen as the ethical standard that justified the hostility the West had exercised against the Soviet model of society, which was characterised by one-party rule and state control of the economy and society. The fact remained that dictatorships were no longer necessary or tolerable as bulwarks against a communist threat. Western interests could more effectively be safeguarded in democratic societies.

The Gorbachev revolution in the Soviet Union in 1980s heralded a new relationship with Third World countries. During the Cold War period even weak and undemocratic states were sustained by Soviet arms and assistance, as the Soviet government tried to challenge the West in its influence in the Third World. Some of these states had no real legitimacy among their people, but remained in power as Soviet allies, for example, Ethiopia, Afghanistan and the Congo. The new thinking in Moscow also discredited the idea of the Soviet bloc. As the Soviet Union liberalised, it pressured its allies to follow. The abandoning of the command economy as a model for development compounded the crisis, as these states faced both an ideological and an economic crisis at the same time. The West was ready to pick up the pieces.

The World Bank

The new Western policy towards the Third World was articulated by the World Bank in the late 1980s. The Bank itself was undergoing a rethink of its economic orthodoxy, as the post-war attempt at bringing development through state intervention was slowly being abandoned as a result of the conservative revolution in the Western countries, especially in Britain and the United States.

The Bank had in the previous decades assumed that the structural adjustment programmes in the economic field would be unpopular and therefore the states that implemented them needed to be insulated from popular pressures and had to have the political determination to see them through. The case for an authoritarian state emanated from the assumption that most development policy in the Third World had an urban bias and largely benefited interest groups in the cities. The most influential book on this thesis was called *Why Poor People Stay Poor* by Michael Lipton, who denounced excessive industrialisation, distorted trade regimes, the failure of redistributive taxation strategies and the neglect of agricultural investment. The argument singled out state bureaucracies, workers and industrialists as the main distorters of development, since they lived off the rent on peasants who provided cheap food for their benefit. The urban parasites had to be bought to heel, with deliberate policies that benefited peasants, including the more popular liberalisation of farm prices. A World Bank researcher, Deepak Lal, even argued that 'A courageous, ruthless and perhaps undemocratic government is required to ride roughshod over these newly created special interest groups'.[1]

Now the message from Washington emphasised the reduction of the state and the liberalising of the society, through democracy. The state was now seen as an obstacle to development, because it regulated too much of the economy. What was needed was deregulation and privatisation. The market was to be the main arbiter in the economy and it had to be opened up to competition internally and externally. As a result tariff walls had to be reduced and currencies devalued. This programme was now linked to multi-party democracy and human rights standards. In addition the administration of the society had to be transparent and severe norms of behaviour on the part of civil service were to be established by the insistence on good governance. The rule of law had also to be respected. The World Bank articulated this policy in regard to Africa:

> State officials in many countries have served their own interests without fear of being called to account. In self-defence individuals have built up personal networks of influence rather than hold the all-powerful state accountable for its systematic failures. In this way politics became personalised and patronage becomes essential to maintain power. The leadership assumed broad discretionary

authority and loses its legitimacy. Information is controlled and voluntary associations are co-opted or disbanded. This environment cannot ... support a dynamic economy. The rule of law needs to be established ... this implies rehabilitation of the judicial system, independence for the judiciary, scrupulous respect for the law and human rights ... transparent accounting for public monies. Independent institutions are necessary to ensure public accountability.[2]

This new intervention had a better chance of success in the circumstance of the debt crisis, especially as the commercial banks virtually ceased to lend to the Third World in the 1980s. This increased the power of the international financial institutions, as they were the only source of lending.

Thinking in Brussels

Because of the economic crisis and the mounting debt burden in many parts of the Third World, the Western powers assumed a dominant influence through economic assistance. In Western Europe, the EU through both the Development Council and the Treaty of Maastricht made democracy a condition of assistance. In effect, the EU made the promotion of human rights and democracy one of the linchpins of its development cooperation policy. It went further by insisting that these democratic principles were vital to a fair, balanced and sustainable development. These links were so important that they were enshrined in the Fourth Lomé Convention with the African, Caribbean and Pacific states (ACP).

The thinking behind this policy was first announced in the Council of Development Ministers in November 1991. It suggested an open dialogue with developing countries to lay down procedures and lines of action to implement democracy in their countries. It also announced assistance to countries who were setting out on the path to democracy, by helping to hold elections, create new, democratic institutions and consolidate the rule of law. Extra development aid was also promised if countries implemented this policy. This assistance reached ECU 16 million in 1993. This aid largely influenced events in Africa and Central America, in El Salvador, Angola, Madagascar, Senegal, Mauritania, Burkina Faso, Lesotho, Guinea, Ghana, Namibia, Kenya, Central African Republic and Mozambique. All these countries were in the process of holding elections or preparing for one.

A secondary thrust to this policy is to encourage the growth of civil society in Third World countries by assisting NGOs and other institutions that counter the influence of the state. Apart from diverting aid budgets towards this end, the EU is also encouraging a stricter adherence to good governance by state bureaucracies. These standards are largely promoted in conferences and seminars or in bilateral aid negotiations. The main plank of this policy is the need for financial strictness, especially in state budgets. The policy of democratisation involved an implied threat of withholding development assistance if human rights were consistently violated. The main lines of this policy were further reinforced in a speech by French President Mitterand in May 1990, when he proposed that these principles would henceforth govern bilateral relations between France and its former colonies in Africa. In June 1990 the British Foreign Secretary suggested that the IMF link further lending to Third World recipients' 'cuts in military spending, movement to democratic political systems and tackling problems like health, education and birth control'. He also stated that, 'political pluralism, respect for the rule of law, human rights and market principles would bring donor support'.[3]

The American Way

In the United States human rights was already a well-established principle in foreign policy actions, as laid out by the Carter administration. The essential shift in policy was towards a regional concentration. The US administrations were largely involved in solving the debt crisis of Latin America and promoting democracy in that continent. In this thrust the more important countries were first Chile, Argentina and Brazil and later the Central American states. The pressures on what were authoritarian clients of the United States were increased as notions of free markets and trade were being circulated in leading foreign policy circles in the US. It was the central policy plank of the Bush administration, which relied on the National Endowment for Democracy to articulate its positions. As in Western Europe, the US also relied on the suspension of military and economic aid to impose its views. The case of Nicaragua became an important test case of this policy. The power of the US was of course greater because of its clout with the major financial institutions that many of these countries depended on.

After the collapse of the Berlin Wall and the emergence of the free East European states, the United States converted its policy into a global crusade, moving from merely a regional concentration. It is in this context that its policy towards China and Russia was articulated. The promotion of democracy and human rights was of course increasingly linked to economic assistance and trade concessions. Under the noble rhetoric was the growing concern about the role of US investment in these new areas of the world economy in the face of European and Japanese competition. The imposition of political conditionality influenced the international financial institutions, who were slowly being made to 'do something' about the debt crisis, by insisting on financial discipline in state budgets and in the handling of loans and grants.

A more recent aspect of US policy has been the defusing of old Cold War conflicts via negotiations and promises of aid, with the co-operation of the Russian government. This has met with partial success in Southern Africa, where through the United Nations the Angolan war was to wind down and elections were held. The fact that a US client, UNITA, refused to accept the result of the vote and returned to the bush to resume its civil war was a disappointment. An escalating and harsh war was the result of this effort, with more people dying recently than in the previous 20 years.

The policy however did succeed earlier in Namibia where an election was accepted by the occupying South African government, who withdrew militarily from the conflict allowing a legitimate government to be installed. The combination of sanctions and the promise of a return to the world economy lead to a painful but successful transition in the Republic of South Africa itself, where an ANC-dominated government took power.

The US-Russia connection has inevitably lead to a greater use of the United Nations to intervene in previous conflicts and impose conditions that would lead to multi-party democracy in the Third World. The case of Namibia has already been mentioned. The earlier UN-supervised elections in El Salvador and Nicaragua, required both an end to a civil war and a slow process of staging elections with legitimate parties competing for the vote. A slower process had begun in Mozambique, where a ceasefire between the ruling FRELIMO and the rebellious RENAMO was agreed. Six thousand UN troops were given the task of disarming the opposing armies and an election was held in October 1994, which FRELIMO won narrowly.

The UN effort has by no means been successful in crucial countries of the Third World. In Somalia, Afghanistan and recently in Rwanda, the UN remains helpless, despite unanimous support in the Security Council for limited intervention, in the face of bitter indigenous and ethnic conflict. The USA and Russia are in the process of reevaluating their policies on intervention, largely as a result of the failure in

Somalia, to include what is termed the 'national interest'. This basically means that US and Russian support will be limited to humanitarian assistance, without the commitment to stop civil wars by the use of troops.

A more curious US policy is unfolding in the Far East and in South East Asia. The democratic rhetoric from US policy-makers is more muted because of the enormous economic interest in the area. Some 60 per cent of US trade now takes place in the area and it has become the major area for US investment. Apart from China, the US and Western Europe seems to have accepted the notion of 'authoritarian pluralism' in the area, since in most countries governments compete politically with officially created opposition parties. The system is highly controlled, and is presided over by oligarchies either based on landed interests or the army, who dominate the economy through an active involvement in economic enterprises. The state is a creation of a leading personality that distributes power through patronage. Cracks have occurred in Thailand, the Philippines and South Korea through popular revolt, resulting in more broadly based governments, but the states are still presided over by the old oligarchies. The US emphasises the respect for human rights in the area, and recently on labour rights, especially in Indonesia. In the case of China human rights are linked to the Most Favoured Nation status in trade. Human Rights organisations in Washington have now also made a strong connection between prison labour and Chinese goods exported to the US market, implying that they should be prohibited.

The policy of linking human rights to economic relations has come under severe criticism in the US policy establishment. Corporate and some government departments are dismayed by the possible harm US interests will suffer if this policy is continued. The argument of the economic interests is that China is more important to the US in the future, since at present levels of growth it could be the largest economy in the world. This is exactly what Japan has been propagating. The Japanese government has protested at human rights violations in China, but has also made it clear that economic relations would not suffer as a result.

The Shift in the Wind

The advent of conservative rule in the United States and Britain brought a sea-change in the post-war ideology of the West in the late 1970s. The ideas of the so-called New Right had been developed in the past, by such academics as Milton Friedman in Chicago and

Friedrich Hayek in London. Both regularly attacked the post-war consensus that had developed in the West, where the state in society was conceived as an arbiter between different interest groups and which intervened in society to protect the weak by providing welfare. The state, as conceived by John Maynard Keynes and especially his followers, also spent resources by taxing citizens to stimulate the economy in periods of recessions, which were inevitable in the complex capitalist system evolving in the West. The New Right argued that the system worked best if the market was the main arbiter in the economy and the state was reduced to a minimum, basically removing itself from the economic domain. What was needed was an environment that encouraged private initiatives, through the profit motive, to meet the needs of society. This means free markets and a judicial system that protected private property. This essentially eighteenth-century view, as propounded by Adam Smith, saw competition as the main force of development in society. The doctrine was elevated as a clarion cry for freedom from the dictates of the state, as a manifesto of the individual against the dark and unfeeling collectivity.

The 1980s saw the ideas of the New Right become official policy under Margaret Thatcher and Ronald Reagan and other Western leaders. Their polices in the US and Britain were conceived as revolutionary and path breaking, as the forces defending state intervention retreated. The general feeling of malaise and decline experienced in both societies during the early 1970s made the 'new' policy more attractive and fashionable, especially in the media and popular culture. In the world of academic economics most Keynesians were subdued if not removed from departments, as the economics became more managerial and business orientated.

This ideological shift permeated international dialogue, especially on North-South issues. The responsibility for the failure of development now fell on the activities of the postcolonial state, that was portrayed as a parasite on society, repressing initiatives of the common man and intervening in national and international markets to distort the true value of commodities and goods. The nationalist project of protecting local resources and interests was seen as a form of socialism that discouraged investment and encouraged corruption by local elites. The failure of development soon began to be linked to the lack of democracy in Third World countries. Authoritarianism was seen as an enemy of economic growth.

The crucial shift in this project was the conversion of the International Monetary Fund and the World Bank to the free market and monetarist ideology, instigated by the Reagan administration and supported by the European powers. As more and more of US aid became security related and the debt crisis crippled private bank lending, the international financial institutions became the main development agents. The credit and loans that they provided became the main source of funds to many Third World countries, and their message on democracy and development became the dominant context in which the dialogue could be conducted. The collapse of 'State Socialism' in the East merely confirmed this tendency. The new generation of economists and social scientists that worked in these institutions were in any case converted to this ideology in the prestigious universities and business schools of the West. Many won their legitimacy because they came from Third World countries.

The international political legitimacy conferred on multi-partyism encouraged some governments and opposition forces in the Third World to push for this project on democracy. In some cases aid was withdrawn by Western powers to force recalcitrant governments to reform, as in Kenya, Malawi, Zaire, Chile and a host of former French colonies. There is, however, no direct link between democracy and structural adjustment programmes (SAPs), though this is what is expected by Western governments. But ironically, the World Bank and IMF know perfectly well that the subscriptions from Western governments are based on this link between democracy and SAPs and the ability of these institutions to carry them through.

Avoiding 'Free Fall'

There is a strand of thinking in the World Bank that suggests that the imposition of SAPs and political democracy could lead to a 'free fall', where both an economic crisis and civil war could ensue. This realisation has constrained the total implementation of many SAPs and has lead to temporising on the democratic experiment. The free fall analysis also betrays the fact that the whole exercise is largely a managerial problem, and any spontaneous revolt against economic reform needs to be suppressed.

The adjustment exercise focuses on restructuring the state in order to make it supportive of market forces and enterprise. In many World Bank documents a central proposition has been the empowerment of civil society and the grass roots, as against the special interest groups that benefit economically from the state. The state in effect needs to privatise enterprises that it controls and also become accountable to the population by being more open and transparent, especially in public finance. The World Bank also calls for an open debate on the merits of adjustment, but finds it difficult to accommodate alternatives to its economic programme. For the Bank, the debate needs to be between people already supporting SAPs.

The more important rural constituency, that still makes up the majority of the population of Third World countries, is targeted by the programmes as the chief beneficiary of adjustment. The participation of local communities in development projects is important to the Bank and so is the earning power of the peasantry. This is brought about by removing the state from projects and liberalising prices on farm products. Subsidies on food for urban consumers need to be abolished or reduced. In its definition of the free civil society, it is talking more of the informal sector and rural communities than the formal wage sector, which forms part of the special interest group in the urban context. This is why adjustment usually means a decline in wage incomes and an increase in unemployment.

The more controversial element of SAPs has been the imposition of user fees for services like education, health, water, transport and electricity. The reduction of the welfare elements of the postcolonial state has made the poor poorer, since it hits both urban and rural populations. The reduction in the subsidies for food has made even basic foodstuffs more expensive, again hitting the poor. The increase in the level of poverty in Latin America, Africa and Asia is a direct result of these policies. In effect the state has not only retreated, but has been delegitimised. At the same time the growth of what is called 'cowboy capitalism' has exposed the economic system as an instrument of the rich, increasing the tensions within society.

Democracy under Austerity

To the powerful in Third World societies the capture of the state power is still essential to its perpetuation. The democratic experiment in many of these societies, under adjustment, has lead to violent transformations, not always for the better. In many instances it has merely legitimised the old rulers, as in Kenya, Ivory Coast, Senegal and Sri Lanka. In all these cases ethnic violence was provoked to crush the opposition. The ruling parties, through their control of the state apparatus, were able to throw up both administrative and physical obstacles to limit the growth of the opposition. However, even if ruling groups follow the formal procedures of democracy, like holding elections, adjustment policies exclude more and more people from the economy, who then remain hostile to the resulting system. In order to control this dissatisfaction repression remains the main tool of the system.

The rolling back of the state in Third World countries is supposed to encourage the growth of civil society that will in turn make state functionaries more accountable. The problem with this scenario is that the growth of grass roots organisations and the civil society associated with it is a result of adjustment itself and have grown in opposition to these policies. It is the *resistance* to structural adjustment that has made societies more democratic, and not the other way round. As Beckman has pointed out, in cases like Poland, Ghana, Argentina and Zambia, the mobilisation for democracy came from forces *opposed* to World Bank policies and not in support of it.[4]

The future of Third World societies remains in flux, as large mobilisations against adjustment win concessions or retreat, according to the degree of democracy established in society. The impoverishment of large sections of the population continues to strengthen the opposition forces, both in rural and urban areas. At the same time, both the legitimacy and capacity of the state is being weakened. The opposition needs to keep democracy in its sight and struggle for alternative programmes that protect the weak against the powerful. Given the evidence in the past 20 years, it is clear in many Third World countries and increasingly in Eastern Europe as well it is Structural Adjustment Programmes that are associated with repression. Contrary to the thinking in Washington, adjustment breeds repression. The banner of democracy is increasingly held by those opposed to an economic project that is against equitable growth, which is dependent on outside forces which are not accountable to the people it is supposed to help.

Notes

1   D. Lal, 'The Political Economy of Economic Liberalization', *World Bank Economic Review*, no. 2 (1987) p. 3.
2   World Bank, *Sub-Saharan Africa: From Crisis to Sustainable Growth: A Long Term Perspective Study* (Washington, 1989) p. 4.
3   *Courier* (March–April 1993) p. 6.
4   Björn Beckman in: *Authoritarianism, Democracy and Adjustment: Seminar Proceedings*, no. 26 (The Scandinavian Institute for African Studies, 1992) p. 17.

11

The World Bank and its Concept of Good Governance

Susan George

When we discuss democratisation, we usually talk about Africa, the Middle East or Latin America. In this chapter, however, I want to discuss the North, more precisely, Washington, where the real power is. This real power is not just in the White House, but also in the World Bank which is situated nearby. Rather than look at the subjects of democracy, in other words, the elites, the people or the countries, the demand side of democracy, I will look at the supply side and ask why it is that an institution as powerful as the World Bank is suddenly so interested in democracy.

I'm not sure I have the answer to this serious and extremely interesting question, but I would like to propose some hypotheses as to why the World Bank has a sudden interest in what it calls, not democracy, but 'good governance'. 'Governance', in English, is a rather archaic word and most people would say 'government', 'democracy' or 'administration'. But the Bank chose the word 'governance' for quite specific reasons.

They can't come out and say 'we want this kind of government' in a particular country. Their charter doesn't allow this. It is officially a 'non-political', a purely economic institution. So they use the notion of good governance as a roundabout way of achieving the same goal. But why now?

The entire notion of development is in crisis. The World Bank has been around now for 50 years and is going through a serious mid-life crisis. The whole narrative of development is one which no longer has a credible or proper direction. In many parts of the Third World it has become difficult to treat it as a serious economic notion. First, there was ordinary development but this didn't work. Then came social development, basic needs development, rural development and participatory development, and now we have sustainable development. They're running out of adjectives.

If you believe in the universalist notion of development on which the World Bank was founded, then you would have to believe that some countries are accidentally ahead in the race, but everyone is running on the same track. Some are behind but they will inevitably catch up if they take the right measures. But this hasn't happened. Over the past 50 years, the gap has actually widened. The difference between North and South in 1945 was perhaps 30 or 40:1. It is now at least 60 or 70:1.

Under its new president, Louis Preston, the Bank has committed itself to reducing poverty. This now appears in all of its documents. We know that the poor are an enduring problem for the Bank. If the slow countries haven't caught up, this is because there are a billion 'absolutely poor' people, to use an expression of Robert McNamara. And their numbers are increasing. None of the Bank's development measures, projects or investments have changed any of this. Up to now, the Bank has been able to make excuses: there was an economic crisis; then there was the problem of structural adjustment and, until quite recently, there was the further excuse that these countries didn't really have their heart in it, didn't apply structural adjustment long enough and hard enough. But this excuse is also wearing very thin. The Bank can also no longer blame Communism, insurgency or Soviet-inspired subversion. Development, as a global notion, is still a failure, in spite of the successes in South East Asia. The old excuses are becoming very thin on the ground. It seems that the new explanation for everything that is going wrong in the Third World is this magic phrase, good governance (or its lack). The responsibility for failure is thus situated in the Third World itself, not in the North.

In reality, however, the World Bank itself is responsible for many of the problems in the Third World. Development, as it has been practised, actually creates poor people and creates the gap. Development, as practised for the past 40 years, has created elites, which it has incorporated into the world system, but it has left the majority of the people in the Third World behind. So the Bank now needs the poor a lot more than the poor need the Bank. The poor would be much better off without the Bank, but the Bank needs them to justify its existence.

Governance is the new, big excuse for everything that will go wrong. Good governance will be the way to cover up its next big failure. The excuse will be that the governments of the Third World have not practised the proper democratic virtues. But this requires a lot of very fancy footwork because the Bank's own charter says that it can only deal with economic development, and that it must not intervene in the political affairs of its members. A lot of lawyers have been working on this question and the Bank has finally come up with a definition of governance: 'Governance is the manner in which power is exercised in the management of a country's economic and social resources for development.'

Good governance, for the World Bank, is synonymous with sound development management. Notice how artistic this is. We go from economic development, through the structural adjustment of the 1980s (in which the Bank began to manage entire sectors, including making many social decisions, in the countries being adjusted), and then into the area of government itself. The Bank believes that, in the last analysis, everything is connected to everything else and therefore everything has something to do with economic development. Therefore the Bank can justify its deep interest in governance. An essentially political area, governance appears now as completely non-political, as something more technical-administrative. The way is thus opened for World Bank interference.

This definition of governance was very quickly amended after 1989. The Bank now demands:

- accountability of government officials through clearly formulated and transparent processes;
- the legitimacy of the government is regularly established through some well-defined open process of public choice such as elections and referenda;
- the safety and security of citizens is assured;
- the rule of law prevails;
- public agencies are responsive to the needs of the public;
- social and economic development is promoted for the benefit of all citizens in a equitable manner;
- information is readily available through freedom of association, freedom of expression, freedom of the press, and so on.

These are good, proper and wonderful goals. But how many in the West could say that they are living under such ideal conditions? I think it would be virtually impossible to say that any of us are living under such conditions of perfect transparency of government, perfect accountability, perfect equality in the dispensing of social and economic advantages, and so on. Perhaps we enjoy the rule of law, but even in this case sharp investors and rich corporations have been known to have more clout in the judicial system than poor citizens.

But while this is what the World Bank is holding up as a demand for governments in the Third World that are under its influence, it is ironic that the Bank itself respects none of these conditions. The Bank is not transparent; it is difficult to get information from it, and its officials are certainly not accountable. They have displaced hundreds of thousands of people with dams, hydroelectric projects and deforestation, and they have never been sanctioned for this. Bank employees continue to be promoted and to draw very nice salaries. There was never a referendum in the countries concerned to see if the people wanted this project. There was also never a referendum in the West to ask us if we still wanted to have the World Bank. If one were to ask the citizens of Germany to name the German executive director of the World Bank, I think very few would be able to answer. And this is not surprising. These people are generally obscure upper middle civil servants, running one of the most powerful institutions in the world without any kind of public control. The Bank stands outside the democratic process.

At the international level, the struggle has to begin all over again to achieve the things that we have fought for, for hundreds of years; in particular to have some control over elected officials, to be able to throw them out when we're not satisfied. The Bank is making decisions that affect far more lives than those of the elected officials of Germany or France, and yet there is no way for any of its actions, when necessary, to be sanctioned.

Non-governmental organisations, especially environmental groups, have occasionally been able, on one project or another, to block or reverse World Bank decisions, such as, for instance, the construction of a massive dam in the Narmada Valley in India. But such changes to particular projects don't really alter the basic structure of the institution itself.

The debate on governance in the Bank was probably triggered by its problems in Africa. The Bank has been failing in a lot of its projects. An internal report from 1992 said that 37 per cent of all projects were failing. Many more are failing in Africa. So Africa has been a particular focus for the whole governance debate. This is what Connable, the previous president of the Bank, said to representatives of the African states:

> Let me be blunt. The political uncertainty and arbitrariness evident in so many parts of sub-Saharan Africa are major constraints on the region's development. I am not taking a political stance here. But I am advocating increased transparency and accountability in government, respect for human rights and adherence to the rule of law. Governance is linked to economic development and donors are showing signs that they will no longer support systems that are inefficient and unresponsive to the people's basic needs.

This is indeed true. The bank is at the centre of a great many consortia of donors. The question of governance, human rights, democracy, all the themes mentioned by Connable, are becoming the dividing line between the North and the South. Countries like Britain and the USA and the other major donors are increasingly using the terminology of 'the carrot and stick'. Good governance has become the criterion for reward and punishment. This policy will sell in the North because nobody can be against good governance any more than, in the USA, you can be against 'motherhood and apple pie'. You can't be against human rights. This will be an argument that works and it will silence a lot of criticism.

This is a very dangerous development. We are entering a period in which the North, in other words, Europe and the United States, is beginning to pull up the drawbridge and retreat into the fortress. The South, in many ways, is cooperating with this strategy. The fundamentalists play right into this configuration. An influential American author, Samuel Huntington, contributes to the phenomenon of separation which he pretends to describe. He writes about the 'new conflicts' that will be civilisational conflicts between 'the West and the rest'. A more analytical French author has written a book with the title *The Empire and the New Barbarians* in which he describes how the empire is beginning to establish a *limes*, as the Roman Empire did between itself and the barbarians. The barbarians are seen as nomadic and chaotic and splintered into dozens of tribalisms, whereas the West sees itself as enjoying the rule of law, order and stability.

Rightly or wrongly, these people are describing a new trend. The question is: How does this whole democracy debate fit into this new and extremely dangerous configuration in international relations? The development myth of the past fifty years, on which many people's lives in the North depend, is in its death agony. And many people in the West are afraid. The West has never, in the past 500 years at least, blamed itself for anything. This failure and the end of this myth is a trauma. But it will, once again, be somebody else's fault.

12

Whose Democracy? Which Democratisation?

Liisa Laakso

Two aspects can be distinguished in the everyday use of the word democracy. The first one refers to the idea of popular power and emancipation conceived as a self-reflexive form of politics. Only in a truly self-commanding social praxis can ideas like equality, participation or institutional design of decision-making have a democratic value. This notion highlights the *substantial* content of democracy, inconceivable without morality and radical in its ability to constantly redefine politics.

The second aspect reduces the meaning of democracy to a certain institutional design of decision-making, which, in turn, is seemingly value-free and neutral concerning different political programmes. When democracy is interpreted as a 'technological innovation',[1] its salient point is no longer emancipation but functionality and effectiveness. In this *instrumental* notion, democracy is seen as a rational way of rule in modern societies. It legitimates the use of power with the concept of general interest or common good emerging from the formal possibility of every citizen to promote his or her own interests.

The substantial and instrumental notions of democracy are intertwined in multiple ways in modern discourse.[2] Still their separation is appropriate from an analytical point of view, because the two notions can neither be really merged into each other, nor deduced from each other. Emancipation and rationality – as they could also be labelled – are ontologically distinct: one referring to moral principles and social creativity in its radical form, the other to abstract or transcendental individual actors conscious of their interests and together capable of solving social problems.

Although both of these notions are present in the scientific discourse on democratisation, it is the latter that has become dominant. Often democracy is simply understood as representing one technique among others, comparable to communication networks, patent systems or free trade. The purpose of this article is to clarify the dominance of rationality, reasons behind it and its implications to our understanding of the political changes taking place in the Third World.

The Concept of Politics and Interests

The instrumentalisation of democracy manifests itself in an institutional definition, like that of *polyarchy*, that is 'rule by many', a term that was introduced by Robert Dahl and has already become classical. According to Dahl, polyarchy is a political system distinguished by the following institutions:

1   elected officials;
2   free and fair elections;
3   inclusive suffrage;
4   right to run for office;
5   freedom of expression;
6   alternative information;
7   associational autonomy.[3]

Dahl emphasises that institutions of polyarchy are necessary but not sufficient for the attainment of the democratic process.[4] However, it is just those institutions – or some of them – that are commonly focused on as distinguishing the democratic systems from others. It is needless to add that these special political systems are those that predominate above all in the West.

The institutions of Dahl's polyarchy constitute a symbolic network, which gives cognitive means of interpreting the political arena and the political game. To what extent these institutions serve as a power-sharing apparatus depends essentially on the ability of the society to employ that symbolic network in conceptualising the use of power. Before people can participate in decision-making they must understand the effects of those decisions on their own lives. Here the notion of interest is crucial.

In the liberal tradition – the roots of which are in the thought of Hobbes, Locke, Bentham and Mill – politics is interpreted above all as a conflict and compromise between different interests. It is not so much about people participating with all their multiple beliefs, values and desires, but about their interests providing the content of politics. Power, then, refers to the ability to promote one's own interests and democracy becomes identified with the fair play of all interests. Competing interests are not only qualifications given to individuals; rather, they define individual political existence in liberal democracy.

In a capitalist, industrialised society the identification of competing interests is usually seen as unproblematic. This does not mean that those interests would always be about profit, accumulation of capital or division of labour. They may as well concern education, health, leisure time or culture as far as these are commodities, that is epitomised in a civilization where citizens are, in the first place, producers and/or consumers. Thus there is a constantly reproduced link between the economic roles of citizens and their political engagement. Citizens' political opinions and activism grow out of their economic conditions. In this sense politics is instrumental to and not in command of the rationalisation of economic processes. Conservative, liberal and the seemingly dissenting socialist rhetoric are only competing expressions of that economic rationalisation. Rather than reflecting utopian thinking about the society that people want to have, they reflect knowledge of economic necessities and promotion of group interests in the context of those necessities.

In other words, instead of representing universal, 'purely rational' aspirations of individuals, interests originate, in the hegemonic Western culture, from historical and social processes centred around capitalism. Obviously the instrumental notion of democracy is not in fact neutral: when created in the context of capitalism, its rationality is capitalist rationality. Above all, it is a strategy to come to terms with social problems caused by capitalism – without challenging it. To answer the question: 'Whose Democracy?' we can conclude that the instrumental notion of democracy is a democracy of interests making sense in the rationalisation of capitalism.

This is illustrated by the idea of growth with equality: the expansion of capitalist rationality is justified by growing wealth, which would finally serve all seemingly competing interests. General interest or common good in these societies becomes almost equal with economic growth, which – though qualified by sustainability – has never been called into question by the existing political systems we call democracies.[5] Moreover, there are good reasons to believe that can never happen.

The process of politicisation in liberal democracies is a relatively closed but nevertheless dynamic cycle. While identities are defined by interests, the promotion of any interests in the framework of Dahl's polyarchy is possible only after they are attached to identities already interpreted as being political. Thus politically significant discussion about gender inequalities requires the feminist movement, not necessarily as a party involved in those discussions, but as a location in the society where the political nature of gender is recognised. But the interests of children or elderly people, for example, are seldom raised. Rather the living conditions of these citizens become politically relevant only as far as they can be related to the interests of politically significant groups, like those of women, or to more general interests, like those concerning the whole welfare system.

The banality and stability of politics in the institutions of polyarchy, such as free and fair elections, freedom of expression or associational autonomy, arise from the fact that political identities are presented and cognitively created by the very same institutions. Usually the political representation of any identity is smoothly coopted by translating it into interests, which place its social signification within one universal, capitalist rationality. While sexual minorities can politicise their identities in relation to issues like discrimination in the labour markets or the legal validation of homosexual partnerships, recognition of difference as such is never an issue of political debate, but entirely left to the sphere of culture and art. Still, aesthetic identities are by no means without political weight, as they, more than interests, refer to human dignity: beliefs of good and bad, respect and contempt, friends and enemies.

This is also the reason why ethnic identities are always more or less problematic in the liberal environment. If multiculturalism – coexistence of different religions, languages and customs within one society – cannot be translated into differing consuming tastes, its representation in the political arena easily freezes the ethnic division into confrontation between the parties, which then clashes with the notion of common good and thus precludes dynamic decision-making.

Nevertheless, at best the instrumental notion of democracy articulates interests as dynamic significations, which can to a certain extent be manipulated by political power. Interests can be discussed and in a conflict situation compromise or consensus becomes possible, such as in an ideal multi-party electoral competition where different parties formulate programmes trying to merge the interests of their particular supporters to those of a wider electorate. With a choice between different programmes, the society represents itself as capable of change and there is no doubt over the meaning of politics. Moreover, settling the dispute of different interests is a task that justifies, once and for all, the existence of the state.

Institutions of Democracy in the Third World

When applied to the social and economic conditions of the Third World, this instrumental notion of democracy faces serious obstacles right from the beginning. While the state may perform the function of settling competing interests through the institutions of polyarchy in the West, this is not so in the Third World. In these societies the economic interests of citizens are not easily politicised in the institutions of polyarchy. These societies are characterised by a dualistic economy, where significant parts of the population are marginalised and delinked from the capitalist and internationalised mode of production. In the current discourse of the structural adjustment programmes this dualism deepens further, while the notion of a truly national economy in most of the Third World tends to lose its meaning.

The economic reality of many Third World countries consists of a growing informal sector with multiple survival strategies that are not controlled by political decision-making, on the one hand, and on the other, of an increasing pressure from international agencies like foreign investors or the World Bank on those sectors of the economy that are linked to multinational production networks and international finance. Furthermore dependency on external aid rather than on a national economy globalises the fulfilment of basic governmental functions like those concerning social welfare.[6] In these conditions, interests of individual citizens or groups of citizens do not compete meaningfully with each other at the level of the nation-state so that the emergence of a common interest through the institutions of Dahl's polyarchy could become possible and provide legitimacy for the use of state power.

On the contrary, democratic institutions – where they exist – have a tendency to facilitate mobilisation of massive political protests highlighting the crisis of the whole state apparatus. These protests seldom lead to a formation of political programmes, in which the masses' interests could positively contribute to the government policy. As the implementations of structural adjustment policies show, authoritarian means to silence political protest have often proved more lucrative for those in power.

Instead of organising themselves into political parties, the marginalised are turning their backs to state power, the incompetence of which they have been disillusioned with for too long. This is evident in the increasing voters' apathy even in countries like Zambia or Zimbabwe where very intensive multi-party competition exists. Those interests that are economically important for internationalised capital, in turn, do not need any mass organisations. The ability of the latter interests to have influence on government policy is dependent on their relations to external actors rather than to domestic ones. For them the people on the top of the ruling party or their 'ideological' commitments matter less than the policy guidance given by the World Bank. Thus if the institutions of polyarchy exist, they do not reflect important differing interests – if the interest of the political and bureaucratic elite to stay in power is not taken into account.

In its most undemocratic form, the state becomes a mere source of personal wealth for those who can attain it and staying in power depends more on the use of coercion and open violence than on popular support. In that case the institutions of liberal democracy cannot be conceived even as rituals legitimating the use of state power for the citizens, although for the international community it is precisely those institutions which are becoming, after the Cold War, increasingly important.

It is no wonder that many scholars who have applied the liberal approach to their analysis of political systems in the Third World have seen authoritarian states if not as inevitable at least as a rational way of trying to resolve conflict between heterogeneous interests and of maintaining state power. Maintaining state power, in turn, is considered as necessary for achieving economic development.[7] Authoritarianism then becomes almost by definition rational for developmentalist states.

Belief in Progress

When the liberal concept of politics as conflict and compromise between different interests clashes with reality in the Third World, then the instrumental notion of democracy as a fair play of interests also loses its meaning there. This brings the universality of liberal democracy into question. In the liberal tradition, it is not appropriate to conclude that institutions of democracy are suitable for some nations but not for others. This dilemma is solved by the idea of democratisation being a part of a universal and historically predetermined progress.

This line of thought has wide currency in the contemporary discourse on democratisation. For example, according to Modelski and Perry, democratisation represents an evolutionary, global process. As they have shown, the growth of liberal democracy has followed a regular pattern of technological change. In the beginning democratisation was experimental, but started to grow in the middle of the nineteenth century. Two hundred years ago no more than two per cent of the world's population lived in democratic communities, a proportion that rose to ten per cent a century later and then to the current level of 40 per cent. Their model suggests that the democratic community will attain a level of 90 per cent around the year 2100.[8]

Modelski and Perry note that the global hegemonies – the Dutch Republic, Great Britain and the United States – became increasingly democratic. But have these powers really served as sources of innovation, diffusion of democracy outside the hegemonies, or nuclei of the emerging global democratic community, as they claim? Colonialism as such was an expression of undemocratic domination, and during the Cold War the United States was too keen to maintain good relations with its allies in the Third World to pay very much attention to their undemocratic domestic performance.

In its extreme form, the instrumentalisation of democracy has led to reductionism, so that countries can be listed according to their levels of operationalised democracy: Iceland 72.8 points, United States 46.1 points, Iran 14.3 points, Gabon 0 points, and so on.[9] These levels of democracy are then analysed by correlations between democracy and development, like education or economic equality – or between democracy and foreign relations. Undemocratic practices are in a way explained, with reference to cases where favourable conditions for democracy do not exist. In this framework, the logic of democratisation is no longer conceptualised in the context of social crises and struggle, but as a parallel process with development and globalisation.

Although the focus of these comparative studies is on the empirical democratisation problems in the South or in the ex-Soviet bloc of the East, the idea of different stages of political evolution implicitly glorifies the West. While liberal democracy with the notion of competing interests is instrumental to capitalism and its expansion is dependent on – although not determined by – the rationalisation of capitalism, it is not a disproportionate amount of world surplus but democracy that differentiates the West from the rest. Indeed, the dominating instrumental notion of democracy has developed for such a long time within a reifying and quantifying capitalist rationality that as soon as the Cold War was practically over it became possible for someone like Francis Fukuyama to equate democracy with capitalism and to conclude that we already live in the best of all possible worlds.

Back to the Substance of Democracy

At a time of globalised financial markets, the instrumental notion of democracy tied to capitalist rationality is pertinent to the discourse of the IMF and the World Bank on good governance. According to that discourse, Third World governments should be, above all, accountable to global financial capital rather than to the desires of the marginalised parts of their populations. For the latter, the prevailing idea of democratisation as an automatic process means nothing else but legitimation of the current global inequalities.

A view opposing that discourse sees these inequalities not as a temporary anomaly interfering with the normal course of development, but rather as a problem with regard to the very notion of development. In this view, development is just another word for Western capitalist rationality. This cultural critique of development describes a growing opposition in the Third World countries against the 'rationalisation and impersonalisation of social existence' inherent in a Western-style nation-state.[10] The centralised, state-based decision-making system is considered as part of the Western 'impersonality postulate' and conducive to decreasing rather than increasing participation of the people in the political system.

The basis of the cultural critique is on the disempowerment experienced by those in the Third World that have been dispossessed of their traditional symbolic networks, or cognitive guides to the universe they live in, during the intentional development intervention that has been going on since World War II. What is needed is a 'decolonisation of the mind' both in Western and non-Western societies.[11]

If the voice of the voiceless is to be heard, if they are to be provided with an institutional and legal arrangement to decide their own destiny, we should 'decolonise' our problem-solving attitude – where the problem is already fixed – into a questioning attitude. Facing the current extremely complicated social, ecological and security obstacles to the expansion of capitalism, we can no longer neglect rationalities that are based on other kinds of social significations – not only traditional but emerging ones as well.

Instead of adjustment to the dominance of compulsory consumption and the economic rationality of growth, democracy should be seen as a radical possibility of institutionalising political decision-making as being in command of economic life. From the grass roots to the global level even cultural and environmental issues could then be discussed regardless of their real or imagined price in the 'free' markets.

This leads us to the substantial notion that democracy was born in ancient Greece together with philosophy, and not with capitalism. Ontologically speaking, democracy was not defined by differing interests but by judging, when every citizen had to be committed to expressing his or her interests and opinions in public discussion. Decisions were to be made on general grounds – not determined by the mathematical proportion of those interests. The essence of democracy became public discussion and a questioning attitude, which provides a basis for emancipation and a more just society.[12]

Although the inheritance of ancient Greece has been ignored for too long, it is still part of our thinking and practically present in some elements of liberal democracy – notably in the institutions of 'freedom of expression', 'alternative information' and 'associational autonomy'. To the extent that these institutions provide legally protected space for critical thinking and action, they also serve as means of making the power of interests more transparent. These are the elements that should be cultivated both in the Third World and in the West, when new rationalities and new civilised forms of political organisation are being looked for. These are also the elements that are most endangered. A culture of silence is promoted as well by a deluge of information, by ignoring important opinions, by coopting opposition or by intimidation.

This approach unveils the nature of democratisation as being essentially a struggle: we are not in a point where history can be ended. When capitalist rationality, with the notion of growth, is reaching its limits, new kinds of normative struggles are in front of us. Providing political space for these struggles requires something more than just the institutionalisation of democracy according to Western models. Moreover, while our problems are global problems, measuring the level of Western-model democracy in different countries makes little sense. If democracy is to be defended, its substantial content as an inherently moral project has to be accentuated. Only then would democratisation be above any particular rationality and have a value in itself.

Notes

1   See G. Modelski and G. Perry, 'Democratisation in long Perspective', *Technological Forecasting and Social Change*, vol. 39, no. 1–2 (1991) pp. 23–24.

2   My terms express a same kind of distinction as substantive and formal rationality in Weber, for whom substantive was related to more values and formal to capitalism. See M. Weber, *Economy and Society: An Outline of Interpretative Sociology* (New York: Bedminster Press, 1968) pp. 85–86. However, the substantial and

instrumental notions of democracy are not contradictory and do not exclude each other like the Weberian types of rationality.

3   Robert A. Dahl, *Democracy and its Critics* (New Haven: Yale University Press, 1989) p. 221.

4   Dahl, *Democracy*, p. 222.

5   For example, the so called *Brundtland Report* gives several proposals for the implementation of sustainable development, but ends up calling for a new era of economic growth. See World Commission on Environment and Development, *Our Common Future* (Oxford: Oxford University Press, 1987) p. 49.

6   See A. Fowler, 'Distant Obligations. Speculations on NGO Funding and the Global Market', *Review of African Political Economy*, vol. 55 (1992) pp. 9–29.

7   See Björn Beckman, 'Whose Democracy? Bourgeois versus Popular Democracy', *Review of African Political Economy*, vol. 45 (1989) pp. 84–106.

8   Modelski and Perry, 'Democratisation', pp. 28–32.

9   T. Vanhanen, *The Process of Democratisation: A Comparative Study of 147 States, 1980–88* (New York: Taylor & Francis, 1990) pp. 94–95. See also A. Hadenius, *Democracy and Development* (Cambridge: Cambridge University Press, 1992).

10 T. Banuri, 'Development and the Politics of Knowledge. A Critical Interpretation of the Social Role of Modernisation Theories in the Development of the Third World' in A. Marglin, F. Marglin and A. Stephen (ed), *Dominating Knowledge. Development, Culture and Resistance* (Oxford: Clarendon Press, 1990) p. 51.

11 Marglin, *Dominating Knowledge*, p. 26.

12 C. Castoriadis, *Philosophy, Politics, Autonomy* (New York: Oxford University Press, 1991) pp. 111–12.

13

Democracy: A Fragile Export

Franz Nuscheler

According to the *Survey of Freedom in the World*, published by New York Freedom House, there has been a virtual 'explosion of freedom' in the world since the global transition of 1989–90. Among 24 global trends listed in the Development and Peace Foundation's *Global Trends 1991*, only three were positive, among them an almost universal 'transition to political pluralism, democracy, and a recognition of political rights'.[1] This was accompanied, of course, by a regression in social rights.

At the end of 'the bloodiest, most inhuman, and most horrific century', as the expert in international law, Otto Kimminich, described the twentieth century,[2] it would seem that 'the gap between, on the one hand, the philosophical and legal development of human rights theory and, on the other, the possibilities of repression by technologically well-equipped (illegitimate) regimes' has continued to widen. But appearances can be deceptive.

The success of the Western model of liberal democracy (with its core elements of political pluralism, competition and the rule of law) appears, at the end of the twentieth century, to be both universal and secular. The Communist regimes of Central and Eastern Europe, as well as their economically and militarily supported offshoots in the Third World (with the exceptions of China, North Korea, and Cuba), collapsed like a house of cards. Throughout Latin America, military leaders withdrew from their government palaces to the barracks and to the 'back seats of power'. In most African states, the one-party system was either replaced by a multi-party system or collapsed with the state itself, largely as a result of the political conditions imposed from outside by the providers of essential aid. Except for the as yet unexplained regressive developments in China, Singapore and Malaysia, the experience of Asia and South East Asia would appear to confirm the interdependence between the economic and political order. According to this theory, success in the development of economic competition promotes the development of political competition. Of course the reverse is also possible.

The 'end of history' as the victory of liberal democracy? The one-time chief of planning in the US Department of State, Francis Fukuyama, has interpreted the changes in Central and Eastern Europe not only as the end of the Cold War but also as 'the end of ideological evolution and the universalisation of Western liberal democracy as the final form of human government'.[3]

In the *International Herald Tribune*, the well-known columnist, Charles Krauthammer, has answered the question posed by every political philosopher since Plato concerning the optimal form of government: 'After several millennia of testing various systems, we end this century with the certainty that, in pluralist capitalist democracy, we have found what we were looking for.'[4]

But these victory proclamations raise a number of questions: does the collapse of the system of 'really existing socialism' really mean the final victory of the Western model of society and democracy? Has the much criticised teleology of modernisation theories, that defines development as imitation of the Western model, triumphed over the cultural-relativist sceptics and the critics of the Eurocentric philosophy of progress? Are the numerous studies of the problems associated with the establishment and survival of democracy in the Third World now only of historical value, for instance the four-volume survey published between 1988 and 1990 by Juan J. Linz and Seymour M. Lipset?[5] Is dictatorship destined to be the 'state model for the Third World'? – a question posed by Hans F. Illy and others,[6] following the growth in dictatorial regimes during the 1960s and 1970s? And, finally, now that the socialist Second World no longer exists as a competing and alternative model, and with the failure, for the time being at any rate, of almost all attempts by Third World states to create their own models of democracy that were capable of promoting economic development, as well as guaranteeing popular participation and respect for human rights, has the consideration of other development models become superfluous?

Rainer Tetzlaff was unable to discover, anywhere in the world, a viable alternative to liberal democracy and he saw:

… good reasons for assuming that, since the division of the world into territorial states, humanity has found itself in a 'democratic world revolution' that is advancing by degrees and always in response to catastrophes. Its twin appears to be the capitalist mode of production …[7]

This is an author who for decades was critical of the Western export model of development but has now come to terms with the 'twins' of capitalism and liberal democracy.

Liberal democracy, as never before, is experiencing a boom almost everywhere. The Western model of democracy – the multi-party system, periodic elections, division of powers, freedom of the press, etc. – appears to have become the universal norm for legitimacy of rule. Not only are the Western victors in the conflict between the two systems celebrating the 'rebirth of democracy' (as the heads of state and the government leaders of the G7 group of nations did at their economic summit in Houston in July 1990) but even the losers in this battle are tripping over themselves to proclaim their faith in democracy and human rights. The successor states of the old Soviet bloc, in the CSCE 'Charter for a New Europe' of November 1990, formally declared their adherence to a pluralist conception of democracy as a universally valid form of government and they accepted a definition of democracy that contained all the key elements of the Western conception of democracy and human rights.

But even more significant, from the point of view of the recognition of liberal democracy as a universally valid system, are three documents that were created partly or entirely by representatives of the South. These are:

1 The Stockholm Initiative on Global Security and the World Order, in which Julius Nyerere and Benazir Bhutto were involved alongside Willy Brandt, Gro Harlem Brundtland and Vaclav Havel. It declared: 'We recognise democracy and human rights as true universal values. They have their origin and their history in societies on all continents.'

2 The Preamble (Article 7) to the strategy document for the fourth UN Decade of Development, passed unanimously by members of the United Nations, stressed the increasing similarity of views on such issues as how democracy and human rights could contribute to the development process. According to Article 13 of the document:

> The strategy should contribute to the creation of an environment that promotes the emergence of political systems based on general agreement and respect for human as well as social and economic rights and also promotes the development of systems of laws that give protection to all citizens.

It may have been the Western industrial nations, with their power of capital, that dictated these sentences but it was the countries of the Third World, with their voting power in the UN, that gave them approval.

3   The Report of the Commission on the South, the 'Nyerere Report', can be seen as a genuine voice of the South (albeit the Southern elite). No other document from the South, prepared by its ruling elites, has formulated so clearly and unconditionally the profession of faith in democracy and human rights. The following passage removes the justification for any form of dictatorship:

> Democratic institutions and the participation of the people in the decision making process are therefore indispensable for development. The interests of the people within the nations are given their due priority only when there is true political freedom. The people have to determine their own system of government and they have to be able to decide who forms the government and what general course it will follow in their name and on their behalf. Respect for human rights, the rule of law, the possibility to change government peacefully are some of the fundamental elements of a democratic society.[8]

The various regional declarations on human rights also provide further confirmation that, since the Declaration on Human Rights of 1948, there has not been such a broad consensus on what constitutes 'good governance'. The consensus, however, is not really universal, as demonstrated by the attacks from the 'Asian bloc', led by China, on the universality principle. The verbal consensus also doesn't mean that states have altered their practice. According to reports from Amnesty International and other human rights organisations, more states are guilty of torture now than ever before.

The Fascination of the Western Democratic Model

Let us also recall that the sometimes hasty retreat of some African states from the one-party system was motivated not so much by a new enlightenment as by a process of economic and political disintegration, accompanied by a threatened withdrawal of aid by the donor nations who were no longer strategically constrained by the East-West conflict.

The second wave of democratisation in Africa, at the end of the 1980s, to the extent that it wasn't just an opportunist adaptation from above to the demands of Western credit institutions, is essentially a protest movement, born of despair, against the unbearable dominance of a bureaucratic, parasitic state class.[9]

The goals of what was essentially an academic protest movement are very informative, much more so than the diplomatically polished and inconsequential declarations of the state classes that were under pressure. A good example is the 'Declaration on Africa' of April 1986, the result of an initiative by the well-known historian, Joseph Ki-Zerbo, from Burkina Faso, which demanded the right to free elections, respect for human rights and the rule of law.[10] Under the much inflated term, 'democratisation', it supported the introduction of a multi-party parliamentary system on the Western model, something which intellectuals, during the period after independence, had declared 'not appropriate for Africa'. They now even pressured the Western donor countries (and one-time colonial powers) to demand certain political conditions, as a way of forcing their various state leaderships to introduce democratic reforms.[11] In the 1960s and 1970s, such political conditions would have been criticised as neocolonial interference because, at that time, there was a 'more or less uneasy consensus around the inevitability of the one-party system'.[12]

The academic debate on the archetypal function of the Western constitutional and democratic model will have to be reopened because, not only are the reform forces of Central and Eastern Europe adopting this model, without the least ideological scruple, but the democratic movements of the Third World, in the absence of convincing alternatives, have also begun to overcome their reservations about Western imports. Even among the left intellectuals of Latin America, there was a growth of constitutionalism during the 1980s, with increasing demands for democratic reform.[13]

Western critics of the export of Western models and of the Eurocentrism of liberal democracy are running out of arguments. How can they continue, with any credibility, to criticise the 'democratic crusade' and political conditionality, when the protest movements of the Third World are demanding precisely what these critics, with their culturally relativist sensitivity, are rejecting? The profound changes in world politics have played havoc with many world images, systems of thought, perceptions of problems, alliances and strategies.

Democracy's Transplant Problems

Professions of faith in democracy, parliamentarism, pluralism and human rights, all made at no cost, still don't provide an answer to the key questions of the old debate: firstly, whether the different societies of the Third World possess the sociopolitical infrastructure and the sociocultural basis on which democracy could flourish; secondly, whether poor societies are at all capable of living up to the high normative claims and expectations of political and social democracy.

The Western democratic model's claim to universal validity as the only organisational form of legitimate rule raises some very fundamental considerations which, for some decades now, have had a very firm foundation in cultural and social anthropology and in the critique of modernisation theories.[14] The essential core of this concern, still valid even after the renaissance of modernisation theories that followed the collapse of alternatives (such as dependency theories), could be summarised as follows: Pluralist parliamentary democracy is a specific end-product of occidental social and intellectual history, of the Enlightenment, and of the development of bourgeois society and the capitalist market economy. This product cannot be transplanted to other societies that lack the necessary social and cultural foundation, even when their elites have been politically socialised at Western universities. These artificial transplants will be rejected.

According to Manfred Mols' somewhat oversimplified account, only small traces are to be found in Latin America of what were the two constitutive events of Western democracy, namely, the Enlightenment and the emergence of a bourgeois state and a bourgeois-led capitalist economy. If this is valid for Latin America, then it is even more so for the other parts of the Third World that had even fewer links with Western civilisation than did Latin America.[15]

What is valid for political democracy could also be valid for the market economy, which the West, through its political conditionality, tries to impose on the Third World. The market economy, in the industrialised nations, was the material foundation for the social democracy fought for and won by the labour movement. But, just as a politically competitive system, with its consensus-building rules and norms, cannot be transplanted, neither can the market economy be transplanted in societies that lack the socioeconomic preconditions as well as the 'spirit of capitalism'. These assumptions are not fundamentally contradicted by any tendency in world history towards universalisation, towards a One World that penetrates and transcends all regions and cultures, impelled by what Immanuel Wallerstein describes as the objective pressures of a 'capitalist world economy'.

The dynamic development within the 'Confucian cultural area' demonstrates clearly that the 'spirit of capitalism' is not tied, as Max Weber thought, to the 'protestant ethic' or to typically Western rationality. Since practical success is more convincing than theory, the West is now pointing to Japan, which, at the beginning of the 1960s, was still receiving credits from the World Bank, and to the other 'Asian tigers', as development models for countries of the Third World: 'Look East, not West!'

The discussion about the transferability of models now has to deal with a number of new variants. The developing countries can learn a lot from the 'big tiger' (Japan), from the other 'small tigers' of East Asia and from the 'big dragon' (China) about, for instance, the importance of agrarian reform or investment in education and training. The secret to these success stories, however, is not something that can be exported at will, namely, the Confucian ethic of work and saving as well as the effectiveness of a 'strong state' that rests on a specific cultural understanding of authority and of the relations between the state, society and the individual. In a group-oriented social organisation and ethics, individual rights have a much lower value than they do in Western individualism, whatever might be written in human rights declarations.

Democracy and Development: Congruence or Antinomy?

At their world economic summit in Houston in July 1990, the heads of state and government leaders from the G7 countries declared: 'We know that freedom and economic well-being are closely linked and mutually reinforcing'. But where did the politicians and their advisers get this 'knowledge' that led them to equate freedom with the market economy? Neither the history of the modern industrial nations nor the success story of the East Asian 'small tigers' which, in the case of South Korea and Taiwan, began under extremely repressive dictatorships, point to a strong causal link between economic development and the level of democracy. China experienced an economic boom and an influx of foreign capital to its flourishing coastal region after the massacre of Tiananmen Square. The history of development of the 'small tigers' and the 'big dragon' rather suggest an antinomy between economic development and democracy, as Richard Löwenthal has claimed: 'Every degree of freedom is paid for with a slow-down in development, and every acceleration of development is paid for with a diminution of freedom'.[16]

There are some experiences, however, where this antinomy has not been the rule. Firstly, most of the dictatorships that sought to justify themselves as 'development dictatorships' turned out to be 'dictatorships without development', unlike South Korea, Taiwan and Singapore, where 'strong states' were adept at promoting development. Secondly, the small number of viable democracies (India, Mauritius, Botswana, Costa Rica and most of the Caribbean island states) fared no worse, from a development point of view, than did the many dictatorships, in whatever ideological garb.[17] Thirdly, the economic success of South Korea, Taiwan and Thailand stimulated a move towards democratisation, while in Singapore and Malaysia, on the other hand, it led to regression from the inherited Westminster model.

The lesson to be learned from these various examples is that any generalisation that attempts to establish a link between economic development and democracy, as the Group of Seven leaders attempted in Houston, is unreliable. What does emerge clearly, however, is that political stability promotes economic development, keeps domestic capital in the country and attracts foreign capital. But political stability is not quite the same thing as democracy. Much more important than the construction of correlations such as these is the question of how these unstable democracies manage to survive at all, in view of the social and economic crises they are experiencing, and how democratic rules can still function under the stressful conditions of mass poverty, ethnic and social conflicts, the problem of debt and the harsh measures of structural adjustment. In many of the 're-democratised' countries, particularly in Latin America, there is a profound disillusionment with the inability of the new democracies to resolve the economic and social crises inherited from the previous military dictatorships. People don't just want to take part in elections, they also want a share of prosperity; they don't just want new faces in government, but changes in their social conditions and improvements in their daily lives. In many cases, the elected politicians soon lead these new democracies into new crises of legitimacy, through corruption, nepotism and their inability to get anything done.

In Africa, the main problem is to prevent the disintegration of the state rather than to develop a multi-party system. The latter results more often from external pressure than from an indigenous development. African countries are confronted now by problems that are even more serious than those that existed after independence, when multi-party systems were declared a 'political luxury'. Now, as then, the new parties are ethnically based and, with this 're-tribalisation' of the party system, they add new burdens to the already fragile state: ethnic rivalry and the struggle over distribution. Under such circumstances, the question has to be asked once again: is the multi-party system really the last word in political wisdom? Many developing countries find themselves in the kind of crisis that the developed democracies could not survive without the use of emergency powers. Their average debt, for instance, is two times greater than that of the Weimar Republic after the Versailles peace treaty. At the time, this was the nail in the coffin of the young German republic. The political conditionality of the international creditors is endangering the stability and the basis of legitimacy of the new democracies.[18]

The economic and social problems that confront the developing countries are particularly acute in Africa, where what is at stake is no longer development, but survival: 'The objective possibilities in Africa today for the gradual implementation of political democracy and the simultaneous achievement of economic progress are extremely limited',[19] according to Rainer Tetzlaff. The democratisation process is being hindered, however, not just by the desperate economic and social situation, but also by the lack of consensus-building structures and rules in those ethnically and culturally fragmented societies. A pluralist democracy won't work without a certain minimum of consensus. Civil society can't be produced from a test tube; it is the end product of a comprehensive socioeconomic and sociocultural transformation process. The present 'wave of democratisation' lacks the structural preconditions that would give it lasting stability. The return to various forms of praetorianism is therefore predictable.

Help for Democracy: But How?

For four decades now, the Western states, guided by their own political and economic interests, have practised a double standard in their policies on development and human rights. They rewarded their pro-Western 'right-wing friends' (even such kleptocratic regimes as that of Duvalier in Haiti, Somoza in Nicaragua and Mobutu in Zaire) and punished 'left-wing enemies' by withdrawing economic aid. Since the end of the Cold War, when such practices became superfluous, they have presented themselves as teachers of democracy and human rights and have attached a 'political conditionality' to their economic aid. African states, in particular, have been affected by this because, unlike prosperous and powerful China, Indonesia or the Arab states, they are not in a very strong position to reject these conditions. This political conditionality poses the question of the legitimacy of exerting this kind of external influence on the internal affairs of another state. The states that are the object of this conditionality reject it as tutelage and political blackmail, and they insist, rather feebly, on their right to determine their own development and to choose their own political system. Critics of this conditionality are caught between support for universally recognised norms, to which the developing countries have themselves subscribed in various human rights agreements, and support for the right of self-determination which, in principle, should apply also to the 'dwarfs of world politics'. Human rights organisations and the states that impose political conditionality can both point to the same declarations of support for democracy and human rights (in the *Nyerere Report*, for instance).

If the human rights conventions have a claim to universal validity, then it is legitimate to impose on despots, of whatever orientation, the pressure of political conditionality, because human rights are not exclusively a matter of internal affairs. But it is neither legitimate nor sensible, beyond a certain indispensable minimum standard of human rights, to use the threat of the withdrawal of aid to force on another country the introduction of particular principles of political organisation, such as, for instance, the multi-party system. And this policy loses all credibility when, as actually happens, this political conditionality is used, for opportunistic reasons, only against the 'have not' countries.[20]

Politically, it would be sensible not to place too high demands on the societies of the East and South. In the socioeconomic and political conditions to be found in many developing countries, a high level of legal security would be of greater value than the mere organisation of what are frequently manipulated elections. The history of the multi-party system in the Third World suggests that it can hardly be regarded as the embodiment of democratic freedom. People have a greater need for protection from state arbitrariness than they do for an electoral choice between a number of different parties. An effective restraint on despots would be a more worthwhile achievement of political conditionality.

The attempt to use political conditionality as a means of exporting the Western model of democracy runs up against a fundamental difficulty, which the Stockholm Initiative described in the following way: 'Democracy develops, not in response to an external command, but as a product of internal "demand". Democracy cannot be set up from the top down, but has to grow up from below'.[21] The industrial countries could, however, in a different way, help to improve the conditions for a viable democracy, firstly, by directing their support to those regimes that are willing to introduce reforms and, secondly, by generously reducing the debt burden, as a way of relieving the pressure on these countries. Felix Ermacora, one-time human rights official for the United Nations, also said that the realisation of human rights and the survival of democracy depended on the creation of decent social conditions.[22]

If welfare and freedom are mutually conditioning, as claimed by the governments participating in the economic summit in Houston, then these governments are doing very little to create the preconditions for freedom. Freedom doesn't just mean the organisation of more or less free elections; it also means liberation from inhuman living conditions. Without the latter, any attempt to revive democracy is destined to fail. According to Rainer Tetzlaff, liberal competitive democracy is 'not a Eurocentric imposition but the rational requirement of an order that is appropriate for the enlightened, mature citizen'. But he immediately restricts this universality thesis by pointing to the exorbitant political demands placed on states with very weak resources. He also makes the realisation of these universal ideals into a 'global task' requiring international cooperation: 'The task of the future is not so much to beat the drum worldwide for pluralist democracy, but to make democracy viable, by means of material assistance and institutional safeguards.'[23]

Conclusion: Against a Standardised 'One World'

The Third World is made up of a number of different social and cultural worlds to which one cannot apply a single standardised set of political organisational principles. Modernisation theory's model of Western societies, with their politically and economically competitive systems, is a one-world model, the realisation of which, if it were possible, would not enrich the world but would rather make it poorer. Insistence on the universality of human rights or the vision of a global community of values do not imply the universal validity of particular economic or political development models. The universal ethics of human rights, as envisaged by Hans Küng, rests on a set of common basic values, but not on a standardised set of organisational principles or decision-making procedures: 'This one world society doesn't need a unified set of rules or ideologies, but what it does need are some binding norms, values, ideals and goals'.[24]

The Report of the Commission on the South (the *Nyerere Report*) declared that participation was 'essential for development', and the *Human Development Report 1993* of the UNDP placed participation at the centre of 'people-oriented development'. But participation, which, according to the UNDP, is not simply voting but a 'way of life', can be organised in a variety of ways. It has to come 'from below'; but liberal democracy which, in essence, is a contest among competing elites, is organised 'from above'. Liberal democracy is therefore not an adequate model for 'participatory development'. This model role attributed to liberal democracy could, in fact, hinder the creative search for alternative organisational models of participation. Every society must, in principle, have the opportunity to develop its own capacities, in its own specific way. There is no rational basis for a single and teleologically predetermined model of democracy and development. A model of democracy which is just a clone of what exists in the West is not the last word in political wisdom. The rejoicing over the 'rebirth of democracy' in many parts of the world overlooks the fact that, in many countries, democracy is only in an embryonic stage, and any kind of external midwifery may well lead to a stillbirth. What is at stake is the security of the basic structure, not the precise detail of the inner architecture. We haven't yet reached the 'end of history'.

Notes

1   Stiftung Entwicklung und Frieden, Globale Trends 1991. *Daten zur Weltentwicklung* (Bonn, 1991) p. 23.

2   Otto Kimminich, 'Menschenrechte', in Peter J. Opitz (ed), *Weltprobleme*, 3rd edn (Munich, 1991) p. 344.

3   Francis Fukuyama, 'The End of History?', *The National Interest*, no. 18 (1989).

4   Quoted from *Die Zeit*, 22 September 1989.

5   Juan J. Linz and Seymour M. Lipset (eds), *Democracy in Developing Countries*, 4 vols (London, 1988–90).

6   Hans F. Illy, Rüdiger Sielaff and Nikolaus Werz, *Diktatur – Staatsmodell für die dritte Welt?* (Freiburg/Würzburg, 1980).

7   Rainer Tetzlaff, 'Demokratie in der dritten Welt: Zwischen normativer Zustimmung und praktischer Realisierungsproblemen', *Jahrbuch Dritte Welt 1993* (Munich 1993) pp. 40ff.

8   Der Bericht der Südkommission: Die Herausforderung des Südens (Bonn, 1991) p. 36.

9   Rainer Tetzlaff, *Demokratie und gesellschaftlicher Wandel in Afrika: Chancen und Gefahren* (Friedrich Ebert Stiftung: Bonn, 1991) p. 7.

10   International Foundation for Alternative Development, *The Declaration on Africa: For Democracy, For Development, For Unity* (Geneva, 1986).

11   See Rolf Hofmeier, 'Politische Konditionierung von Entwicklungshilfe in Afrika', *Africa Spectrum*, no 2 (1990), pp. 167–70.

12   Reinhart Kößler and Henning Melber, 'Afrika vor der demokratischen Frage', *Blätter für deutsche und internationale Politik*, no. 9 (1990) p. 1052.

13   See Barbara Töpper, 'Die Frage der Demokratie in der Entwicklungstheorie, *Peripherie*, no. 39–40, pp. 146ff.

14   ibid., pp. 129ff.

15   Manfred Mols, *Demokratie in Lateinamerika* (Stuttgart 1985) p. 21.

16   Richard Löwenthal, 'Staatsfunktionen und Staatsformen in den Entwicklungsländern' (1963), reprinted in Franz Nuscheler (ed), *Politikwissenschaftliche Entwicklungsländerforschung* (Darmstadt, 1986) p. 266.

17   See Franz Nuscheler, 'Erscheinungs- und Funktionswandel des Prätorianismus in der dritten Welt', in Franz Nuscheler (ed), *Politikwissenschaftliche Entwicklungsländerforschung*, pp. 177ff.

18   See Leopoldo Mármora, 'Was haben Demokratisierung und Außenverschuldung miteinander zu tun? Das Beispiel Argentinien', *Peripherie*, no. 33–34 (1988).

19   Rainer Tetzlaff, *Demokratie und gesellschaftlicher Wandel*, p. 22.

20   See Franz Nuscheler, 'Menschenrechtliche Doppelstandards in der Entwicklungspolitik', in Rainer Tetzlaff (ed), *Menschenrechte und Entwicklung* (Bonn, 1993) pp. 79–95.

21   Stiftung Entwicklung und Frieden, *Die Stockholmer Initiative zu globaler Sicherheit und Weltordnung: Gemeinsame Verantwortung in den 90er Jahren* (Bonn, 1991) p. 56.

22   Felix Ermacora, *Menschenrechte in der sich wandelnden Welt* (Vienna, 1974) pp. 32ff.

23   Rainer Tetzlaff, 'Demokratie in der dritten Welt', p. 47.

24   Hans Küng, *Projekt Weltethos* (Munich, 1990) p. 14.

25   *UNDP: Human Development Report 1993* (New York and Oxford, 1993) p. 23.

Notes on Contributors

Jochen Hippler is a political scientist and Director of the Transnational Institute in Amsterdam. His main areas of research are regional conflicts and democratisation in the Third World, and questions of World Order and he is the author of *Pax Americana?: Hegemony or Decline* (Pluto Press 1994).

Joel Rocamora is a Fellow and former Associate Director of the Transnational Institute. He is a Philippine political scientist and activist living in Manila. He is the joint editor of *Low Intensity Democracy* (Pluto Press 1993).

Peter Schraeder is Associate Professor of political science at Loyola University of Chicago. His research areas are Africa, and US foreign policy. He is coordinator of a TNI project on the foreign dimension of Third World Democratisation.

Claude Aké is a political economist, Professor of Political Science and Director of the Center for Advanced Social Science, Port Harcourt, Nigeria. He has published numerous books and articles on the political economy of Africa.

Xabier Gorostiaga is Rector of the Central American University in Managua, Nicaragua and TNI Advisor. He is working on questions of development on peace in Central America.

Niala Maharaj is a journalist and writer from Trinidad. She is working on development and human rights in the Third World and lives mostly in Amsterdam.

Achin Vanaik and **Praful Bidwai** are journalists and TNI fellows, living and working in India.

Joe Stork is Editor of *Middle East Report*, Washington. His main interests are the US policy towards the Middle East and the developments in Palestine and Israel.

233

Azmy Bishara is a Professor of Philosophy and Cultural Studies at BirZeit University, Palestine. His research topics include: state and religion, politics and myths, Marxism, Eurocentrism. He lives in Jerusalem.

Basker Vashee is a TNI Fellow and former Director of the institute working mostly on African development. He is a Zimbabwean living in Amsterdam.

Susan George is an Associate Director of the Transnational Institute. She is author of *The Debt Boomerang* (Pluto Press 1989) and numerous books on Third World debt and the World Bank.

Liisa Laakso is a researcher at the Institute for Development Studies of the University of Helsinki, working on questions of Third World Democratisation.

Franz Nuscheler is a Professor of Political Science at Duisburg University, Germany, and Director of the Institute for Development and Peace.

Index